STEPHEN ALFORD

London's Triumph
Merchant Adventurers and the Tudor City

ALLEN LANE
an imprint of
PENGUIN BOOKS

ALLEN LANE

UK | USA | Canada | Ireland | Australia
India | New Zealand | South Africa

Allen Lane is part of the Penguin Random House group of companies whose
addresses can be found at global.penguinrandomhouse.com

First published 2017
001

Copyright © Stephen Alford, 2017

The moral right of the author has been asserted

Set in 10.5/14 pt Sabon LT Std
Typeset in India by Thomson Digital Pvt Ltd, Noida, Delhi
Printed in Great Britain by Clays Ltd, St Ives plc

A CIP catalogue record for this book is available from the British Library

ISBN: 978–0–241–00358–9

www.greenpenguin.co.uk

MIX
Paper from
responsible sources
FSC® C018179

Penguin Random House is committed to a
sustainable future for our business, our readers
and our planet. This book is made from Forest
Stewardship Council® certified paper.

For my parents, with love

O London, thou art great in glory, and envied for thy greatness: thy towers, thy temples, and thy pinnacles stand upon thy head like borders of gold, thy waters like fringes of silver hang at the hems of thy garments. Thou art the goodliest of thy neighbours, but the proudest; the wealthiest, but the most wanton.

Thomas Dekker, *The Seven Deadly*
Sinnes of London (1606)

Moved by the good affection . . . and much more by that good will, which of duty I bear to my native country and coun-trymen, which have of late to their great praise (whatsoever succeed) attempted with new voyages to search the seas and new found lands . . .

Richard Eden, *A Treatyse of the*
Newe India (1553)

Contents

The Triumph of London

This book tells a story that breaks all the rules of historical probability: how one city grew in spite of huge and recurring demographic crises of mortality and disease, coped with massive levels of immigration and, on top of all this, found the confidence by the late sixteenth century to explore, trade with and colonize far parts of the world unknown only two generations before. It is a story about money, wealth, poverty, self-confidence, greed, tenacity and remarkable happenstance and accident. It is the story of Tudor London, the city William Shakespeare knew.

As much as this is a book about a single city, it also explores significantly changing worlds of experience, knowledge, possibility and imagination within and beyond London. To say that English horizons were opened up between 1500 and 1620 would be a severe understatement. Where for centuries London's merchants had been content to send their ships to and from the Low Countries (today Belgium and the Netherlands), France and the Baltic, by 1620 they knew Russia, Persia, the far eastern Mediterranean and Africa, and had bases from the Red Sea to Japan, as well as colonies in North America. Their ambitions were without limit; they built vast trading corporations and entertained hopes of trans- and inter-continental business that would circumnavigate the globe. Hand in hand with this was the discovery by ordinary people of faraway places through books printed in London. In 1500 the keenest bibliophile would have struggled to fill even a modest shelf with books printed in the city. A century later, thanks to a combination of a thriving industry and readers eager for new knowledge, the same shelves would have heaved with pamphlets and volumes of explorations, navigations, exotic peoples, sermons, foreign languages, histories, poetry and drama. Add to this what was effectively the quadrupling of London's population in just over a century and the physical reshaping of a city bursting with people, and it is no wonder that we are left with the exciting task of trying to understand (or sometimes frankly to keep pace) with a dizzying story.

We need right at the beginning to leave behind some big modern assumptions. The first is that the kingdom of Tudor England was a major player in Europe; the second (a hard notion to let go of today) that to speak English counted for anything. In European terms, England in 1500 was a marginal backwater, London a solid enough but broadly unspectacular city. English was a minor language spoken by some, but by no means all, of the inhabitants of what today we call the British Isles. Survey the various fields of European endeavour in 1500 and England barely registered; its cultural pulse was very faint indeed. The great names of the day in art (Sandro Botticelli and Albrecht Dürer, for example), church power (Giovanni di Lorenzo de' Medici, later Pope Leo X), finance and banking (Jakob Fugger), navigation and exploration (Christopher Columbus), political analysis (Niccolò Machiavelli), science and human knowledge (Leonardo da Vinci) and university scholarship (Erasmus of Rotterdam) all had, as well as their brilliance, at least one other thing in common: they were not English. The most powerful royal courts and most impressive seats of learning were to be found in Italy, Spain, France and Germany. The Tudor Henry VII, king of England in 1500, was able to punch above his weight diplomatically by signing international peace treaties and marrying off his children to fellow princes. But Henry's wider influence was as nothing compared with the kings of France and Spain and, pre-eminently, the Holy Roman Emperor Maximilian I, who ruled the great agglomeration of territories that make up modern Germany and central Europe. To be understood abroad, an Englishman had to speak either another European vernacular or, ideally, Latin. English was a language whose furthest reach was Calais, at least when Calais was still an English possession (but it was lost by battle to the French in 1558).

In terms of trade and navigation, England was a very long way behind other European powers. As we will see, the great entrepôt of north-western Europe, where the riches of the Middle East and Asia were bought by English merchants, was Antwerp; before that it had been Bruges. The Italian cities of Genoa and Venice were formidable commercial powers in the eastern Mediterranean, and Naples was much larger even than Paris in terms of its population (and Paris in turn was considerably bigger than London). Banking houses of Augsburg like the Fugger and the Welser dominated the financial scene of western Europe, lending huge sums of money to kings and emperors, including (a little later) kings of England. London was a modest satellite of a European system of international trade whose weight was settled firmly in the middle of the continent.

When it came to the wider world, by 1500 Spain and Portugal had well-established global ambitions. Blessed by the papacy, those two Iberian powers had practically carved up the whole world between them, as in 1493 Pope Alexander VI divided the globe by a meridian drawn north to south 370 leagues west of the Cape Verde Islands. Spain's western imperial ambitions were just at that point beginning to develop. Already by 1500 Portuguese explorers knew Africa and the Middle East and were establishing bases in the East Indies to import pepper and valuable spices into Europe. Within a few decades the vast riches of Mexico would be opened up to plunder and exploitation; the silver fleets returning across the Atlantic by way of the Caribbean became the greatest prop of global Spanish power. In 1503 the Casa de la Contratación, a department of Spain's central government, was set up to process the immensely valuable cargoes returning from the other side of the world. It was also a highly regarded school of navigation that developed ever more advanced techniques of further exploration. In this new world, English merchants and navigators were nowhere to be seen. To say 'empire' or 'colony' to such a merchant in 1500 would be to invite a puzzled look at words which had no obvious relevance to his life and business. Equally, English navigators would take another half century even to begin to catch up with the advanced skills of Portuguese and Spanish sea captains.

If the rise of London looks all the more remarkable in the light of the utter marginality of England at the beginning of the sixteenth century, then just as confounding is the fact that the city flourished as, in the decades that followed, continental Europe was torn by religious war, massacre and revolt.

Europe at the best of times was a hotchpotch of kingdoms, provinces, dukedoms and city-states. Even relatively settled kingdoms like France and England had all kinds of semi-autonomous regions and princedoms. Notionally Europe was bound together by the idea and structures of Christendom, in which the formidable multinational spiritual corporation that was the Catholic Church, with its pope in Rome, offered to all Christian Europeans the keys to heaven and gave a sense of unity to an otherwise disparate and diverse continent. In 1500 the enemies of Christendom were firmly on the outside: the Ottoman Empire in the far eastern Mediterranean (always a danger), or Muslims forcibly pushed out of southern Spain in the late fifteenth century. Other than isolated heretics and heresies here and there, there were few enemies within. But all that changed in 1517, when the lectures of an Augustinian monk and university teacher called Martin Luther escalated into a movement that shook Christendom to its foundations.

What became the Reformation is one of the great backdrops to this book. After 1517 the whole of Europe was turned upside down by Protestant ideas that unravelled the fabric of Christian Europe. There was more than one kind of Protestantism and many Protestant leaders of different generations: Luther, Ulrich Zwingli, Johannes Oecolampadius, John Calvin, Theodore Beza and others. What each of these movements and theologies had in common was the power to challenge not only the Catholic Church, but also the authority of kings and princes: the Bible as God's unimpeachable word could be used to challenge fundamental assumptions of who was in charge of kingdoms and peoples. For a century Europe was convulsed by wars between and within its greatest powers. After the 1560s France was all but paralysed by periodic and vicious bouts of religious civil war. In the same decade, patriotism and faith combined together in the Low Countries to stimulate resistance to the rule of the imperial Habsburg family, and the greatest king of his day, Philip II of Spain, son of the Holy Roman Emperor Charles V, would spend a fortune on sending armies of crack Spanish troops to crush the rebels. Nothing in Europe between 1517 and 1600 stood still for very long. For more than eighty years, every assumption about religious faith and political order and authority was shaken to its core.

In all this, England sat slightly apart. Its own Reformation was of a strange kind. Not provoked by a popular movement, it was Henry VIII – emphatically no Protestant but rather a highly idiosyncratic kind of Catholic – who for reasons of politics, dynastic statecraft and raw ego broke away in the 1530s from the Church of Rome. With the exception of the years between 1553 and 1558 (the reign of Henry's older daughter, the Catholic Mary I), the England ruled by his son Edward VI and younger daughter Elizabeth I was a Protestant state whose monarch was the spiritual leader of his or her people. Queen Elizabeth's advisers believed that England was a model kingdom and a beacon of hope in a continent soaked in the blood of martyrdom and persecution. To Catholic Europe, however, Tudor England was a pariah state, isolated and embattled; Philip II of Spain in particular thought England's heresy an abomination. A plausible counterfactual history of the later sixteenth century might comfortably imagine Elizabeth I's Protestant England by 1600 crushed and beaten out of existence. Instead, it clung on to survival.

London was not insulated from the storms battering Europe in the later sixteenth century. True, in so many ways Londoners were fortunate. They enjoyed a civil peace that in 1572 Parisians could only yearn for: in that year Catholics in Paris massacred thousands of their Protestant neighbours. Yet in their own way Elizabethan Londoners felt the challenges of the age. They wrestled with domestic and foreign immigration, a fact of life over decades as thousands of displaced refugees and émigrés made new lives for themselves in the city. Ordinary Londoners had to come to terms with outsiders who threatened their livelihoods. At times the city crackled with hostility and threatened violence. Equally, London had in the sixteenth century an impressive ability to absorb new arrivals into its social fabric.

London's merchants had no choice but to trade with a Europe where little seemed truly stable. Over the decades they became used to having their goods and ships seized in diplomatic spats between monarchs, or being denied access to the ports of the Low Countries by Spanish military blockades and diplomatic embargoes. With English sailors and troops fighting Spain at sea and on land in the Low Countries in the 1580s and 1590s, they learned to adapt to war conditions, lending money to a royal exchequer squeezed almost to exhaustion. Merchants thought about money in new ways, shrugging off centuries of church teaching about the evils of usury, pragmatically embracing the benefits of interest. They began to look for new markets and opportunities. In part prodded by circumstances beyond their control, they went very much further afield than western Europe, helped by geographers and navigators who were convinced that it was possible to sail vast distances and build new trading links, emulating – perhaps even surpassing – the achievements of Portugal and Spain. Odd though it may seem in a book on London to write at length about voyages to Asia and Russia, America and the East Indies, it would be impossible to understand what made the city's mercantile elite tick without taking in the whole globe. And it just so happened that in this formative time in London's history the businesses of merchants and the policy interests of the monarch's advisers meshed: this book shows how effortlessly money and power can sit together. Without looking closely at what was going on in Elizabethan London, we would struggle to understand how a global trading organization like the East India Company, which in later centuries built an empire, came into being. If the world helped to reshape London, then London helped in turn to change the world.

This is an ambitious book; there is, I hope, no other quite like it in terms of approach and method. Certainly there are already plenty of books about London. Some tell the city's story in a vast historical sweep of two millennia. Others, impressive models of close scholarship, explore London's government, its merchant elite and trade guilds, its archaeology, its demography, its religious reformation, its print culture, its architecture and its literary life. Though much of the academic substructure of *London's Triumph* is buried away in my notes and references, I should say at the beginning how acutely conscious I am of just what I owe to scholars who have devoted their careers to these specialist fields of study.

My wish was to do something different, pushing forward the subject (and also pushing myself) by trying to capture London's life in three dimensions: to explore the city and its buildings, certainly, but to look above all at its people, trying to make out a little of the texture of their lives. I give as much importance to woodcuts, fabrics, letters and gravestones as I do to portraits, letters, plays and poems, sermons and books of travel adventure. All of these sources help to bring back to life, imaginatively, Elizabethan Londoners. Exploration and encounter are two words that occur and recur. This book is in part about how people come to terms with a world changing all around them. For Londoners of the sixteenth and early seventeenth centuries those changes – physical and material, intellectual and imaginative – were real, and there was no escape from them.

At the beginning we have to take into account what was lost in the Great Fire of London. Most of the buildings and places I describe were reduced to ashes in 1666, when most of the Tudor city was razed. We rely for our knowledge of sixteenth-century London on archaeology and those books, papers, maps and pictures that did survive the fire, and have since survived wartime bombs and the gradual erosions of time. There is still so much to work with, and it is striking how far we can bring the Tudor city into light and focus. There is all the difference between the simple woodcut of London's church spires from a medieval chronicle and the way we can use later plans, sketches, engravings and surveys to explore every nook and cranny of the Elizabethan city. That city developed a sense and understanding of itself; it is as though Londoners and others came to recognize the vastness and substance of everything around them, and set about recording London in new ways – here, for example, the drama of the Elizabethan playhouses gives us the sights, sounds, colours, fashions, pastimes and manners of a city developing a new and arresting cultural self-confidence.

Some of the greatest names of Elizabethan history, like Sir Walter Ralegh, Sir Francis Drake or even Queen Elizabeth I herself, are purposely on the margins of this book. I have given much more space to characters who otherwise lurk too much in the shadows of the familiar. Some are remarkable and deserve to be better known, like the younger Richard Hakluyt, geographer and theorist of colonial plantation, whose magnum opus, *The principal navigations*, is one of the glories of English prose. Another is the explorer and merchant Anthony Jenkinson, who carried the name of London and the interests of its trade to Russia, Persia and beyond. Sir Thomas Smythe, who bridged the sixteenth and seventeenth centuries, was the consummate mercantile bureaucrat whose skills gave shape to English trade and plantations in the East Indies and America. Other characters are less spectacular; and yet they made up the complex weave of

London's life, whether they were workaday merchants trading with Antwerp, ordinary Londoners worshipping in their parish churches, foreign immigrants who came to the city to find safety and work, angry young apprentices kicking against authority, or preachers calling Londoners to repentance. This book spends more time on the streets of London and with its merchants abroad than it does walking the corridors of power at the Elizabethan court, and deliberately so.

People have helped me to bring something of Tudor London to life. Indeed, it is impossible in its story not to be struck by the sheer cumulative weight of human life, energy and experience, the rich variety of community, the sheer force applied to far parts of the globe, all in one city.

Author's Note

Dates are given according to the Old Style Julian calendar. Though Elizabethans exchanged New Year gifts on 1 January each year, the calendar year began in Europe on the Annunciation of the Blessed Virgin Mary or Lady Day (i.e. 25 March). Throughout the book I have adjusted all dates to a calendar year that begins, as ours does, on 1 January.

Money is given in its pre-decimal form in use until 1971. There are 12 pence in a shilling (modern 5p or US 6 cents) and 20 shillings in a pound (£1 or US$ 1.30). Given the effects of inflation, currency devaluations and so on, modern equivalents for sums of money in the sixteenth century are practically impossible to calculate. A very rough estimate may be obtained by multiplying all the numbers by a thousand.

For a sense of the relative values of amounts of money, readers might like to bear in mind some of the following prices and wages in Tudor and Jacobean London. In 1506 a quart (two pints) of red wine cost 3 pence and a kilderkin (a cask containing between 16 and 18 gallons) of high quality ale 2 shillings. In the 1550s the price of a boat ride across the Thames between Westminster and Lambeth was a penny; a gentleman's haircut 8 pence; a loin of veal 1 shilling; a dozen rabbits for the table 4 shillings and 4 pence; and a hogshead (63 gallons) of claret 40 shillings. By 1610 a London 'ordinary' (a fixed price meal) cost 12 pence, for which the diner could eat goose, woodcock, stewed mutton and a dessert of fruit and cheese. The day wage of a London labourer in 1563 was 9 pence (or 5 pence if he was also given food and drink) and the same in 1588. In those years a carpenter employed by one of the city companies earned 4 shillings a week, a brewer likewise employed £10 a year and a shoemaker and a fletcher £4 a year.

Act, scene or line references to drama and poetry are taken from the following editions: *The dramatic works of Thomas Dekker*, ed. F. Bowers, 4 vols (Cambridge, 1953–61); *The Cambridge edition of the works of Ben Jonson*, ed. David Bevington, Martin Butler and Ian Donaldson, 7 vols (Cambridge, 2012); *Thomas Middleton: the collected works*, ed. Gary Taylor and John Lavagnino (Oxford, 2007); and *The Riverside Shakespeare*, ed. G. Blakemore Evans (Boston, MA, 1974). Reference to other works, literary and otherwise, will be found in the Notes at the end of the book.

The map illustrations in the book are taken from Edward Wright's world map of 1599 (sometimes known as the Wright-Molyneux or Hakluyt-Molyneux map) in the first volume of the second edition of Richard Hakluyt, *Principal navigations, voiages, traffiques and discoveries of the English nation*, 3 vols (London, 1598–1600) in the Special Collections of the Universiteitsbibliotheek in Leiden (shelf-mark (KL) 1370 C 10): 'Thou hast here (gentle reader) a true hydrographical description of so much of the world as hath beene hitherto discovered, and is comme to our knowledge.'

CHAPTER ONE

A Merchant's World

In about 1533 the artist Hans Holbein the Younger made two imposing decorative murals for the hall of the London base of the German
Hanse merchants. Their headquarters on the River Thames was known
as the Steelyard, a rectangle of real estate west of London Bridge
in the parish of All Hallows the Great, a small portion of the City of
London in the preciously guarded jurisdiction of its lord mayor and
aldermen, where the Hanse merchants were old and privileged guests.
The *Stahlhof* was a working base, with a great half-timber-framed
warehouse on the waterfront and a crane on Easterlings quay used to
load and unload boats. An imposing tower crowned by a blue cupola
looked out over the neighbouring wharves and jetties of Queenhithe,
Three Cranes and Coldharbour. Like so much else in London, the
Steelyard was an unapologetic statement of mercantile power and
money.

Holbein, a fellow German, knew some of the Hanse merchants
very well. He painted their portraits – young men held for us vividly
in a moment of time: alert, confident and self-assured in their chambers and counting houses, expensively dressed and well used to good
food and wine. In the murals he made for the Great Hall, by contrast, Holbein's technique and purpose were very different. Large
and striking, the murals were painted on fine linen cloth with a blue
background heightened with gold. They were allegorical – big, bold
and morally challenging. One had Poverty personified as a woman
raggedly dressed sitting in a rickety cart, leading a rabble of artisans,

labourers and vagabonds. The second showed Plutus, the Roman god of riches, elderly and stooped, enthroned in a chariot piled high with treasure.

At first glance Plutus's procession looked like a great celebration of wealth and material comfort. It was instead a cheerless march of the doomed, for trudging beside Plutus, burdened by their riches, were the unhappy figures of Cleopatra, Croesus, Midas and Tantalus, with Fortune, her eyes bandaged, blindly throwing out gold pieces. Hovering above was Nemesis the avenger, ready to chastise those whose hubris offended the gods. Holbein presented for his merchant clients a hopeless scene, as stark in its way as those medieval carvings of devils swallowing down into Hell unrepentant sinners. Behind this ambitious allegory was the uncompromising judgement of God. Riches, it was clear, were as much a way to Hell as they were to worldly success. Like the priest and the preacher, Holbein knew that the sin always catches up with the sinner.

The murals had inscriptions. One read: 'Gold is the father of blandishment and the author of sorrow/Whoever lacks it dies, whoever keeps it, fears it.' The other: 'He who is rich . . . fears hourly that the inconstant wheel of fortune may turn.'

Holbein's allegory had a double title. The first was *The Triumph of Poverty*, the second *The Triumph of Riches*.[1]

* * *

We begin not very far away from the Steelyard, a little way north of the wharves and landing steps of the River Thames and across the close tangle of the city's streets, in the parish church of St Antholin, with a man who knew it all so well and was buried there in the early months of the year 1500. Both are markers: St Antholin's of a pre-Reformation London proud of its churches and monasteries, a modest city in European terms; and our parishioner as a sort of merchant Everyman, typical of his kind in a city on the eve of a new century. In this book such markers are important – for London, and for the lives of the people who lived there, changed in the following twelve decades almost beyond recognition.

St Antholin's was a church like so many others in the city, neat and small, with a compact tower and some striking stained glass, sitting humbly yet solidly in its plot on Budge Row. Founded in the twelfth century, a generous lord mayor paid for it to be rebuilt in about 1400, and over the generations dozens of other rich benefactors and parishioners had shaped the church, repaired its fabric, added new chapels, beautified it with glass, and filled it with their tombs and memorial brasses. Somehow only an old church can capture in the present moment that deep sense of time past.

On a day early in 1500 the corpse of a London merchant of middle age was lowered into a grave in the church's chapel of St Anne. There was nothing unusual about this; the same kind of burial took place every week across the city, as it had in the decades that, by the compound interest of time, had accumulated into centuries. And there was nothing so unusual about the merchant, for there were hundreds just like him in London. Successful and respected, well up the rungs of the ladder of city responsibility, his name was Thomas Wyndout.

Death was not a surprise for Wyndout. He had prepared for eternity much as he operated his business trading in fine textiles – with care and thought. He had made his will in good time, in July 1499, the fourteenth year of the reign of the Tudor king Henry VII, when John Percyvale was London's mayor and Stephen Jenyns and Thomas Bradbury were its sheriffs. Wyndout made all the provisions he felt were necessary for the well-being of his family and posterity and for his kinsmen and friends. As a pious Catholic, he made a solemn reckoning with God, recommending himself to Our Lady St Mary and all the holy company of heaven in the hope and expectation of eternal life.[2]

Wyndout was a freeman of the Mercers' Company and a citizen of London. The London citizenry in the sixteenth century was an exclusive club. Only a fraction of the city's inhabitants belonged to it, and those who did – the privileged few – had a voice in the government of their city that was denied to so many other Londoners. The route to citizenship was freedom of a city livery company, which brought both seniority and respectability. These livery companies were the bodies that organized and supervised the various trades of London, companies like the clothworkers, drapers, goldsmiths, skinners, tallow chandlers, vintners, butchers and so on. Each had a clear hierarchy, with wardens, masters and other officers, a governing court that regulated the activities of members and disciplined those who broke a company's rules and laws, a hall for common feasting (the social life of any company was hugely important) and often a chapel for worship. Livery companies built almshouses and handed out charity, and sometimes they built and founded schools. They formed the tough sinews of London's body politic: they stood for money and power. Company and city government fused together, as London's sheriffs, aldermen and lord mayors were all senior company men, and there was no other route to city influence. Power in Tudor England rested for the most part in the hands of a landed elite of Crown, nobility, gentry and Church, but in London the key to influence and high office was mercantile success.

Wyndout enjoyed the prestige of belonging to the Mercers' Company. With its origins in the twelfth century, out of all the London companies it was pre-eminent, a fact that becomes clear when we look at the profile of London's top job. Twenty-two mayors held office between 1480 and 1500. One was a senior man in the Fishmongers' Company, one was a haberdasher, one a skinner, one a merchant taylor, two were goldsmiths, two were grocers, and three were drapers. Eight were mercers, and one of those mayors, Henry Colet (a man Thomas Wyndout knew very well), served twice.[3]

Wyndout ran his business from Cheapside, the greatest mercantile thoroughfare of London, the showcase and window display of a vibrant trading city. Lying in the shadow of St Paul's Cathedral, Cheapside bustled with the shops and stalls of haberdashers selling their caps, hats, threads, tapes and ribbons, and mercers their cloths and luxury fabrics just in from Antwerp. Close by was the headquarters of the Mercers' Company in the hospital of St Thomas of Acon (or Acre). Centuries earlier, this had been the base of the Knights of St Thomas of Acre, a semi-religious military order similar to the Knights Templar (hence the word 'hospital', from 'hospitaller', a monk under military discipline fighting for Christianity). St Thomas of Acon was further imprinted with special spiritual significance, for on the same site in 1120 Thomas Becket had been born, the martyr archbishop and saint, known for centuries as 'lux Londoniarum', 'the light of the Londoners'.[4]

St Antholin's church and St Thomas of Acon were two places in London of enormous significance for Thomas Wyndout. In the first he took the Christian sacraments, in the second he ate and drank with his fellow mercers, and sat too in the company's court. Faith and business were hard at times to tell apart, something true also of Thomas's responsibilities as a citizen. Here a third site in London, not far away from Cheapside, stood out in Wyndout's life. This was the Guildhall, which for Thomas was a familiar walk from St Antholin's to St Laurence Lane and Catte Street, where the gate to Guildhall Close was tucked in tight against the eastern wall of the church of St Lawrence Jewry.

The whole of London was governed from Guildhall. Decisions that affected every aspect of life in the city were made in a great pile of fifteenth-century Gothic architecture built self-consciously and deliberately as a statement of both London's wealth and its chartered rights to independent self-government. Guildhall was a splendid maze of halls, courtrooms, undercrofts, a chapel and a library. Throngs of people walked through its beautifully carved porch to attend courts whose sometimes mysterious names spoke of London's long and rich history: the court of the mayor, the court of the aldermen, the court of husting, the court of orphans, the court of the sheriffs, the courts of hallmoot and wardmoot, and the court of requests, also known as the court of conscience. This was very much Thomas Wyndout's world, for he was one of the two city sheriffs (for the year 1497–8) and in the last months of his life alderman for Cripplegate, one of London's twenty-six electoral wards. As alderman he would have worn a striking gown of scarlet.

* * *

Like so many of the Tudor city's merchants, Thomas Wyndout was a Londoner by adoption, not by birth: he was a native of Hertfordshire. His parents were buried in the small village of Buntingford on Ermine Street, the old Roman road that years before had taken their son south to London.

Sixteenth-century London was a city of immigrants: some lucky, some, as we shall see, much less fortunate. The lucky ones were boys who had the stamina to serve out the better part of a decade in a demanding apprenticeship before settling themselves in their own businesses. Young Thomas was lucky that his master was the mercer Henry Colet, an influential man in the company and later a lord mayor.

A merchant's career went through a number of typical phases. First there was apprenticeship, the success of which rested on the relationship between apprentice and master. An apprentice, usually a teenager, was a member of his master's household – really a member of his extended family – and Colet's family was a very large one. We have to assume, given his later success, that Thomas's years with Colet gave him a superb entrée to city life.

A second phase was freedom of the company. This was probably as challenging as apprenticeship. The young merchant needed the right kind of sponsorship and advice (here again there was no better master than Colet), as well as enough money to start trading. Any merchant, as a pragmatic man of the world, was on the lookout for a wife, ideally the daughter of a rich mercantile family, who would bring to the marriage a large dowry, or maybe a widow whose former husband's fortune (though not straightforwardly hers) could be used imaginatively by a new spouse. Sometime after 1480 Thomas Wyndout married Katherine, the daughter of Thomas Norlande, a London grocer, an alderman and a former sheriff. With Henry Colet's support, the connections of Katherine's family and a growing constituency of influential friends in the tiny world of the London mercery trade, Thomas Wyndout was set up for life.

But that was not how it had looked in January 1480, when Wyndout's career had hung in the balance, and he was brought before the court of the Mercers' Company accused of a business agreement that looked to outsiders highly suspicious and even criminal in nature. More than this, the accusation even suggested that Thomas, then still single, had designs on a woman already married to a senior mercer. Disciplined by his betters, Thomas Wyndout learned a hard lesson.

Thanks to the official paperwork of the Mercers' Company, the story of Wyndout's indiscretion was put on record. Whether it was fully told is not clear: there is just a sense that some of the awkward details were fudged for the archive. What we know, however, is this. In 1478 Wyndout owed a large sum of money to a fellow London mercer called John Llewelyn for some cloth that he had bought. In Antwerp in

September the two men had drawn up a contract for the repayment to Llewelyn of the 540 Flemish pounds borrowed. Here was the odd twist of the agreement: Wyndout would pay the money back 'at the time that I, the said Thomas Wyndout, mercer, be wedded unto the wife of Thomas Shelley, mercer of London'. When they were married, Wyndout bound himself and all his goods to pay to Llewelyn the sum in full.[5]

It was a deeply peculiar contract. It was worrying, too, for it had the whiff of a conspiracy. How, after all, would Wyndout be able to marry Mistress Shelley without getting her husband out of the way first? Probably through Master Shelley's information, the government of King Edward IV got wind of the agreement. Over a year later, in December 1479, the Mercers' Company received a stiff letter from the king. This looked like a murder plot: the bargain could not be kept 'but upon assurance' of Thomas Shelley's demise, 'Whereby it may appear evidently that the said bargainers fully conspired and imagined his said death'. Thanks to the intervention of Shelley himself, the king allowed the Mercers' Company to examine the matter and punish the offenders. But royal officials let the company know that if it did not act in 'an offence right pernicious' royal justice most certainly would.[6]

The mercers' court heard the case in February 1480, determining the facts of the 'divers controversies, stirs, debates and demands of late had and sprung' between Shelley and Wyndout. Llewelyn seems to have played no part in the hearing: at contention was Shelley against Wyndout. Wyndout was very lucky. The court decided that the bargain had been made out of great 'simpleness'. It was a word that the senior officers of the company had chosen with great care: it suggested naivety, not malice. For Thomas it must have been an excruciating experience. One of the presiding mercers was his former master Henry Colet, another was Thomas Shelley himself. Wyndout was ordered by the court to go down on his knees before Master and Mistress Shelley to ask their forgiveness, and he was fined the then huge sum of £40, £30 of which went in damages to Shelley and the remaining £10 to the company's coffers. Here was decisive disciplinary action – and no wonder, given the seriousness of the allegation.[7]

Following this thoroughly sobering episode, Thomas Wyndout's counting house must have been emptier than it had been before the court's judgment, though probably worse must have been having a private indiscretion made the public business of his company. In mercantile London tongues wagged freely and easily.

So far as we can tell, Thomas Wyndout never again put a foot wrong. He and Katherine had a son, Bartholomew, and a daughter, Joan. In the 1480s and 1490s his business grew and diversified. He traded in luxury fabrics, even supplying the royal household with textiles; seven yards of Wyndout's black velvet were used to make a short gown for Henry VII. He exported fleeces and wool into the Mediterranean and imported wine from France. He was ambitious for office and government. Friends and partners in business sponsored his election as alderman, just as during his year as sheriff Wyndout had supported them.[8] In this tiny world of money and influence, merchants knew as much about cooperation as they did competition.

When he made his will in the summer of 1499, Thomas Wyndout's career in city government had just taken off. Ahead of him might have been years of office – perhaps he even aspired to be Lord Mayor. As it was, he had at best months in the court of aldermen. And yet he was a success: his business interests flourished; he knew rich and powerful men whom he counted as allies and friends. Wyndout was international in outlook, yet he was rooted firmly in London. He was one of the fortunate and established: a mercer, a citizen, a sheriff, an alderman, elected to the House of Commons for London in 1497. Trade, family, friendships: in mercantile London in 1500 – as in 1600 also – it was impossible to disentangle the three strands of life and career so closely interwoven.

Saturating Thomas Wyndout's world was a late medieval Catholic Christianity that marked out in long-established ritual the rhythms of life and death. In a city of tens of thousands of people jammed together in urban congestion, existence was precarious and uncertain: faith, by contrast, was reassuringly fixed in belief and practice. Even over the busy, hectic and jostling world of the city there hung the promise of the peace of heaven. Wyndout needed to attend to his soul just as much as any other Tudor Londoner.

He wanted to be buried in the thirteenth-century chapel of St Anne in St Antholin's church. It was all prepared: in 1499 a blank stone was waiting there for the appropriate inscription. In so many ways, the church contained Wyndout's London life. In its stained glass he saw Henry Colet and Colet's sons and daughters, Thomas's first family in the city.[9] His own family worshipped there, surrounded by the memorials of men just like him. And he knew that in St Anne's chapel his corpse would lie until the day of his bodily resurrection.

Tudor Londoners could not afford to take life for granted. They were fond of memento mori – so much in the city reminded them of their own mortality. They lived under God's scrutiny and they prepared for heaven. The stone tombs and brass plaques that Thomas, Katherine, Bartholomew and Joan saw in St Antholin's week in and week out both celebrated the material success of the parish's merchant benefactors and reminded the living that life was fleeting and temporary. On his memorial, Thomas Knowles, the lord mayor who had rebuilt the church, was celebrated in rhyme: 'Here lieth graven under this stone/Thomas Knowles both flesh and bone'. 'Such as I am, such shall you be', said the tomb of a fifteenth-century grocer. Even more uncompromising are the words of another inscription:

> Example by him ye may see
> That this world is but vanity:
> For whether he be small or great,
> All shall turn to worms' meat.

There was no escape from death even for the greatest and the richest of the city: no one was spared the judgement of God.[10]

When the end came for Thomas Wyndout, he was buried in St Anne's chapel to the light of eight torches and four tapers. We can imagine St Antholin's on that day: incense hanging heavily on the air, the familiar Latin liturgy, the lights burning at the graveside and on the altars of other chantry chapels. It was a city event, the church full of London's worthies from the livery companies and government, aldermen in gowns of violet, with the sword-bearer in black processing before the Lord Mayor. For the London elite, strict protocol and long tradition meant everything. The torches at Thomas's grave marked his journey from this world to the next; they were symbolic of memory and obligation – for Wyndout himself and for those members of his family who had lived and died before him. In his will he bequeathed torches and tapers to the church in Buntingford where his father and mother were buried.[11]

Wyndout asked his executors to commission a priest to sing at his burial the office of the dead 'with other orisons accustomed . . . and mass of requiem' for his soul. He left money to pay for nearly 400 requiem masses for the souls of his father and mother and instructed his executors to find a 'good honest priest' to pray for him, his parents and all Christian souls for a period of twenty years. Charity was essential for a Catholic Londoner of Wyndout's generation, and for a Protestant a century later too, though the emphases were different. For Wyndout, Christian generosity would help to ease his way through a purgatory that Protestants later did away with.

Wyndout's charitable bequests show the rich patterning of institutional life in London, as well as all the obligations to others that men of substance felt they needed to make. It was a kind of spiritual quid pro quo. Religious houses and churches were high on his list of beneficiaries. Thomas gave money to the Carthusian priory at the London Charterhouse near Smithfield, to the Charterhouse at Richmond, to the high altar of St Antholin's, and to the mercers' chapel in St Thomas of Acon. In the same spirit of Christian duty and civic obligation, he left money for the repair of the city's roads, for its poor, for its prisoners, for scholars in Oxford and Cambridge, and for the marriages of poor maidens, expecting their prayers in return for his charity.

In preparing for death, Wyndout looked above all to his family: to the security of his wife Katherine, to their children, and to his servants. He appointed as executors and overseers of his will and estate seasoned and experienced men. They were men of his own kind, each one a freeman and citizen of London, each a member of a powerful and privileged livery company. Some were his friends and partners in business, heavyweights in the city; others former servants, loyal to the end.[12]

Thomas Wyndout's obligations were manifold: to God, to family, to the Mercers' Company, to his fellow Londoners. They found expression in the ordering of his affairs and in charity. The passage of a life was part of an inextinguishable human continuity, something Wyndout articulated most powerfully when he wrote in his will of his family and inheritance, and of 'my fellowship of the Mercery of London'. Fellowship was belonging.

To Thomas Wyndout, the Mercers' Company was more than just a club or a trade guild: for him (and for others) it was a way of life bound by long tradition – something instinctive to him, part of his being. This is why he wanted to make a gift to the company of a fine cup in silver gilt, eventually presented, with great ceremony, by his executors to the company's wardens in 1503. It was a celebration of the mercers' past and present. And it was something, too, for the future, a reminder of Wyndout in the years to come. Friends remembered him in prayers to be said annually in the mercers' chapel, and there was more to this than good form or routine. When in 1506 the company's priests found it difficult to squeeze Thomas's memorial prayers into a busy chapel schedule, his widow Katherine went to the wardens to suggest a neat solution, and they were moved instead to the feast of St Katherine – simply and touchingly because that was her own name.[13]

Katherine Wyndout lived a quarter of a century beyond Thomas's death. Fairly quickly she remarried. Her new husband was Sir Richard Haddon, a widower himself, and one of the powers of the city: a sheriff and an alderman like Thomas, in 1506–7 lord mayor, and a senior official of the Mercers' Company. By his first wife Sir Richard was a brother-in-law of Wyndout's great friend and former business partner, the goldsmith John Shaa – a single but far from unusual example of how intricately interwoven were ties of friendship, business, blood and marriage for families like the Wyndouts and Haddons and very many others like them.[14]

The women of mercantile London helped to bind together the city's elite. Marrying, having children, seeing to the welfare of their sons and daughters and their families, the women are often in the background and taken for granted. But they are most certainly there, sometimes in the precarious conditions of a marriage, where their value might be measured by a dowry, or sometimes as widows. Remarriage was common for younger widows with family and a dowry. Marriage was an efficient and necessary way of moving capital between families and businesses. In making their wills and testaments, husbands often made sure that their wives were set up securely for the rest of their lives with a home and income, while upholding the principle of patrilineal succession. Sons inherited houses, money and businesses; daughters helped to build mercantile dynasties.

It is hard not to be impressed by Dame Katherine Haddon. She was scrupulous in honouring both of her husbands. For the sake of Thomas's soul, she went, as we have seen, to the Mercers' Company in 1506, and when Sir Richard Haddon died in 1517, she maintained his prayers and charities. For his part, Haddon never avoided his duties to Katherine and her family, especially to her daughter Joan, who was also, through Joan's marriage to his son and heir William, Sir Richard's daughter-in-law. Haddon had to take urgent action against William to protect Joan in what was a painfully stormy marriage.[15]

In 1499 and 1500 Thomas Wyndout, citizen, alderman and mercer of London, had made his final reckonings. He had looked to his soul, provided for his wife and family, saluted his friends and his fellowship, and tried to ease the burdens of the poor in the hope that they would pray for him. He had prepared for Heaven, settled his affairs, and made his confession, with only the slimmest sense of what the future might hold for his children, grandchildren and great-grandchildren.

CHAPTER TWO

Londoners

Thomas Wyndout brought miraculously back to life in 1600 would have boggled at the numbers of people then living in London. About 50,000 people lived in the city he knew; that figure rose to approximately 75,000 in 1550 and somewhere in the region of 200,000 by 1600. No other urban centre in England came remotely close to that scale or pace of growth. Bristol and Norwich, jointly second in size to London, had populations of about 10,000 people in 1500 and 12,000 a century later. London was a leviathan, massive and overwhelming – and it ranked in European terms. In the middle of the sixteenth century it was the sixth largest city in Europe. By 1650 only Paris was bigger, London having overtaken major ports and commercial centres like Antwerp, Lisbon, Naples and Venice.[1]

In many ways, the city's population was merely catching up with itself after the horrors of the Black Death in the middle of the fourteenth century. That generation of Londoners had known cataclysm: of perhaps nearly 100,000 inhabitants, some 48 per cent had died of bubonic plague. The city's elite was cut down with savage speed; the poor were even more vulnerable.[2] It is a wonder that London was able to function. It took two hundred years for the city to recover itself, a recovery that began in the middle decades of the sixteenth century.

With roughly 115 male to 100 female births, there were more men than women in Tudor London, a trend further exaggerated by the high numbers of young men coming to the city to apprentice themselves to merchants. Early middle age as we know it was the beginning of a fairly brisk journey to the grave, so Thomas Wyndout's death in around his middle forties was no great surprise. Here we have to rely on the complicated mathematics of population models that, because of the nature of the records kept, work better for men than they do for women. Of all the male infants, boys and men in the city in about 1550, a fraction more than six out of ten were under the age of thirty-four years. According to this model, the proportion of men in the city aged over thirty-five shrinks quickly, and only a handful of Londoners were over the age of sixty, meaning that there were very few greybeards in the city Shakespeare knew. On the face of it, the demography of Tudor London was much more like that of a society in the developing rather than developed world in the twenty-first century.[3]

Two blunt realities stalked Londoners in the sixteenth century. One was the very high level of mortality in the city, the second its persistently low birth rate. For the seventy years between 1580 and 1650 there was fewer than one (0.87) baptism for every burial in the city, and that number is unlikely to have been higher for the years before 1580. What struck the city hardest were epidemics of disease. In 1563 plague killed 17,404 men, women and children, just over 85 per cent of all Londoners buried that year, and probably somewhere in the region of 20 per cent of the city's entire population. Though the city government could do almost nothing to stop the spread of infection, it was at least assiduous in recording the numbers of dead.[4]

All of this means, of course, that London should have shrunk and contracted. But when we look at what actually happened – the quadrupling of the population – we see at once that something very important was going on. That something was migration into the city: migration that was heavy, sustained and necessary. The city's mercantile elite had no choice but to renew itself by means of recruitment from outside London. In the 1550s, fewer than two in ten of new freemen in the city's livery companies had been born in London. The rest came from throughout England, nearly 30 per cent of them from Yorkshire, Lancashire and the other northern counties.[5] London was able to draw young men, especially, and young women from across the whole kingdom, who came to the city to change their lives. What they found when they arrived was, we can be sure, an intensity of human society on a scale beyond their experience.

Elizabethans themselves pondered the reasons for London's success, sensitive to the charge that it was massively overbearing, and that its merchants were ruining the trade of other English towns. The antiquary John Stow, the greatest Elizabethan expert on the city, summed up the case in five words: situation, estimation, service, government and benefits. Decoded, Stow meant that London was ideally placed geographically, that it had played a long and distinguished role in English history, that its reputation as a city was unparalleled, that it enjoyed excellent government, and (an argument as controversial in Stow's day as it is in ours, at least for anyone living outside London) that it benefited the whole realm.[6] It is easy to see what Stow was driving at. London was undoubtedly England's chief city, and for most of the time the king's or queen's court, from where the kingdom was ruled, was close by. Royal courts, which needed provisions, were good for business, just as courtiers, with houses near the city, had expensive tastes for fine things. London benefited, too, from the purses of the country gentlemen lodging there when they had business in the law courts of Westminster.

Most significant of all were the Thames and the merchants who used it to send out ships to the ports of mainland Europe. As formidable as the great river were the livery companies of London: they were extraordinary concentrations of money, mercantile dynasty and privilege. Together, London's merchants were a powerful constituency that could help to make up the minds of monarchs and their councils.

Londoners were used to seeing foreigners and strangers on the city's streets. Foreign merchants and financiers had long had outposts and offices in London, though it had not always been in the premier league of Europe's great trading cities. Best known are the Hanse merchants of the London Steelyard, whose league was founded in Lübeck in the fourteenth century, and whose international European trade connected London to Hanse bases in the Low Countries, the Baltic and Russia. Resident Italian merchant bankers had made loans to English medieval kings. The Pope's Head on Lombard Street, one of the great taverns of Tudor London, had its origins in the fourteenth century as a house owned by the Bardi merchants of Florence.[7] Italian ships docked on the city's quayside in the fifteenth century, bringing from the Mediterranean wines, spices, sugar and fine cloths, their crews recruited from the coast of Dalmatia, the Peloponnese and the Greek islands, as well as southern Spain.[8] Merchants from France and the Netherlands were also frequent visitors to London.

Some Londoners stood out more than others. The slaving voyages of Sir John Hawkins in the 1560s brought about 300 Africans to the city.[9] In 1588 'a man blackamore' was found dead on a street in the parish of St Olave, Hart Street, not far from the Tower of London. He was buried in its churchyard, as were two black women, Mary and Grace, who had lived in the same parish as servants to the physician and merchant Hector Nunes (or Nuñez).[10] Nunes was a Portuguese Jew by birth whose family had been forcibly converted to Christianity. He lived in London for over fifty years, practising as a doctor to the nobility at the queen's court and trading as a merchant with Spain, Portugal and Brazil.

Striking in London's sixteenth-century story (and a subject to be picked up later in this book) is the arrival in the city of thousands of Protestant refugees. Fleeing war and persecution, families from France and the Netherlands settled in London. On one level they were welcomed as fellow Protestants. On another, many Londoners were troubled by fears of competition, especially given that many of the émigrés brought skills in clothworking, metalworking, printing and brewing. The city's elite prickled at the notion of outsiders challenging the privileges of citizens. Occasionally the atmosphere of the city was heavy with violence against the strangers, as young men roamed the streets in gangs looking for a way to vent their frustrations and resentments.

This was London's diversity: French merchants, Dutch craftsmen, Italians who kept seedy bowling alleys, a handful of Africans, foreign teachers and printers, refugee doctors, promenading gentlemen, wide-eyed boys and girls from across England, rich, poor or middling – the city was a complex and sometimes volatile human patchwork made up of many thousands of individual pieces.

Most Londoners had to work hard to survive. Illustrations on maps and plans of the Tudor city show laundresses laying out clothes to dry on frames, milkmaids with pails, water-bearers with buckets and drovers with their cattle. The wharves and docks of London were always busy, with an armada of wherries, barges and rowing boats moving up, down and across the Thames. There were gun foundries at Houndsditch near the Tower and on the corner of Water Lane and Thames Street. Lime and brick kilns pumped out smoke. Windmills, built on top of rubbish tips in Finsbury Fields, ground corn. Throughout the city there were shops and buildings for dyeing, brewing, butchery and tanning, foundries for making bells and factories for making pottery.[11]

The city's merchants lived in grand townhouses built of stone, slate, timber and plaster. These often served as their business headquarters as well as family homes. Life for merchants was comfortable. They were able to furnish their chambers with tables, beds, cupboards, chests, fine carpets and tapestries and silverware.[12] Many merchants had houses and estates in the countryside outside the city. All of this was a very long way removed from those Londoners who scratched a living and found themselves in overcrowded and filthy tenements. London was both a triumph of riches and a triumph of poverty. And yet there was an equality of sorts to be found in the city's parish churches, where records were kept of the baptisms of the sons and daughters of gentlemen, merchants, serving men, carters, joiners, glaziers, wool-packers, bakers, porters, musicians, cloth-workers, smiths, chandlers, tailors, labourers and strangers – all Londoners united by a church and a font.[13]

Dress in the sixteenth century was a quick and effective way to identify and classify others. It would have been impossible to mistake a labourer or a craftsman for a freeman of a livery company. Aldermen and sheriffs wore gowns of scarlet and violet, with velvet hoods and furred capes. The codes of dress were clear – by law as much as by fashion – with sumptuary statutes setting out restrictions according to social rank, limiting to the elite the wearing of velvets, satins, damasks and furs. Merchants and their wives wore caps and long gowns often trimmed with fur, ruffs and elegantly worked gloves. The proper balance of taste and authority was neatly expressed in the merchant's suit of black: modest, discreet and unostentatious, certainly, but also very expensive given the complicated process of dyeing black cloth.[14]

By modern standards, Londoners owned very little. A London priest called John Haigh was comfortably off and in 1514 left a black gown to his mother, his horse to his brother Roger, and his best bow to a gentleman called Master Henry West. Haigh's possessions were those typically listed in the wills and testaments of the time: gowns, jackets and doublets; a bed with bolster, pillow and coverlet; blankets, sheets and hangings. Possessions like these (or the single brass pot left by a London yeoman, John Gyllyke) were precious, and in their wills testators used them to honour friendships. For those who could afford them, mourning rings with a death's head were especially popular.[15]

London in the sixteenth and early seventeenth centuries was in many ways a confederation of much smaller communities – the city's electoral wards and, of more significance to ordinary Londoners, the city's parishes.

The sense of communal life could be powerful. There were times of festival and celebration, with bonfires in the streets and the ringing of church bells. The provision of charity by the wealthy helped a deeply unequal society to cohere – it also reminded the poor of who was in charge. Feasts were important events. When John Barnaby, the rector of St Matthew's church near Cheapside, made his will in 1517, he left money for food and ale to be served at his burial service.[16] London's parish churches were expressions in stone of common belonging and the continuity of community life. They stood for ritual and routine, year in, year out: the auditing of parish plate and books, repairs to family pews, bell-ringing at funerals, provisions for the poor, the holly and ivy brought in at Christmas, the scouring out of the pissing place in the churchyard, the annual walking of the parish boundary followed by breakfast in a local tavern.

Food and drink mattered, of course, and London was full of inns, taverns and beer gardens. Some Londoners bought food cheaply from cookshops: for the poor, without the utensils, fuel or money to cook their own food, a cookshop offered hot fast food. Early Tudor Londoners could dine out on a range of meats, fish, eggs, cheese and fruit, eating salmon, oysters, herring, sprats, lamb and rabbit, and drinking good wine, ale and beer. A Venetian merchant visiting London in 1562 wrote: 'if anyone wishes to give a banquet, he orders the meal at the inn, giving the number of those invited, and they go there to eat.' The inns were clean and hospitable, and women dined out just as frequently and publicly as men. Above all the merchant was staggered by the amount of meat Londoners consumed: 'for those who cannot see it for themselves, it is almost impossible to believe that they could eat so much meat in one city alone.'[17] It was mainly beef (the Tudor staple), with some lamb and mutton and a little pork. Even elite dining was not necessarily marked by refined table manners. At a dinner given for an embassy from the Holy Roman Emperor in 1567 – a banquet of bacon and salted or pickled cows' tongues – there 'was such eating and drinking that . . . the house was marvellously bepissed and bespewed to the great shame of those banqueters'.[18]

They drank ale, beer and wine. A merchant's cellar would have stored away casks and bottles of malmsey, sack, other white and red wines and claret from France and southern Europe. Ale, made out of malt, water and yeast, was the common and traditional drink. Hopped beer came to England from the Low Countries in about 1400, distrusted for a long time because of its foreignness, but a taste happily acquired over the course of the Tudor century.[19] The Dutch were famed for both brewing and drinking beer, and it was no surprise that the city's Dutch strangers ran many of London's breweries. But if it was easy to tut at the drunkenness of foreigners, the English themselves were developing a reputation for drinking to excess. Some astute social commentators, like the dramatist Thomas Dekker, believed they saw a change in habits: 'drunkenness,' he wrote in 1606, 'which was once the Dutchman's headache, is now become the Englishman's'.[20]

The taverns and inns Londoners used were familiar parts of the city's topography: the Angel on Bishopsgate, the Bear on Basinghall Street, the Bolt and Tun on Fleet Street, the Cardinal's Hat on Lombard Street and the Mermaid on Bread Street. Supplying the taverns and inns were brewhouses like the Harts Horn in West Smithfield and the James brewhouse that made ale for the Castle, Bull and Swan taverns in Southwark.

To keep London fed was a huge effort, especially in times of harvest failure, when the city's needs trumped those of the surrounding countryside. Practically the whole of the south of England supplied the city with food, and the malt used to brew Londoners' ale came from as far away as Norfolk. Londoners shopped and traded at Stocks Market for fish and meat, Smithfield for livestock, and Leadenhall for poultry and other commodities. The city government held huge stores of wheat, barley, oats and malt on London Bridge and at Bridewell hospital just in case of emergencies, and the lord mayor monitored and sometimes fixed the prices of essential foodstuffs.[21] When there were shortages, Londoners were highly sensitive to rumours about the city authorities and private individuals hoarding grain for profit.[22] Food could easily become a highly charged political topic.

Life in the city was uncertain. Slum housing, contaminated water supplies and the physical hazards of the city meant poor health and accidents for a great many inhabitants. The number of houses and factories burning fuel in London meant that levels of sulphur dioxide in the city were about thirty times greater than those in the countryside.[23] London was dirty: as one well-travelled English diplomat wrote in the middle of the sixteenth century, it was 'such a stinking city, the filthiest of the world'.[24] Effluence was a fact of city life, particularly for the occupants of London's 'rents': in 1579, for example, only three privies served eighty-five people living on Tower Street, the occupants of tenements and others in alleys round about. Neighbourhood disagreements over cesspools and leakages were common.[25] Given that the population of the city was at this point steadily marching up to 200,000 people, Pissing Alley was not merely a colourful name, but a fact of urban life. In about 1612 Ben Jonson, embracing the poetic possibilities of London's stench, celebrated in mock-heroic verse the boat journey made by his friends up the toxic Fleet river, a tributary of the Thames that ran from Holborn to Bridewell Palace and Blackfriars. Unable to resist a pun of puns, Jonson rhymed 'A-jax' (Ajax, the hero of the Trojan war) with 'a jakes' (a flushing privy).[26]

Epidemic disease was inevitably London's regular visitor, for which Thomas Dekker and Thomas Middleton blamed the unwholesome country just outside the city walls:

> From bogs, from rank and dampish fens,
> From moorish breaths and nasty dens –
> The sun draws up contagious fumes

> Which, falling down, burst into rheums
> And thousand maladies beside,
> By which our blood grows putrefied.[27]

Elizabethans had no proper understanding of what caused disease, and it was only by long experience that the city authorities and parishes learned to isolate those infected. Plague was the city-dweller's grim familiar. In most years it claimed lives, and it was recorded by the parish clerks of St Botolph without Aldgate, one of the city's poorest parishes, as the cause of a quarter of deaths for the years between 1583 and 1599.[28] There were particularly brutal plague epidemics in 1563, 1593, 1603 and 1625.[29] In 1551, Londoners had been killed in their thousands by a sweating sickness which took its victims with terrifying speed.[30]

The statistics give a sense of the scale of deaths. But Londoners saw the human cost to their own friends and families extending out over weeks and months. The records of St Olave, Hart Street, for 1563 show normal life almost at a standstill. In September and October of that year, five babies were baptized in the parish church and one or two couples married. But fifty parishioners were buried in September alone, and October was worse, with burials nearly every day and seventeen in a single week.[31]

Whatever killed their families, friends, servants and neighbours, for all Londoners the words of burial service in the Book of Common Prayer were tangible and immediate: 'In the midst of life we be in death: of whom may we seek for succour but of thee, O Lord?'[32] Or as the poet Thomas Nashe wrote in 1593:

> Adieu, farewell earth's bliss!
> This world uncertain is:
> Fond are life's lustful joys,
> Death proves them all but toys.
> None from his darts can fly;
> I am sick, I must die –
> *Lord, have mercy on us!*[33]

London had a vibrant underworld of brothels, bowling alleys and gambling dens, as well as a more public life of inns, taverns and playhouses. The earliest theatres were in the suburbs north of the Thames like Shoreditch (the Theatre and the Curtain theatres), in Stepney and Whitechapel (the Red Lion and the Boar's Head) and in Clerkenwell (the Fortune). South of the Thames in Southwark were the Rose, the Swan and the Globe.

For fun, Elizabethan Londoners squeezed themselves into the playhouses of impresarios like Philip Henslowe and enjoyed the pleasures west of London Bridge on the south bank of the Thames. This was the city's entertainment strip, where they went to watch bears and bulls being baited and killed. In Elizabethan maps and views, this stretch of the Thames has a rustic look of neat gardens, ponds and grazing cattle, close to the manor house and wooded parkland of Paris Garden. Innocently bucolic, however, it was not, for in Elizabeth I's reign Paris Garden was a notorious haunt for secret agents, unscrupulous foreign ambassadors and conspiring Catholics, perfect for unobtrusive meetings and encounters thanks to a maze of passageways where the heavy planting of trees made it too dark to see anything even on an evening in high summer.[34]

For the moralists, the popular entertainments of London invited God's righteous anger. One great accident – a judgement of providence – stood out: on a Sunday in January 1583, while bear-baiting was taking place in Paris Garden, the gallery collapsed, killing and seriously injuring many. 'When the scaffold cracked (as it did once or twice) there was a cry of "Fire! Fire!", which set them in such a maze . . . so that as destitute of their wits, they stood still, and could make no shift for themselves, till the scaffold was overturned.' Killed were a baker, a clerk, the wife of a pewterer and a number of servants, some from the city and some from Southwark. The injured, with broken legs, arms and backs, were carried over London Bridge in chairs or led by friends. This was what happened, the preachers said, when Londoners profaned the Sabbath. The cry from the pulpit was a familiar one: 'O London repent'.[35]

The preacher who celebrated the disaster in Paris Garden found moral desolation all about him: 'There is gadding to all kind of gaming, and there is no tavern or alehouse, if the drink be strong, that lacketh any company: there is no dicing house, bowling alley or theatre that can be found empty.'[36] But these spectacles were as much a threat to public order as they were an offence to God. The city's government and the queen's Privy Council saw in the playhouses the double menace of lower class disorder and infection.[37]

Prostitution was very well established in the city. Tudor Southwark was famous for its 'stewhouses' or 'stews'. For centuries the attitude of city and church authorities to sex for money was a balance of high morality and pragmatic acceptance. This changed with the Reformation, and a fear of moral contagion. In 1538 the city authorities complained about 'the evil example of the gorgeous apparel of the common women of the [Southwark] stews to the great temptation of young maidens, wives and apprentices', and by the reign of Elizabeth I there was an outright ban on all forms of commercial sex.[38] Needless to say, London's brothel-keepers, pimps and procurers, prostitutes and their clients stayed as busy as ever. Most of London's prostitutes were young single women, many of whom were new arrivals in the city, facing a choice between crime and sex in order to survive. Their customers were mainly journeymen, servants, unmarried apprentices and the lower clergy. A brothel-keeper called John Shaw admitted in 1577 to dozens of clients in the London Steelyard, various servants, clothworkers, and even a son of the Lieutenant of the Tower of London.[39]

And so Londoners turned on its head the upright morality of the godly minister. Crime, poverty, gambling, drink, sex and (from the late 1570s) theatrical entertainment were deeply embedded in the life of the city, offering (doubtless to the further righteous anger of the preacher) rich material for the stage. As Ben Jonson wrote in the Prologue to his play *The Alchemist* (1610):

> Our scene is London, 'cause we would make known
>> No country's mirth is better than our own.
> No clime breeds better matter for your whore,
>> Bawd, squire [pimp], imposter, many persons more,
> Whose manners, now called humours, feed the stage
>> And which have still been subject for the rage
> Or spleen of comic writers.[40]

The 'Rome' of Jonson's play *Catiline, His Conspiracy* (1611), with its suburb-brothels, bawds and brokers (pimps), was in reality the London his audience knew.

The elite worried, as elites tend to do, about theft, robbery and begging. London's pamphleteers gave entertaining and sensationalized accounts of an organized underworld that all at once mirrored, inverted and subverted ordered society. A pamphleteer, writing under the name of Martin Mark-All, set out what he called 'the canters' dictionary', a whole criminal lexicon of theft, begging, prostitution, deception, drink, criminal law and punishment. Decent London society seemed a fragile thing indeed.[41]

If crime was understood to be subversive of property and order, so too was deliberate and contrived poverty. London had charitable hospitals to look after those who could not be held responsible for their own straitened circumstances: St Thomas's in Southwark, St Bartholomew's in Smithfield and Christ's Hospital. Bethlehem Hospital (better known as Bedlam) near Bishopsgate was a hospital for the insane. The thriftless poor of 'rioters', vagabonds and dissolute women went to Bridewell, a former royal palace next to the Fleet river, to be confined and disciplined.

Some Londoners who fell on hard times found the help of others. They were the fortunate ones. Most fell through the flimsiest of social nets, often to find themselves on the wrong side of the law. By the end of Elizabeth I's reign, parishes supported their deserving poor and maimed soldiers returning from war abroad, but they also saw to the whipping of vagabonds. Punishments for criminals were severe: the stocks and the pillory, with noses slit, ears cut and skin branded, or worse still the gallows. For many in the city, life was brutal and cheap. Walking around London was to be struck forcefully by contrasts. Poverty and wealth were obvious enough; they were neither disguised nor subtly coded. At times of greatest anxiety – in periods of food shortage, plague, war or disorder – the authorities cracked down ferociously hard on the poor. In the 1590s, out of fear of robberies and murders, vagabonds in London were put under martial law and those who evaded constables and justices were summarily executed.[42]

When Hans Holbein the Younger made his two murals for the Great Hall of the Steelyard, he had only to look out of the window of his studio to find his subjects for *The Triumph of Poverty* and *The Triumph of Riches*. Every kind of type and character walked the streets of

London, a city in which riches and poverty, success and failure, and life and death were shackled together. But the tableau was never fixed; Londoners kept living and dying.

Some historians have argued that the society of Tudor London was broadly stable and secure; others that the city was riven by deep rumblings of discontent and division. But somehow London defies neat categorization. F. Scott Fitzgerald once suggested that the test of a first-rate intelligence is the ability to hold two opposing ideas in the mind at the same time and still retain the capacity to function: perhaps then the test of a first-rate city is to harness the opposing energies of unity and division and to make out of them something irrepressibly creative. And that was sixteenth-century London, a struggling mass of people fighting to live their own lives, out of which existential struggle a city was transformed.

CHAPTER THREE

Landmarks

Tudor Londoners believed that the origins of their city lay far back in the mists of recorded history. The story retold again and again was that London had been founded eleven centuries before the birth of Christ by Brute (or Brutus), descendant of the demi-god Aeneas. Brute had called it 'Troynovant' – the New Troy – in memory and celebration of the great city of King Priam, destroyed in the Trojan wars.[1] The Brute myth was as familiar to the Elizabethan antiquary John Stow in the 1590s as it would have been to Thomas Wyndout a hundred years earlier. Stow, who knew Livy's masterful history of Rome and the story of Romulus and Remus, understood that great cities needed to be able to boast of their founding by heroes.[2]

Modern archaeology describes a less exciting, though more believable story. On the site of modern London, Neolithic stone implements and metal objects and pottery from the Bronze Age have been unearthed, and there is plenty of evidence of Iron Age settlement all along the River Thames. But it was the Romans who founded the city we know as London, soon after the invasion of the armies of the Emperor Claudius in AD 43. The Roman historian Tacitus called it Londinium, and it served first as a trading centre, then as a military barracks and eventually as a capital for the remote province of Britannia. It suffered two early disasters. In AD 60 or 61 the first Londinium was destroyed in the uprising of Boudicca and her tribe the Iceni, and seventy years after that a second London was burned to the ground. We have the tenacity of the Romans to thank that the city was not only rebuilt but also thrived.

John Stow picked up from Tacitus a few words full of significance for him and other Elizabethan citizens of London. Tacitus had described the town as 'crowded with merchants and filled with merchandise', for which Stow gave his own paraphrase: London was 'most famous for the great multitude of merchants, provision, and intercourse [trade]'.[3] Stow, the citizen son of a citizen father in trade, was quick to point to this reassuring continuity. Prosperous Elizabethan Londoners, proud of their traditions of citizenship and self-governance, embraced the idea of their ancient city of merchants.

Still, Tudor Londoners would have been amazed if they had known what lay beneath their feet. Guildhall precinct was built above the site of London's amphitheatre. There had been a grand Roman house under Lower Thames Street near Queenhithe, one of the great Tudor docks. The mysteries of the god Mithras had been performed in a temple close to the later site of the medieval church of St Stephen Walbrook. The remains of the Roman provincial governor's house were below Candlewick Street and Thames Street. The officials of the senate and people of Rome transacted their public and private business in the great forum and basilica that lay beneath Gracechurch Street between Cornhill and Fenchurch Street. A few metres below Tudor London there was a kind of shadow city, the sights of which were lost and forgotten. And when the Romans left Britain, the city was reinvented all over again, with others coming to inhabit the shell of Londinium, doubtless wondering what to make of the ruins, like the Anglo-Saxon poet: 'Splendid this rampart is, though fate destroyed it, / The city buildings fell apart, the works / Of giants crumble.'[4] Over a thousand years, settlers and conquerors made it their own and gave it new names, though all were variations on that first syllable – 'Lon' or 'Lun' – whose meaning is lost.

Yet the Roman stamp on London was so deep as in a sense to have become fixed. Where the River Thames gave Tudor London one of its two boundaries, the old Roman wall of the third century AD gave it the other. This much patched and embellished wall was far from what it once had been, neglected for generations, wrangled over by householders and the city government, and in Thomas Wyndout's day only just about defensible. But it was still very much a part of the city's identity.

The fact that sixteenth-century London extended out further than the Roman wall meant that Londoners were always using the old gates through it – Ludgate, Aldersgate, Bishopsgate and Aldgate, with the medieval additions of Cripplegate and Moorgate. In Londinium these points of entry into the town had taken major Roman roads straight to the forum, fort and basilica. Roman efficiency was lost in the congested tangle of Tudor London, though the gates still marked the ends and beginnings of the big city thoroughfares – 'the capital streets of Troynovant', as Thomas Dekker called them – like Newgate, Cheapside, Bishopsgate Street and Aldgate.[5]

London's great natural boundary was the Thames, which divided the city proper on the north bank of the river from the suburb of Southwark on the south. The course of the Thames had changed considerably in over a millennium, but the Roman and Tudor ports were in approximately the same place. The river was one of the keys to London's success as a trading centre. Wide and easily navigable – maps and views of the city show galleons sailing right up to London Bridge – it was protected from the storms of an exposed sea coast, and yet it was close enough to the sea to make it ideally situated for trade across the English Channel to France and, especially, to the Low Countries, as well as into the North Sea and on to the Baltic.

Connecting London to Southwark was London Bridge. Extending out beyond the old wall were other suburbs: Moorfields and the Barbican to the north, Smithfield and Holborn to the north-west, Fleet Street to the west, leading eventually to the Strand and the separate cityscape of Westminster. Today, even this extended London would seem tiny. Settlements that are now part of the city and its great conurbation – Paddington, Knightsbridge, Islington and Barking – were then mere villages in the country.

London's government was proud of the royal charters that allowed the lord mayor and corporation to govern the city. The city elite – of which, as alderman, Thomas Wyndout was a member – bristled at any effort to trespass on its jurisdiction. In a way, the proximity of Westminster only emphasized the privileges of London's citizens. Westminster was the preserve of royal power, with great palaces like St James's and Whitehall, and the ancient complex of Westminster Palace where the law courts sat and, when they were summoned, parliaments met. London's government prided itself on the city's loyalty to whichever monarch was on the throne. And yet London was different, set slightly apart. Its elite knew that theirs was a city of immense weight and consequence; they experienced not a moment of doubt as to their importance.

To guide us in making sense of the sights and landmarks of the Tudor city, we are lucky to have the work of a Flemish-speaking artist called Anthonis van den Wyngaerde, who in about 1544 sketched on fifteen sheets of paper a great panoramic view of London. Looking north across the Thames from his vantage point in Southwark, he saw before him a city dense and compact, with row upon row of steeply pitched roofs of shops and houses, great halls and public buildings, and a skyline jagged with dozens of towers and steeples.[6]

Wyngaerde's sketches offer the contrast of city and countryside. This is probably the greatest surprise for someone used to today's cities, where conurbations often stretch for tens of miles. Just outside London – a stone's throw from one of the most heavily populated cities in Europe – were quiet villages. Wyngaerde visited them, sketching small settlements around Bermondsey: impressionistic rural scenes formed by movements of the pen whose effect is to contrast the angularity of London with the softness of the country. There he found the trees in full leaf, animals grazing in fields and a carter driving his team of horses. He saw houses; in one or two of them ghostly figures looked out at the artist from an upstairs window. As Marcus Gheeraerts' later and glorious painting of an early Elizabethan fete in Bermondsey also shows, even the south bank of the river could feel a long way from congested London. But this was so much more an imaginative distance than a geographical one: densely packed city and countryside were separated only by a few hundred metres.

Towering above London was St Paul's Cathedral. In Wyngaerde's panorama, the cathedral's spire dominates the city: every Londoner lived in some sense in its shadow. Tudor St Paul's was as different a building from Sir Christopher Wren's baroque masterpiece as it is possible to imagine. It was huge: at nearly 600 feet in length, it was almost a third longer than the cathedral of Notre-Dame de Paris, and from transept to transept nearly twice as wide. It was indeed a shade larger than Wren's St Paul's. Wyngaerde struggled to fit so massive a building on to his paper; he had to crop the nave from eleven to five bays to fit it on his sheet. Equally, the cathedral's spire was in reality even taller than in Wyngaerde's sketches. Yet what he was able to show speaks for itself: with its flying buttresses, transepts and a huge rose window in the eastern wall, St Paul's was an ancient leviathan. Even the loss of its spire to a lightning strike in 1561 blunted its magnificence only a little.

Cavernous St Paul's was filled with chapels and altars dedicated to apostles, saints and martyrs, one of whom, Thomas Becket, had been born in the cathedral's shadow. But St Paul's was also the great social centre and meeting place of the city, and Londoners had for centuries gone there to walk, talk, beg and exchange money, activities of which the church took a very dim view. Preaching after the fire of 1561, the Bishop of Durham discerned in the destruction of the steeple God's sharp punishment for 'the profanation' of St Paul's, 'of long time heretofore abused by walking, jangling, brawling, fighting, bargaining etc'.[7] Yet for Londoners, for whom the cathedral was a kind of Roman basilica or forum, it was a hard habit to break. As incongruous as it may seem, fashionable gentlemen even used St Paul's as a kind of catwalk for the struttings and preenings so wonderfully satirized in *The Meeting of Gallants at an Ordinarie: Or, The Walkes in Powles* (1604), a work attributed to Thomas Dekker and Thomas Middleton. Here, London is a city scarred by plague and pestilence, and death throws into ironic relief the vanities of well-dressed gentlemen like Signior Shuttlecocke and Signior Ginglespur: 'But see how we have lost ourselves, Paul's is changed into gallants, and those which I saw come up in old taffeta doublets yesterday, are slipped into nine yards of satin today.'[8]

The whole site of the cathedral was more or less rectangular, bounded on its four sides by the city's streets. There was Old Change and Little Carter Lane in the east and to the south Paternoster Row. Ave Mary Lane and Creed Lane entered the cathedral's precinct (known as the Atrium) at its west end. Nearby was the Bishop of London's palace and all the administrative buildings for the cathedral, as well as the chapter house and cloister, and its various churchyards. Snug against the cathedral's south-west corner was the small parish church of St Gregory by St Paul's.

Also in the cathedral's shadow was the churchyard of St Paul's Cross, more generally and colloquially known as St Paul's Churchyard. This too was a popular city meeting place, and had been for generations. It was to Paul's Churchyard that medieval Londoners had been summoned by the bell of the Jesus Steeple to the Folkmoot, the city's early consultative assembly, but by the sixteenth century that was long gone. What endured was the pull of the churchyard as a place to walk, buy, sell, loiter and beg, as well as two other activities – to listen to sermons and buy books.

Paul's Churchyard was famous amongst other things for Paul's Cross, the octagonal pulpit from which were preached the great sermons of the day. From Paul's Cross clergy earnest about saving Londoners' souls addressed matters of faith and God and the sins of a decadent city, as well as – given the close relationship between religion and politics in Tudor England during the fraught decades of Reformation – urgent questions of national politics and the affairs of monarchs. These portentous sermons were often printed, and Londoners could buy them from the printers' and stationers' stalls and shops within earshot of the pulpit. One example was Bishop Pilkington's sermon upon the lightning strike of 1561, which was sold from William Seres's shop near the west end of the cathedral, marked out from all the other shops by the sign outside of a hedgehog.

Indeed, Paul's Cross churchyard became the bookselling centre of London. By 1620 there were many hundreds of titles to choose from on all kinds of topics. What a contrast this was from the days of Thomas Wyndout, when only a handful of pioneers had set up their workshops in the city – printers like William Caxton, Richard Pynson and the wonderfully named Wynkyn de Worde. Even by the 1550s the London book trade was transformed, with dozens of printers and stationers busy in and around the churchyard. They organized themselves into a trade body called the Stationers' Company, whose headquarters was just to the south of the cathedral.

The printers of Tudor London are the unacknowledged heroes of sixteenth-century England. Without them and the books that came off their presses we would understand only a tiny fraction of the life and culture of their times. It was a trade demanding skill and labour: imagine setting by hand the individual letters of a folio volume of 500 pages, possibly in different languages set out on the same page (English, Latin, perhaps some Greek or even Hebrew), and one has an idea of just how huge and intricate a task printing a book was. Not surprisingly, the more important printers employed large teams of highly skilled craftsmen, a fair number of whom were Dutch strangers who settled in London in the 1540s and 1550s, bringing with them experience gained in Antwerp and other towns. London's printers were craftsmen, scholars, linguists and businessmen all rolled into one.

The printers' shops, like those of other businesses, were identified by colourful signs: there was Seres' hedgehog, for example, or the mermaid, the sun, Our Lady of Pity, and the Bible. (Londoners had a highly visual mental map of all kinds of shops and residences – there were, after all, no street directories for the city, and probably no obvious signs, so topographical familiarity and memory were essential.) London's printers produced books for their readers, not for twenty-first-century scholars (something perhaps modern scholars tend to forget), and they had a canny eye for the market. In a highly competitive trade, they effectively copyrighted their productions by securing exclusive licences to print titles they had registered, naturally for a small sum of money, with the Stationers' Company. Any book too controversial might be censored and suppressed by the Bishop of London or even the monarch's Privy Council: 'Seen and allowed', words which commonly appear on the title pages of Elizabethan books, really meant something in a trade which was as heavily regulated as it was brilliantly innovative.

By 1550 it was possible for only a few pennies or shillings to pick up in Paul's Churchyard hundreds of titles on all kinds of subjects, including bibles, big chronicle histories, poetry and drama, sermons, law books and so on. Much more popular – and more ephemeral – were the cheap prints of songs and ballads, lurid tales of murder and sensational wonders of nature. Elizabethans loved a good story told with pace, colour and drama, just as they enjoyed the woodcut illustrations and images to complement the heavy black-letter gothic typeface of so many of their books. Books like these offered Londoners realms of new imaginative possibility; they spoke to a city that was beginning to encounter and make sense of the wider world. A bibliophile walking from shop to shop in Paul's Churchyard in 1620, for example, would find books as diverse as the first translation into English of Boccaccio's *Decameron*, Sir Francis Bacon's philosophical study of nature, and an account of the nurture of silk worms and mulberry trees in the English colony of Virginia.

Only a very small minority of Elizabethans could read and write, and education for most people was limited. But given the size and density of the city, few Londoners would have missed out on the news and information offered by the city's booksellers. The most important pronouncements, the city and royal proclamations, were read out loud across London, and copies of books of parliamentary statutes, bibles and martyrologies were kept – sometimes chained – in the city's parish churches.

For the lucky few, there were schools: for boys of course, and not girls, though generally boys from poor to middling families for whom the private tutors of the elite were not a possibility. Some of London's parishes paid for schools to be set up, or at least allowed schoolmasters to teach children in church porches. Sometimes a parish might support a boy at a boarding school or at university. Close to Paul's Churchyard was St Paul's School, founded in 1512 by John Colet, dean of the cathedral. One of the leading humanist scholars of his day, a friend of Thomas More and Erasmus of Rotterdam, Colet was the son of Thomas Wyndout's master Henry Colet; Thomas and John knew each other well. Other schools in or near London were Christ's Hospital, Westminster and Charterhouse, each one giving in return for a spartan life the kind of education that might prepare a boy for Cambridge or Oxford.

Catering for the education of other boys were freelance tutors in the city who taught grammar, mathematics and foreign languages – teachers like Pierre du Ploiche, a French refugee who lived on Trinity Lane near Queenhithe at the sign of the rose, or later his fellow countryman Claudius Hollyband (Claude de Sainleins), who taught for a time in a printing-shop in Paul's Churchyard and then at the sign of the golden ball. Du Ploiche published a French and English phrase-book perfectly suited to the young Londoner off on his travels abroad:

> Neverthelesse it is good to have company and lighte, especially in the nighte; you cannot tell whoo you may mete.

> *Toutesfois, il est bon d'avoir compagnie, et lumiere especiallement de nuict; vous ne scavez pas quy povez rencontrer.*[9]

For those engaged in trade, modern languages like French, Italian and the various 'Dutch' dialects of the Low Countries and Germany were essential; no European would think of speaking English. Latin was the international language of European religious debate, the universities and diplomacy, though most boys would have had at least a foundation in Latin grammar (and boys fortunate to have had a full grammar school education, like Shakespeare, would have known Latin to what we would understand as degree standard). Typically, a boy destined for trade and the mercantile life would be educated up to the age of about thirteen and then sent off to work as an apprentice to a merchant's factor (or representative) in London or Antwerp: it was an invigorating and tough vocational training in the ways of the world.

From his vantage point in Southwark, Anthonis van den Wyngaerde saw the spires and towers of over a hundred churches in London. The ringing of their bells would have been one of the defining sounds of the city.

St Lawrence Jewry and St Mary le Bow were two of these churches, both landmarks of London – the first close to Guildhall, the second on Cheapside – enjoying the patronage of wealthy parishioners and the livery companies. By contrast, Holy Trinity the Less on Knightrider Street was by 1600 in such a poor state of repair and so in danger of falling down that it was propped up with stilts.[10] Less precarious but undoubtedly modest were other little churches like All-Hallows-on-the-Wall, St Peter Le Poor and St Gregory's by St Paul's, each at some point on a scale between the inconspicuous and the anonymous, tucked away in corners of the city or built abutting far grander foundations.

London's parishes made the city a kind of federation of urban villages. Its churches offered to their parishioners the hope of God and eternity; to wealthy benefactors the opportunity for patronage, to craftsmen and artists commissions for beautiful objects of devotion, and to priests very modest livings. Over the sixteenth century the churches changed as the Reformation did away with chantry chapels, altars, stained glass and colourful wall paintings, preferring the austerity of God's true word to what reformers dismissed as Catholic idolatry: instead of altars, plain communion tables; instead of wall paintings of saints' lives, instructional texts like the Ten Commandments. To walk into a London church in 1500 and then again in 1600 was to enter the same building, but to experience a wholly different apprehension of God.

The parishes of London were a frantic patchwork of shapes dividing apparently at random streets, shops, houses and tenements, a growth over time of ancient boundaries and jurisdictions. Most of the parishes within the wall were small – and some were tiny – covering only a couple of streets and a few alleyways. Those outside the wall, like St Sepulchre-without-Newgate and St Giles-without-Cripplegate, were very much larger and tended also to be poorer.

Fixed in the spiritual life of the city for centuries were London's abbeys, priories and friaries – a strange thought, perhaps, when today we often think of the surviving ruins of monasteries tucked away in secluded spots in the countryside. Here Wyngaerde's panorama is suggestive: he drew it at a time of huge change, a few years after King Henry VIII had suppressed the monasteries. While Wyngaerde was occupied in making sense of London's fabulous cityscape, powerful and aspiring families were busy buying up former monastic properties to turn them into either grand townhouses or tenements for London's ever-growing population. Wyngaerde's bird's-eye view necessarily misses the transformation at street level, but to Londoners some old, great and familiar institutions were being broken down before their eyes by the aspirations to power of a king's government.

In 1530, a decade and a half before Wyngaerde drew London, the city's religious houses were still wealthy and powerful. In the far western corner of the walled city was the Blackfriars, London's Dominican friary founded in the thirteenth century, used on occasions for meetings of Parliament and, in 1529, for the legatine court that heard the case made by Henry VIII to annul his marriage to

Queen Katherine of Aragon. The preaching friars were also common in London: the Franciscans (or Greyfriars) near Newgate, in a complex founded in the thirteenth century and greatly enlarged in the fourteenth and fifteenth; the friars of the Holy Cross next to Tower Hill, whose house, the Crutched Friars, was founded at the very end of the thirteenth century and whose church was rebuilt in about 1520; and the Carmelites (or White Friars), part of whose church and precincts, the Austin Friars, later became London's Dutch church. Inside the city wall at Aldgate was Holy Trinity Priory; outside it at Bishopsgate was the priory and hospital of St Mary Bethlehem. Also beyond the wall was the vast Augustinian priory and hospital of St Bartholomew in Smithfield, and north of that a Carthusian monastery known as the Charterhouse. Charterhouse was founded in 1371 on the site of a plague cemetery, and over the centuries it grew ever larger, with the Carthusians adding chapels, conduits for water, cloisters, courts and cells. Thomas More knew the London Charterhouse well, and it was in this contemplative and ascetic house that he lived for three years between 1501 and 1503. Before their very visible and deliberate destruction by Henry VIII, the London Carthusians were a commanding moral presence in the city.

More or less hidden in Wyngaerde's panorama, given its angle, are London's streets, of which there were hundreds. A few of them – the big thoroughfares running north and south – we can make out from Wyngaerde's quickly sketched lines of steeply pitched roofs. The streets had apparently no order to them, seeming to make sense only on their own terms. Some of their names are striking: Ave Maria Lane and Bladder Street, Broken Wharf, Conyhope Lane and Seething Lane. These names came to be settled after centuries of changing and often erratic spelling. Seething Lane was once Sydon Lane, 'Babeloyne' (Babylon) of the late fourteenth century became London Wall, and Black Raven Alley was lost to the much duller-sounding Pope's Alley. London so often reinvented and renamed itself – it was oddly fixed and fluid at the same time.

But out of the tangle the eye begins to see some kind of pattern to the city's thoroughfares. There was a very rough rectangular arrangement to the relationship between some of the streets in the western portion of the city. Upper and Lower Thames Street, Fish Street, Knightrider Street, Candlewick Street, Catte Street and Cheapside ran broadly in parallel with the line of the River Thames, and they were intersected by roads, streets and alleyways running at an angle of more or less ninety degrees to the waterfront. Of course there were all kinds of twists and turns and weird and wonderful lines and curves in the city too; but nevertheless there is a sense – or at least a hint of a sense – of some very deeply buried notion of arrangement, like builders' Chinese whispers played over centuries. One shape that does stand out strongly is the dividing of Cheapside and the Poultry into Threadneedle Street, Cornhill and Lombard Street. This was right at the centre of the walled city, and it was here, close to the Poultry, that in the 1560s one of the greatest merchant princes of the Tudor century, Sir Thomas Gresham, built London's bourse, the Royal Exchange.

When Anthonis van den Wyngaerde positioned himself in Southwark near the end of Henry VIII's reign, he saw before him London Bridge connecting Southwark to the city proper, sitting on nineteen huge piers driven into the riverbed of the Thames. After a long history of rebuilding and repositioning, by the sixteenth century London Bridge had become a grand city street itself, within the lord mayor's jurisdiction and a symbol for citizens of their city's greatness. Piled upon it were a chapel, many houses and shops and (an amenity to boast of) a public privy. The northern end of the bridge was in the parish of St Magnus the Martyr; its southern end in the parish of St Olave in Southwark. The chapel on the bridge was dedicated to St Thomas, for centuries Thomas Becket, but from the 1530s St Thomas the Apostle: Henry VIII resented any churchman who questioned the power of a king, as Becket had done. King Henry sent men like that to the block and put their heads – Thomas More's was one – on display over the bridge's gateway.

Between the claims of God and the king was the city. And that is what London Bridge really stood for: London's power and corporate independence, its wealth and mercantile prowess, its separateness and self-government. Coming into London from Southwark, it was impossible to miss the city government's coat of arms high up on the gateway, and of course the bulk and scale of

London beyond the bridge; it was the urban profile that Wyngaerde saw in the middle 1540s – massive and complex. Leaving London for Southwark would have affected the senses in a different way, though Southwark too, with its churches, houses, bear gardens and (a few decades later) theatres, was impressive enough. But nowhere in England was quite like London, and any traveller heading south must have known that they were leaving behind them one of the great cities of Europe.

CHAPTER FOUR

In Antwerp's Shadow

To understand Tudor London fully and properly we have to take account of the pre-eminent mercantile and financial centre of Europe in whose shadow it sat for a very long time. That centre was Antwerp on the Scheldt river, a town English merchants had known for generations. We need to make sense, too, of exactly the kind of London merchant who thrived in Antwerp and who took his success and ambitions back to London. And we have a model in the career of Richard Gresham of Milk Street in the parish of St Lawrence Jewry, a London merchant prince with impeccable political connections, who was able to rise through the city establishment to become lord mayor, with great ambitions for a talented son.

Antwerp was made rich in the fifteenth century by a happy combination of Portuguese spices from the East Indies, precious metals from the mines of southern Germany, and English cloth. A nexus for global trade and an essential marketplace for the merchants of London and other English towns, Antwerp's great fairs were the biggest events in the European mercantile calendar. High finance followed on from the trading of commodities. The major bankers of Europe like the Fugger, the Welser and the Höchstetter had offices and agents in Antwerp, and with their loans they kept imprudent and ambitious governments in power and at war with one another. Art, music and printing all flourished in cosmopolitan Antwerp, which meant that merchants with full purses bought tapestries and pictures for their houses, altarpieces for their local parish churches and books for their private libraries. It was impossible to imagine English mercantile life in the fifteenth and early sixteenth centuries without Antwerp.

Antwerp's fairs were the Sinxen mart held in late spring and the Bamis mart in late August. Those at nearby Bergen-op-Zoom (a port town powerfully under Antwerp's influence) were the Passmarkt held at Easter and the Cold mart in early winter. During these fairs Antwerp's streets, squares and cloisters were full of sellers' stalls. The fairs guaranteed freedom of movement for foreign merchants, as well as an opportunity for fun and spectacle, especially dazzling for young men just out of London.[1]

Through Antwerp, English producers and merchants were able to reach the whole of Europe and beyond. In the 1530s and early 1540s fashionable lightweight woollen cloths called kerseys were bought by German merchants and sent as far as Hungary, while Italian firms from Ancona and Genoa traded them to the eastern Mediterranean. These firms used the Antwerp fairs and also operated through their own agents living in London.[2] To get an idea of Antwerp's importance as a hub of European trade, and of London's reliance upon it, we need to multiply those transactions and movements across the continent – and of course the money made from them – many hundreds of times over.

International trade in the sixteenth century was difficult, dangerous and expensive. The risk of losses through accident, weather, theft or piracy was very high. Crossing the borders of kingdoms, merchants had to negotiate Europe's various currencies. The mints of Augsburg, Frankfurt, Nuremberg, Württemberg, Salzburg and Regensburg, Prague, Ulm, Denmark, Poland, Lübeck, Switzerland, Venice, Paris, Antwerp and of course London produced hallers, guilders, shillings, groschen, marks, pounds, ducats and crowns.[3] Merchants had to be skilled in what looks to us like a chaos of coins and a nightmare of exchange. They had to know one another's languages and employ agents and factors abroad. They had to endure the vicissitudes of travel, and they had to be able to trust fellow merchants to honour the paper bills of exchange that, rather than moving around great chests of coin, did the job of carrying money to different countries. And they had to hope for stability in a Europe where international politics and internal peace rested on the often precarious treaties and alliances between the great powers of the day – the Holy Roman emperor and the potentates of his empire, the pope, the king of France, the king of Spain and the king of England. Situated close to the emperor's court at Brussels, Antwerp was particularly exposed to the shifting of great power politics.

Merchants in early sixteenth-century Europe wanted and needed peace – war and political and civil unrest upset the operation of trade and business. Merchants had an international view whose values and interests sometimes transcended those of Europe's sovereign powers struggling for supremacy and initiative. At the same time – and in contradiction – merchants were instinctively protectionist. They wanted to secure for themselves privileged conditions of trade that others did not have, especially foreign merchants. Joining with fellow traders of the same town, city, trade or nationality helped to share out the risks and dangers, and special privileges in paying reduced customs duties, for example, meant that profits were not entirely consumed by the expense of travel and carriage. For these reasons, national and city guilds and companies of merchants throughout Europe had for centuries used collaborative muscle to negotiate exclusive trading rights abroad.

In Antwerp it was the Company of Merchant Adventurers who looked out for the interests of English merchants. By the fifteenth century this powerful organization was dominated by London's mercers. The adventurers negotiated and protected the charters they had secured from successive dukes of Brabant since the late thirteenth century. These privileges inevitably nourished local grumblings and grievances, and even minor incidents could precipitate crises that called for emergency talks and renegotiations. One, for example, was the disagreement that took place at the Sinxen mart in 1457, which began with an argument over a bale of madder (a plant used for dyeing cloth) that had split during weighing. This was followed by a hot-tempered exchange of words between a young English mercer named John Sheffield and one Martin van Hove of Antwerp, in which van Hove is alleged to have used the well-known insult that the English were born with tails like devils.[4] But if beneath the surface calm of trade there simmered national rivalries and prejudices like these, there was an obvious mutual interest too, certainly between England and the Low Countries. Antwerp needed English cloth just as

English merchants owed their businesses to Antwerp, and so the merchant adventurers were a fixed feature of the Antwerp scene. From the early fifteenth century they had a permanent salaried governor living in the town, and in 1474 Antwerp gave the company a house on the Wolstraat as a mark of the 'special love and friendship' between the town and the company, a place known simply as the English House.[5]

Many of London's merchants knew Antwerp as well as they did their home city, and it would have been difficult for them not to draw comparisons between the two. Antwerp's town hall faced northwards onto its great marketplace; it was a building of the early fifteenth century with an impressive façade of niches for statues, and instinctively Londoners would have compared it to their own Guildhall, a complex of buildings in English Gothic. Grandest of all was the New Bourse, or merchants' exchange, which opened in the city in 1532. One report says that 5,000 people congregated at its sessions, 'some of whom had to stand outside halfway into the street, not to talk or to hear the news, but only to do business'.[6] Merchants in London, by contrast, met together out in the open on Lombard Street whatever the weather.

In some ways, London was not so very different from Antwerp. Both were river ports. Antwerp's population, like London's, was rising quickly: 40,000 people in around 1496, about 55,000 in 1526, and about 84,000 in 1542–3, a little way ahead of London.[7] Both places had very high levels of immigration, and the townscapes of Antwerp and London changed considerably in the early decades of the century. For any town or city, a population of such size and density offered opportunities as well as challenges: there were benefits to the sheer mass of energy of human activity, just as there were sometimes problems in having so many people jammed together in such close proximity. Antwerp was for decades pre-eminent, the great entrepôt of Europe, but that changed in the sixteenth century. London was enjoying the outstanding benefit of civil peace, while by contrast both the economy and population of Antwerp were hit very hard indeed by the war and religious turmoil of the Dutch Revolt, which began in the 1560s.

At the height of its glory Antwerp was prosperous and cultured, and that prosperity was shared widely. Art and architecture flourished.

Visiting Antwerp in 1520, the artist Albrecht Dürer praised the beautiful stonework and tower of the collegiate Church of Our Lady, the town's spiritual focus as well as the largest parish church in the Christian world, where music and lay guilds and confraternities flourished. Dürer described the procession on the Sunday after Assumption:

> the whole town of every craft and rank was assembled, each dressed in his best according to his rank. And the ranks and guilds had their signs, by which they might be known. In the intervals great costly pole-candles were borne and their long Frankish trumpets of silver. There were also in the German fashion many pipers and drummers. All the instruments were loudly and noisily blown and beaten.[8]

Several hundred artists and craftsmen worked in Antwerp, making and selling the luxury goods that London's merchants bought to take home to furnish and beautify their town and country houses: paintings, sculpture, jewellery, tapestries and stained glass. Antwerp's art market boomed when its economy did and when the merchants of Europe were doing good business.[9]

The printers and booksellers of Antwerp were also prolific. London's book trade took a long time to catch up with the scale and sophistication of Antwerp's. Between 1500 and 1540, sixty-six printers were active in the town, producing well over 2,000 titles, or 55 per cent of all the books printed in the Low Countries.[10] Paul's Churchyard was busy with activity by the 1560s partly because so many of Antwerp's exiled expert printers had settled in London. For decades, English merchants were able to read books in Antwerp that were impossible to buy in London. Works by Martin Luther were on sale in Antwerp as early as April 1518, only months after his famous protest in Wittenberg against the Catholic Church's sale of indulgences. Before London's print trade was fully developed, Antwerp's printers knew that merchants from England were a key market for new ideas and contentious debates about church and religion: Antwerp was probably the largest producer of Protestant literature in English before the 1540s.[11]

So for centuries English merchants had breathed the air of Antwerp, depended upon its markets and money, known its people, heard news and gathered information there from all over the known world, seen its sights and absorbed its rich culture. Generations of English merchant adventurers had negotiated and renegotiated charters and privileges. They had seen Antwerp in all its mercantile glory. They would see it fall too, and their own city rise.

Like other Europeans, Antwerpians loved the kind of predictions of the future that offered at least the promise of security in a challenging world. Jaspar Laet's 'prognostication' for Brabant and Antwerp in 1520, the year of Albrecht Dürer's visit, was a skilful and judicious blend of likely challenges and predictable happenings. The duchy of Brabant, he said, would do well, 'peradventure a little dissension may arise there'. It would experience sickness, but no pestilence – though (to cover all eventualities) perhaps there would be just a little pestilence in March, July or August. Moisture or rain might cause corruption in some places. There would be no war in the duchy, 'but rather peace by reasons of astrology'. The noble town of Antwerp would behave itself wisely, profiting in 'lucre and substance'.[12]

It was Richard Pynson of London who printed the *Prognostication*, Laet's readers being those hundreds of merchants in the city who traded with Brabant and Antwerp. Though men of the world, merchants were as nervous as anyone else of the operations of the heavens. Only a fool ignored news and intelligence from whatever sources it came – and for a very good reason. International trade was profoundly uncertain; fortunes made could quickly be lost. Any number of things might make economic life in Antwerp and elsewhere deeply uncomfortable: wobbles in currency exchange, the debasement of a kingdom's coinage, defaults on loans and national bankruptcies, wars, rebellions and uprisings, and the making and breaking of international treaties.

Tit for tat between major powers was fairly common. In 1545 the Emperor Charles V, in one of his tussles with Henry VIII, seized English goods and shipping and arrested English merchants. In Antwerp at the time was Stephen Vaughan, the king's financial agent and go-between with brokers in arranging bankers' loans for Henry. Vaughan was having lunch with the governor of the merchant adventurers at the English House when an officer of the emperor marched in and wanted to know what and who they were. 'We answered "Englishmen",' Vaughan reported, to which the officer had replied, 'I arrest every one of you by commandment of the emperor'. Nothing was to be removed from the English House, and throughout Antwerp merchants' counting houses were sealed up. Before long the Antwerp exchange was in a panic and business on the New Bourse came to a standstill.[13] A single order from the Holy Roman emperor had managed to paralyse the financial centre of Europe.

Merchants always operated in the knowledge that politics between princes could disrupt or even ruin their businesses. This was a fact of mercantile life. The arrest of the English merchants in Antwerp in January 1545 took three months of hard negotiations in Brussels to resolve. But if kings and emperors could push around the merchants, the merchants – or, at any rate, those of them who lent money as well as trading in commodities – exercised their own kind of power. Financial agents like Vaughan worked to negotiate loans with the great banking houses, and the bankers set the terms. The irony is that the emperor who brought the Antwerp exchange to a standstill in 1545 was the same Charles V whose imperial crown had more or less been bought for him with Fugger loans thirty years before. Probably the notion that any state was absolutely sovereign was really a myth: each, the greater as well as the smaller, depended upon inescapable financial interests. Kings and emperors dressed up in armour, led armies and made treaties – but it was banking houses like the Fugger and the Welser that in effect paid those armies and kept kings and emperors in the business of looking and sounding magnificent.

For the prudent merchant and banker, reliable, good intelligence about what was going on was everything. Information gathered from throughout Europe was its own kind of currency, a fact shown brilliantly by the famous newsletters of the Fugger.[14] Antwerp, as well as being a powerhouse of money, was also a processor of intelligence: trade, finance and knowledge constituted power, and they were impossible to separate from one another. Antwerp was well known as a centre of rumour and speculation. Only a few hours' ride from Brussels, merchants brought news to the exchange and took it away with them. In 1553, for example, it was 'reported for a truth and many wagers laid' in Antwerp that King Edward VI of England was dead, a rumour with apparent substance that was quickly relayed to the imperial court in Brussels.[15]

The experienced politician and the canny merchant saw at once the mutual good they could do for each other. Where the merchant provided information, the politician offered protection. The best merchants were skilled at telling powerful men what they needed to know. One such merchant was the Londoner William Lok, who sent to Henry VIII's minister Thomas Cromwell detailed political, commercial and military intelligence from the Low Countries and Germany, passing on news that came from his own sources. If Lok hoped to catch Cromwell's eye, he also knew his place in the great scheme of things, as Cromwell saw them, ending his letters: 'Yours to his little power, William Lok, mercer of London'.[16] There was literary and social convention here, but for Lok a hefty dose of reality too.

Few English merchants knew Antwerp as well as Richard Gresham, and only a fraction of those merchants got anywhere close to his wealth and influence. Richard and his brothers John and William were of the elite of mercantile London.

In their own minds, no doubt, the Greshams were merely the kind of gentlemen whose gentility was enhanced by the dignity and chartered standing of the city of London. They were proud of their roots as solid Norfolk landed gentry. In fifteenth-century East Anglia, Richard's grandfather James had adopted a grasshopper as his family's crest. Over a century later it was the outstanding symbol in Elizabethan London of the Greshams' wealth and influence.

Richard Gresham was himself born in Norfolk, near Holt, around 1485, later going off to London to serve his apprenticeship with the mercer John Middleton. Admitted to the freedom of the Mercers' Company in 1507, he went into partnership with William Copeland. Their trade flourished. Making full use of cheap credit on the Antwerp exchange, between about 1508 and 1517 they bought silks, velvets, satins, taffeta and sarsenet (a type of very fine and soft silk-like material often used to line doublets and gowns) and exported a huge volume of English cloth. Copeland's death brought to an end a successful partnership, but his money was kept in the family by the strategic marriage of his widow to Richard Gresham's elder brother William. The business went from strength to strength. John Gresham had important trading interests in the far eastern Mediterranean, while the family operation more generally, under Richard's direction, pursued a trade in Italian silks and woollens and tapestries from the Low Countries, with a niche sideline in importing armour and weaponry, something carried on by his son Thomas into the 1550s.[17]

By 1520 Richard Gresham was writing letters to Cardinal Wolsey in which we discover his talent for nourishing a reciprocal interest between a clever merchant and the consummate politician-diplomat – Richard working for Wolsey ('your own servitor'), and Wolsey, the king's powerful minister, able to direct his influence in Richard's favour. In October 1520, after measuring up eighteen chambers in Wolsey's new palace of Hampton Court, Gresham was arranging to buy and ship hundreds of pounds' worth of tapestries for the cardinal, as well as 'certain cloths of golds for to hang' in Wolsey's new private chapel there.[18] This kind of elite procurement had benefits for both parties. For Wolsey, we can be sure, London merchants like Richard Gresham were ten a penny, but for Gresham the great cardinal's favour and patronage really mattered. His strenuous efforts to please Wolsey were worth every moment of his time.

Richard Gresham had always an instinctive eye for an opportunity. Recognizing in 1520 the likely consequences for England of a poor harvest, Gresham filled his ships with wheat. They left Antwerp and went on to Zeeland. When he ran into political difficulties there, he asked Wolsey to intervene on his behalf with the government of the Low Countries.[19] Five years later Gresham found himself arrested at Nieuport by the Emperor Charles V's officers. His words to Wolsey had the breezy confidence of an experienced man who knows he can call upon a powerful patron. It was a routine matter of presenting his documents in Brussels, he wrote: 'That done I trust in God to be at my liberty, who ever keep your grace in good health.'[20]

When Cardinal Wolsey fell from Henry VIII's favour in 1529, Richard Gresham simply shifted his attentions to Wolsey's protégé Thomas Cromwell. It seems likely that Gresham and Cromwell already knew each other. Cromwell had spent at least some of the years of his obscure early career in the Low Countries. He was at the Sinxen mart in 1512, and he may have worked at the English House in Antwerp, possibly as a clerk or secretary, at the time Richard Gresham and William Copeland were building up their successful business.[21] Gresham probably saw at first hand the extraordinary rise of Cromwell – at first the young man of little account who became a broker of power at Henry VIII's court in the 1530s.

It was in the 1530s that Richard Gresham decided to stand back from his Antwerp trade. He was a brilliantly accomplished international merchant with a keen political instinct, rich, and one of London's leading citizens – and still only in his late thirties. He began to concentrate instead on property and finance, lending money to powerful men in the king's government and the Church. One of his early debtors was Cardinal Wolsey himself, who on his death still owed Gresham a substantial amount of money. Gresham treated Wolsey's debt like any other: he would have his money and he asked Cromwell to press Henry VIII to make good the sum.[22] It was a bold pitch – to ask the king himself to honour the debt of a disgraced minister by then dead for three years. Gresham would have said, no doubt, that he was merely being assiduous in balancing his accounts, but others had a different view of his activities as a moneylender. On his death in 1549, a popular 'epitaph' described him as a man who had turned away from the poor and driven young men into bankruptcy; the men of Cheapside praised God that Richard Gresham was now with the devil.[23]

Gresham wanted to serve in the city's highest offices and he became a grandee: sheriff of London and Middlesex in 1531; alderman in 1536; and, at the apex of city government, lord mayor in 1537.

The office of lord mayor was hedged about by all kinds of very old traditions. One was the ancient custom that on entering office, he should shave off his beard. It caused quite a fuss when one Elizabethan lord mayor chose to keep his, though his eccentricity was offset just a little bit by his willingness to adopt the four-cornered bonnet traditionally worn by his predecessors.[24] The lord mayor pursued a demanding round of ceremonial duties: the election of the sheriffs in August at Guildhall and their swearing in at Michaelmas; the appearances at fairs, holy days, dinners, sermons and funerals; the mayoral election itself on Michaelmas eve. There was intricate protocol on dress, with all kinds of permutations and changes of gowns, hoods and cloaks to be worn by the sheriffs, mayor and aldermen on different occasions. It was a performance the purpose of which was to celebrate the dignity and importance of the city, emphasizing rank and office and the exclusivity of London's mercantile hierarchy.

But the lord mayor of London was more than a tailor's dummy who spent his year in office at dinners and suppers. Behind the protocol and ceremony was the fact that any good and effective mayor had to be a political operator of the first rank. He represented a powerful constituency of citizens and livery companies, and they expected him to defend the chartered interests and liberties of the city of London. The lord mayor was their spokesman at the king's court; his credibility was everything, and he had to be a persuasive diplomat. But he was at the same time the king's man in London, who saw to the efficient execution of royal governance, negotiating and navigating the city's corporate will. Etched deeply into London's history were the events of June 1381, when the mayor and his ceremonial sword-bearer had, with King Richard II, faced down Wat Tyler (using the alias of Jack Straw), the leader of a peasants' revolt. The sword-bearer had insisted that Tyler pull down his hood in the presence of the king, at which Tyler, going for his dagger, was killed by the lord mayor himself: 'William Walworth, mayor of London, drew his baselard [a long dagger or short sword] and smote Jack Straw on the head.'[25]

The ceremony of his election, oath-taking and confirmation spoke to the lord mayor's challenging double role and expectation. He took his oath to London's citizens in the hustings court at Guildhall, after which he received the sceptre, keys, purse and seal of the city. On the following day the new lord mayor and his entourage took a barge from the Vintry, an area on the Thames waterfront with warehouses that stored wine from Bordeaux, and were rowed up the river to Westminster. In their scarlet gowns and cloaks, the mayor and aldermen entered the ancient and cavernous Westminster Hall, where in the king's Exchequer the mayor took an oath to the monarch. There followed a tour of the law courts of King's Bench and Common Pleas before a formal visit to the tombs of England's kings in Westminster Abbey, then a barge back to the city and the grandest dinner of the year at Guildhall with all the livery companies in attendance.[26]

Freshly dignified by a knighthood, Sir Richard Gresham – as lord mayor – was all at once London's man and the king's. He was helped by nearly two decades' worth of political and international experience, as well as a relationship with Thomas Cromwell in which Gresham knew his place: Cardinal Wolsey's 'servitor' became Baron Cromwell of Wimbledon, 'Your own, at your lordship's commandment, Richard Gresham'. The voice of dignified and humble service was an important one for any lord mayor to practise.

Sir Richard Gresham was scrupulous in two other aspects of his own business and the city's corporate life. His mayoralty coincided with the dissolution of England's religious houses, and with Cromwell's influence and help Sir Richard gathered up for himself a handsome portfolio of dissolved monastic property all over the kingdom, coming more or less to control the market in lead stripped from former religious houses.[27] This made him a further fortune. To the city and to the Mercers' Company he was a public benefactor, supporting the foundation of a hospital for the poor at St Mary's Spital in Bishopsgate, as well as using his influence to buy outright for the Mercers' Company the hospital and chapel of St Thomas of Acon on Cheapside.

A brilliant merchant, an unforgiving moneylender, a city politician, a patron benefactor, a political facilitator: Sir Richard Gresham was all of these things. In his letters to Wolsey and Cromwell he was always attentive, always alert. Only in one thing did he fail, and that was to build for London an exchange to rival Antwerp's. This was a 'bourse' or 'burse' – a word believed in the sixteenth century to have originated from the name of a meeting place for merchants in medieval Bruges, Antwerp's predecessor as the great mercantile city of Europe.

London's citizens had for years felt the indignity of having to transact business in the open air – and in all weathers – on Lombard Street. Other cities had specially built exchanges, the grandest of them all being Antwerp's New Bourse. London could only hope to catch up. But in the 1530s there was a spark of interest. In 1534 the Court of Common Council at Guildhall began to discuss the project, and three years later the aldermen chose a site near the Pope's Head tavern on Lombard Street.

During his year in office as lord mayor, Sir Richard Gresham pushed and pressed Thomas Cromwell on the project, showing him the 'plat' (plan) for the site, and suggesting a cost of £2,000 'and more' to build a beautiful exchange 'for the honour of our sovereign lord the king'. At first, only the curmudgeonly Sir George Monnocks stood in the way of progress, refusing to sell his property on the intended site. But even when Monnocks gave way, under pressure from the king himself, nothing happened, and the city's records fall silent.[28]

Had the exchange been built in 1538, it would have been a great feather in Sir Richard Gresham's mayoral bonnet. But a purpose-built bourse for London had to wait for the better part of thirty years – and its builder and founder would be Sir Richard's son Thomas.

In fact Thomas Gresham was his father's greatest legacy. With fantastic wealth, Richard Gresham was the friend of very powerful men, the toast of the city and the Mercers' Company, the giver of charity – to his fingertips the merchant prince. Of his three sons, Thomas was the young man who would continue and develop his father's business. Sir Richard's training of Thomas was meticulous. And it was worth every penny, for no other merchant in early Elizabethan London would be grander than Thomas Gresham.

CHAPTER FIVE

'Love, serve and obey'

Our first impression is of a handsome and commanding young man with a long straight nose, high cheekbones, cropped brown hair and a light beard. He is calm and composed, fixing the artist eye to eye. Of that artist we know nothing at all, beyond the fact that he was a painter of talent whose studio was in or near Antwerp. Of the sitter, however, we can be certain. The letters and numbers stand out clearly: '1544. Thomas Gresham. 26', with the addition of Gresham's monogram, as well as two sets of initials – A. G. and T. G. – and the motto 'Love, serve and obey'.

It would have been impossible for the artist to contrive a plainer setting for young Thomas Gresham's portrait. The colours are muted – greys and browns and the dark shadows of a wall, of a human skull laid on one side, and of the subject himself. Gresham's cap, doublet, gown and hose are black: the only relief is provided by the white of his shirt collar and cuffs and the plain brown leather gloves he holds in his right hand. Decoration is sparing: the delicate lace of his shirt, the leaf patterning of his doublet, the rings on his left index finger and on his right little finger. He stands at the slightest of angles to the artist, his left leg just in front of his right. His left hand rests on his waist, its thumb tucked halfway into his doublet. He wears no sword.

And yet for all the plainness and the studied lack of anything ostentatious, this was a portrait that spoke powerfully of Thomas Gresham's ambition. No other merchant in London had one like it, and for such a young man it was a remarkable commission. Here was a merchant in his twenty-sixth year, painted in the style of Europe's monarchs – not the usual study from waist or shoulders up (and that was rare enough for any London merchant in the 1540s), but a portrait in full length. Here, it says, is a grandee in the making. The picture speaks of sobriety, earnestness and taste, and of a merchant's comfortable austerity, for Gresham wears a dark merchant's suit of the finest possible quality.

The year 1544 was a highly significant one for Thomas Gresham. The portrait most likely celebrated his marriage to a wealthy merchant's widow, Anne Ferneley – as Anne Gresham, the 'A. G.' bound to the 'T. G.' through a shared motto. With his father Sir Richard more or less in retirement by this time, Thomas was running the Greshams' successful family business. The future belonged to him, and it promised exceptional things.

Thomas Gresham was born around 1518 at his father's house on Milk Street, a couple of minutes' walk from Cheapside and close to the Guildhall. The family's parish church was St Lawrence Jewry, which young Thomas would have known in the 1530s, just as young Thomas More had done a few decades earlier, for More too had grown up on Milk Street. The church was well known throughout London for two mysterious objects on display to parishioners: the first, the tooth of an enormous fish 'hanged up for show in chains of iron' on a stone pillar; the second the reputed shin bone of a giant. The Elizabethan antiquary John Stow saw the tooth when he was a boy, though it had disappeared by the time he came to write his Survey of London in the 1590s. The bone – Stow thought it might once have belonged to an elephant – was still in the church, and presumably was destroyed when St Lawrence Jewry went up in flames during the Great Fire of 1666.[1]

Of Thomas Gresham's early life we have the basic shape. He had an elder brother, John, and two sisters Christian and Elizabeth. Their mother, Dame Audrey, died in 1522, when Thomas was three or four years old, and she was buried in St Lawrence Jewry. Sir Richard married for a second time – to Isabelle Taverson, who brought her daughters to live at Milk Street.

In October 1530 Thomas was sent by his father to study at Gonville Hall in Cambridge, a small foundation of university scholars 200 years old with strong connections to the Greshams' ancestral county of Norfolk. Thomas was thirteen or fourteen years old when he left London for the fens. He stayed in Cambridge for at least a year and perhaps a little longer.[2] He was a 'pensioner', a kind of extra-mural student whose family paid for his room, food and drink, and who enjoyed the privilege of dining with the college fellows at high table, separated and elevated from the other, poorer boys.

Life at Gonville Hall was a long way removed from the comforts of Richard Gresham's house on Milk Street, however. The college was in essence an austere and tiny boarding school of twenty-five to thirty boys and young men mostly in their late teens and early twenties whose lives together were governed by unyielding routine. The community worshipped in the college chapel at five o'clock every morning, taking their meals in hall: an early breakfast, dinner at about ten o'clock, supper at about five. They studied in a library filled with books and manuscripts going back to the foundation of the college in 1349. They heard lectures in the university's teaching rooms next door to the college, and gave scholarly disputations in their own college hall. For someone of Thomas's age, the curriculum was the 'trivium' of advanced grammar, rhetoric and logic, building on the Latin he would have been taught from the age of about seven. At Cambridge, teaching was in Latin and, for the boys more advanced in their studies, Greek.

At Gonville Hall there was no whisper of luxury. Chambers were sparsely furnished. The hall, unlike anywhere else in the college, was heated, though a brazier or two represented only the barest of nods to the winter cold. Meals were taken in silence, with a college fellow reading aloud passages from the Latin Vulgate Bible. On holy days like Christmas, stringent rules were relaxed just a little so that fellows and students could enjoy themselves with plays and music.

The monastic feel of Gonville Hall in the early 1530s was accentuated by the familiar presence of young monks on study leave from the great religious houses of East Anglia. For a boy used to the bustle and news of London, Cambridge must have felt like a place out of time, small, self-contained and inward-looking. But in 1530 and 1531 the rumble of change was being felt even in the fens. In 1530 the university gave its collective opinion on Henry VIII's 'Great Matter' – the legitimacy or not of his marriage to Katherine of Aragon – on which (with no great surprise) it decided in favour of the king.

At Gonville Hall, as throughout Cambridge, reform was in the air, though for many it stank of heresy. There were efforts in 1531 within the university to suppress the writings and ideas of controversial theologians and translators like Jan Hus, Martin Luther and John Wyclif. There were suspicions that Gonville Hall was something of a hotbed of new and dangerous theology. Nicholas Shaxton, one of its Fellows, was a convinced supporter of the king's Great Matter and a protégé of Anne Boleyn. Richard Taverner was a scholarly refugee from Oxford: accused of heresy there in 1529, he moved to Cambridge with the intervention and protection of Thomas Cromwell. A less controversial contemporary of Gresham at Gonville Hall was John Caius, then a twenty-year-old student of theology and an enthusiastic follower of the great humanist scholar Erasmus of Rotterdam. Caius later became the best-known physician in England. And it is just possible that Gresham knew William Gonnell, a pensioner at Gonville Hall from 1531, who, at the time of Thomas's birth, had been the brilliant tutor to the children of Thomas More.

Given our knowledge of Thomas's later success, we might imagine that his short stay in Cambridge was part of Sir Richard Gresham's master plan for his son's brilliant career. Perhaps it was – a university education was highly unusual even for the grandest of London merchants. But most likely Richard just wanted Thomas to have a thorough grounding in grammar and an acquaintance with the academic study of rhetoric, logic, the classics and history.

Richard Gresham allowed his son no easy short-cuts. Thomas valued his father's discipline, later explaining why he had served an apprenticeship of eight years to his uncle John. His father's position within the Mercers' Company could have spared him those years, 'Albeit my father Sir Richard Gresham, being a wise man, knew . . . it was to no purpose except I were bound prentice to the same, whereby to come by the experience and to the knowledge of all kind of merchandize.'[3] This was the Gresham way: hard work, attention to detail and steady application.

The years 1535 to 1543 were a period of startling changes in Church and State, of Sir Richard Gresham's mayoralty and of the family's ever-increasing fortune. They were years, too, of Sir Richard's careful placing of his son on the outer wings of the political and diplomatic stage, for Thomas's apprenticeship was no ordinary one. In 1538 Sir Richard supervised the visit to London of French dignitaries, making sure to let the powerful Thomas Cromwell know that 'My son hath waited upon them and doth keep the same company by the way to the intent to see them well entertained and used by reason of his language' – he was a kind of chaperone translator.[4] By 1543 Thomas was playing a minor role in diplomacy between England and the Holy Roman Empire, carrying letters between the royal courts. It was important to be noticed as a young man of promise.

In some ways Gresham's Antwerp portrait of 1544 is not representative of his very delicate edging forward into political and diplomatic life. Thomas was a man with a fine mind for business, with a father who was not afraid to tout his son's talents, but he was neither a nobleman nor a diplomat. The picture speaks powerfully of Thomas's own instinct of self-presentation. He was a kind of merchant-courtier hybrid, positioned by his father to become the head of a powerful family business; he was the son of a former lord mayor, with at least a taste of a Cambridge education, experience of international mercantile diplomacy, and some talent for languages. A true courtier, as Gresham would have known, was made as well as born. Baldassare Castiglione, in his *Book of the Courtier* (translated into English in 1561), laid out the essential criteria: of good birth and stock, favoured with the right kind of body (well proportioned and not too tall), amiable in countenance, curious, well spoken, wise, musical, knowledgeable about affairs, an accomplished linguist, honest, educated, clean and well dressed. He was to look much as Thomas Gresham looked in his Antwerp portrait: 'To make his garments after the fashion of the most, and those to be black, or of some darkish and sad colour, not garish.'[5]

Thomas Gresham's life in London in the late 1540s was that of a rich gentleman merchant. His house on Basinghall Street, close to Guildhall, was both a home and a business headquarters, buzzing with servants, factors and extended family. In March 1547 his wife

Anne gave birth to a son Richard, and she was a frequent attender at the christenings of her friends' children. Minstrels played for the family over the Christmas of 1547, and Thomas celebrated the election of his uncle John, Sir Richard's brother, as lord mayor for the year 1547–8. For relaxation, Thomas played dice for money, along with a game called 'bank notes'.[6]

By the time of Sir Richard Gresham's death in 1549, the Greshams had been in the first league of the city establishment for nearly thirty years. Sir Richard's will contained all the usual provisions for family, charity and livery company, and just a hint of the extent of his property portfolio: money for the poor as well as for grand commemorative dinners for his fellow mercers, and big houses in Middlesex, Norfolk, Suffolk and Yorkshire. But most striking of all were the breadth and depth of his political connections. His will was a Who's Who of the government of King Edward VI, who had succeeded to the throne on the death of his father Henry VIII in 1547. Privy councillors, courtiers, judges and law officers all received Sir Richard Gresham's mourning rings. The most prominent among them was King Edward's most powerful adviser, Edward Seymour, Duke of Somerset. Thomas Gresham's sister Christian was married to Sir John Thynne, one of Somerset's household officers. It could not be clearer that the Greshams were firmly embedded in the Tudor elite. Thomas's future looked very bright indeed.

In December 1551, Thomas Gresham had the most important interview of his career. It took place because of the refusal of the king's agent in Antwerp, William Dansell, to return home to explain why English royal finance in Antwerp was in such a mess. Gresham later explained that Edward VI's Privy Council had sent for him 'to know my opinion (as they had many other merchants) by what way, with least charge, his majesty might grow out of debt'. Clearly Gresham's performance before the council was impressive. There and then he was given the job of replacing Dansell in Antwerp, without, as he later put it, 'my suit or labour for the same'.[7]

For decades, Crown expenditure had far outpaced the ability of the government to raise sufficient sums of money effectively. Tudor taxation, whether by the king's prerogative or through parliament, was as unpopular as it was inefficient and periodic. Even the extraordinary windfall provided by the dissolution of the monastic houses had not been enough to pay for Henry VIII's ambitions. In the early summer of 1544, Henry had been preparing a military expedition in France, for which the sum of £250,000 was needed just for the first three months of the campaign. Stephen Vaughan, Henry's financial agent, went to work with those whom he called the 'foxes and wolves' of the Antwerp financial world, using as his intermediary the hard-nosed Italian broker Gaspar Ducci of the international syndicate of Neidhart, Seiler, Ducci and partners. It was the Welser banking house of Augsburg that supplied the loan to King Henry of 100,000 crowns at an interest rate of 14 per cent, with the promise of 100,000 crowns more two months later. The Welser would accept security only from the Anglo-Italian mercantile houses of Vivaldi and Bonvisi in London.[8]

As a proportion of the amount of money spent by Henry on campaigning in France and Scotland (characteristically he had opened up a war on two fronts at the same time), the Antwerp loan was modest. The total came to a little over £2 million. Parliamentary taxation, forced loans, the sale of ex-monastic lands (to families like the Greshams) and the debasement of England's coinage covered the bulk of expenditure. But what was crippling about the Antwerp loan, particularly for a royal exchequer now drained dry, was the rate of interest being charged on it. In 1548 the sum owed to the Welser amounted to almost £240,000, rising quickly to £325,000.[9] When Edward's Privy Council interviewed Gresham, the books could not be made to balance. The king's government desperately needed a pause for breath, and it was Gresham's task somehow to manage the crippling repayments. In 1551 he was invited to take up what must have appeared to many an impossible brief.

What made it worse were the policies being enforced by Edward's Privy Council. Terrified that England's economic fragility would lead to 'the great impoverishment' of the realm, the council ordered that no gold or silver in the form of 'bullion, money, plate or vessel' should leave the kingdom, forbidding also exchange dealings in England. At the same time the government introduced a devalued currency in the form of copper shillings, as a result of which prices in the kingdom rose and the value of sterling fell. Merchants were in uproar, and nine months later, after lobbying the government with their 'lamentable complaints and humble suits', the prohibition on exchange was at last lifted.[10]

With Edward's councillors floundering, Thomas Gresham could afford to be both brisk and blunt. His aim was to clear the king's debts, and his approach was strictly commercial. Gresham lived and breathed Antwerp, and it was his mastery of the exchange and its processes that gave him the sort of advantage he would need to balance the kingdom's books. His house in Antwerp was a stone's throw from the New Bourse. He knew the Antwerp market inside out: its merchants, its deal-making bankers, the intrigues between the town and the emperor's court at Brussels, the changing and often febrile world of big money. He knew that regular and accurate information was everything. He lived by numbers and data; probably he dreamt of exchange rates. As he wrote in 1553 with a self-important flourish: 'No bourse passes wherein I am not furnished with a statement of all monies borrowed on that day.'[11]

And yet, even for Thomas Gresham it was intense and demanding work. As skilled, able and obsessive as he was, he found himself stretched to his limits. The job he had been given called for all the persuasive skills of a merchant-courtier both suave and purposeful. Gresham, after all, was making deals with the foxes and wolves of international moneylending, where a banking house like the Welser could lend 800,000 crowns to Charles V and still have plenty of capital left over to make other loans in the hundreds of thousands of crowns – and the Welser were not as rich as the Fugger. There is nothing at all in Gresham's style to suggest over-excitement or fretful anxiety – merely a command of every detail, with ever a plan, always a strategy, and an honest and unvarnished assessment of his negotiating hand.

Still, the pressures and expectations were huge. A few years later Gresham wrote of the sacrifices he had made in the king's service: taking his whole family and household to Antwerp; travelling forty times in two years between the Low Countries and the king's court in England; the close negotiations; the intricate book-keeping; and 'the infinite occasion of writing' to the Privy Council – letters prepared without the help of a secretary 'for mistrust in so dangerous a

business'.[12] Here he was undoubtedly playing up for effect the travails
of his work. But he had had to fight for his plan for settling the king's
debts. At least once, when he was not getting his way, he had floated
the suggestion of his own resignation, 'For otherwise I see in the end
I shall receive shame and discredit.'[13]

So it was Gresham's way or nothing. But for all the plain speech,
he possessed a courtier's talent for self-promotion, later claiming
for himself sole credit for paying off the Crown's debts and securing for King Edward 'such credit both with strangers and his own
merchants that he might have had for what sum of money he had
desired'. He was fully confident in his skill at playing the Antwerp
exchange in the king's favour.[14] In fact, on Gresham's side were
forces beyond the range of even his talents: in 1552, a crisis in silver
production in central Europe caused the value of silver to rise at the
Antwerp exchange, which is precisely what Gresham needed to be
able to settle the king's debts with the least amount of pain.[15]

Nevertheless, Gresham's plan in 1552 to pay off the Crown's debt
was audacious. It was nothing short of a forced loan imposed on the
Company of Merchant Adventurers, whereby the adventurers would
pay the king's debt out of their sales in Antwerp, to be compensated
within three months by the royal exchequer. Already bruised and bat-
tered in 1551 and early 1552, the adventurers knew that such a
deal was hardly in their favour, but later, looking back on his plan,
Gresham himself was satisfied that everyone benefited from it, however much the merchants had grumbled at the time. He wrote: 'there
was touched no man but the merchants for to serve the prince's turn,
which appeared to the face of the world that they were great losers,
but to the contrary in the end when things were brought to perfec-
tions [sic] they were great gainers thereby'.[16] The adventurers must
have fumed at Gresham, one of their own. In a remarkable coup,
Gresham was able – just – to satisfy two constituencies: king and city.
He was not shy of trumpeting his own success. Thomas Gresham was
ever a master of businesslike self-congratulation.

The deal was done at Syon Palace on Monday, 3 October 1552.
That it was necessary was clear from the huge sums of money set
out on paper by the king's secretary, Sir William Cecil. He knew the
scale of the repayments to be made: £48,000 on 9 November 1552,

followed by £21,000 in February 1553, £14,000 in July and £26,309 in August. Edward's Privy Council intended to do everything it could to pay off the debt, selling Crown and chantry lands, bullion, church plate and lead. The reason for Gresham's plan was that the money had to be raised quickly: the next repayment to foreign creditors was due within weeks. The sum to be borrowed in the short term from the merchant adventurers was £30,000.

It was clear the adventurers had very little choice but to agree. At Syon Palace they met Gresham and Edward's Privy Council. Cecil's minute of their meeting records with magnificent understatement what must have been a frank exchange of views. 'Upon much communication and treaty', the merchants 'agreed for themselves' (Cecil was keen to make that clear for the record) 'that they would pay in Antwerp by the end of December of every cloth they had twenty shillings to the discharge of the king's debt, requiring repayment within three months after the delivery thereof.'[17] Thus the merchants were heavily leaned on by the Privy Council to offer the Crown short-term credit on terms wholly favourable to the government.[18] The scale of the plan is hard to ignore. It was an audacious gamble, a naked political interference in the conduct of international trade on big scale. A whole adventurers' fleet ready to sail out to the winter mart of 1552 was held back: thirty to forty ships carrying up to 40,000 pieces of cloth worth up to £150,000.[19]

In their negotiations at Syon, the Merchant Adventurers' Company was able to offset just a little the damage about to be done to their purses. With Edward's government they agreed a quid pro quo. The ancient privileges of the Hanse merchants of the Steelyard, for a long time deeply resented by the adventurers, would be abolished. Only a week after the Syon meeting, the Privy Council recorded in pungent language the king's decision to deprive the Hanse of their accustomed trading freedoms and liberties: the foreign merchants' 'disorders, colourable and deceitful dealings' deserved 'both in law and conscience the deprivation of their said liberties heretofore enjoyed'.[20] The council's formal language and high moral tone covered an instance of naked mercantile politicking.

It was not quite the end for a medieval trading organization that had been in London for centuries: they would return in the reign of

Mary I and Philip (1553–8), just able to cling on, embattled by a predatory city establishment, until their final expulsion from London in 1597 (and even then they returned in the seventeenth century). But perhaps in 1552 – and then again at intervals over the following four decades – the German merchants in London looked up at *The Triumph of Poverty* and *The Triumph of Riches* in the Great Hall of the Steelyard: 'He who is rich . . . fears hourly that the inconstant wheel of fortune may turn.'

Thomas Gresham himself knew as much about the inconstant wheel of fortune as he did about strategic planning. He relied, like any courtier, upon the favour of his monarch. Young Edward VI, who was himself interested in money, exchanges and markets, recognized the value of Gresham's work for his prince and government, giving him the honour of a favourable audience and a royal pension.[21] But when Edward died in 1553, his successor Queen Mary removed Gresham from office. As the agent of what had been an aggressively Protestant government, he was not trusted; it was a frankly political dismissal. He defended his success and his service, but did so almost with a shrug of his shoulders, simply returning to his business as a merchant.

In fact it turned out to be more a period of leave than it was a permanent retirement. Months later, Gresham was back in Antwerp to act for the new queen, picking up the pieces of a poorly judged loan negotiated by his successor, the inexperienced Christopher Dawntsey, with the German banker Lazarus Tucher. On the loan of 200,000 guilders, Dawntsey had agreed a particularly high rate of interest. Gresham's speed and command of detail were formidable, making Dawntsey look feeble. Within hours of arriving in Antwerp at nine o'clock on the night of 17 November 1553, Gresham knew the terms of the loan, having spoken personally to Tucher. Their relationship was an old and complicated one: Gresham called Tucher a friend, but also described him for Mary's Privy Council as 'a very extreme man, and very open-mouthed'.[22] Probably Tucher was no different to any other agent, broker or banker in Antwerp – outwardly friendly and amiable and a purposeful gossip, but behind all that hard as steel, well able to take advantage of Christopher Dawntsey. Gresham himself showed off his talents to the council: with apparently no effort at all he was able to give a full account of what was happening in Antwerp, including his view of the financial standing of the emperor and the King of France.²³

Thomas Gresham was in his element. He knew precisely who to talk to and what to do. It was evident that Tucher, no doubt irritated by the silence from Mary's government, had been gossiping: the bargain between the banker and the queen, Gresham reported, was open knowledge amongst all the merchants at the exchange. A week later, Tucher came up to Gresham at the bourse and asked him plainly 'whether his bargain should take place or not'. Gresham's answer was as deft as it was diplomatically evasive and non-committal: 'I could take it but in good part, and that there was no fault in me, for that I knew not the queen's majesty's pleasure afore my present coming away.' He could not resist wondering out loud to Tucher why Dawntsey 'would give so great interest'. He said that his own commission did not extend 'to so high a price'.²⁴ It was the subtlest of pokes in the eye for Mary's Privy Council. But Thomas Gresham was back – skilled, subtle and indispensable as ever.

When Lazarus Tucher and Thomas Gresham met at 'the bourse', Gresham meant Antwerp's New Bourse in the centre of the town between the great thoroughfares of the Meer and New Street. The first exchange for Antwerp's merchants was built in 1515, a grand enough building on Garden Street, with a gallery or portico over two of its four sides. Before that merchants had met in a large courtyard off Wool Street, close to Market Place and the English House. By 1530 even the Old Bourse was too small for the fantastic volume of business in Antwerp, and so in 1531, at a cost to the town of 300,000 crowns, the architect Domien de Waghemakere built a new one.²⁵

The New Bourse was one of the wonders of Europe, a rectangular court around which there was a portico resting on thirty-eight decorated columns, each unique, with two great towers and four double doorways leading in from the streets that look from contemporary woodcuts like elegant boulevards. Where geographically and symbolically it was at the heart of Antwerp, economically the New Bourse was at the heart of Europe.

Thomas Gresham knew it intimately – its stone and mortar, its men and its business. The New Bourse was as much a part of his world as

Milk Street, St Lawrence Jewry, Basinghall Street or Guildhall. It was the definitive mark of Antwerp's pre-eminence in European trade and banking. By the 1560s Gresham had a clear ambition: with the New Bourse as his model, he would complete what his father and the livery companies of London had attempted to do in the 1530s. London would have its own exchange, and Thomas Gresham would be its patron.

Gresham's career captured something of a shift of focus in the mercantile life of Tudor London. Like every other London merchant for generations, he knew Antwerp. But perhaps he had seen the city through different eyes, measuring the possibilities of London against the achievements of Europe's greatest mercantile and financial centre. If English merchants had for decades gone to Antwerp, then perhaps it was time for London to fix its own ambitious claim in the European mercantile world.

Thomas Gresham was aware, too, of a way of linking up money and political power, of getting merchants and governments to work together. For centuries there had been a delicate and pragmatic trade-off: kings recognized and confirmed in their charters London's liberties because they needed to have its merchants on their side. Gresham's hope by the 1560s was to wean the English Crown off its dependence on loans made by foreign lenders, and indeed Elizabeth I would look for security to her own city. Gresham wrote: 'I would wish that the queen's majesty in this time should not use any strangers but [instead] her own subjects, whereby . . . all other princes may see what a prince of power she is.'[26]

And perhaps London's merchants could look to opportunities and horizons even beyond Europe. The mercantile elite of the city, though to some extent hidebound by tradition and the ancient ways and structures of its livery companies, possessed a remarkable energy. The wobbles in the trade between Antwerp and London in the early 1550s were deeply unsettling. In difficult times merchants might even strike out to distant oceans and continents: to test maps and sea charts, to find new markets, to build a different kind of trade with a new kind of organization, made up not just of merchants but investors also. For many years navigators had wondered about routes to the oceans of the Far East and the wonders of the fabled empire of Cathay. Just beginning to come into focus was a brave new world of adventure and encounter.

CHAPTER SIX

Searching for Cathay

No place on earth came to fire the early Tudors' imagination like Cathay. It was, so they believed, the most formidable power in Asia, whose ruler, the Great Khan (or Cham or Chan), was a descendant of Noah. His empire was as far from London as it was possible to travel, in 'superior or high India', north of China on the coast of what was known as the Scythian Sea, approximately what is today the East Siberian Sea.[1]

Cathay was an inspiring fantasy, skilfully deployed by a Venetian-born Anglophile called Sebastian Cabot, who wanted to take English ships to the other side of the world to find the great empire. Cabot, an expert sea pilot who had taught in the elite school of navigation in Spain's Casa de la Contratación, arrived in England sometime after 1547, bringing European skills and ambitions to a kingdom that was lagging well behind the achievements of Spain and Portugal. He brought, too, an innovative business model for long-distance trade that helped to change London forever.[2]

The enduring popularity of Sir John Mandeville's medieval *Travels* (it was printed in Westminster in the 1490s) certainly helped Cabot's cause, lending an exotic texture to the Far East: 'Cathay is a fair country and rich, full of goods and merchandizes; thither come merchants every year for to fetch spices and other merchandizes more commonly than they do into other countries.'[3] Translators, scholars and mapmakers added layers of detail and authority to the existence of Cathay, an empire of so 'many provinces, people and princes, and innumerable islands in

65

the great east sea, called the Great Ocean'. The Great Khan, who sat upon a throne of precious stones, was enormously rich and powerful. His mighty capital city was Cambalu, which was described in 1553 by the cosmographer and translator Richard Eden, though even Eden's formidable literary talents struggled to describe just how wealthy and impressive the court was: 'What great pomp, glory, and furniture of all things, is observed in the emperor's court, it cannot be spoken.'[4]

And so Cathay was the golden key to trade with Asia, 'rich, full of goods and merchandizes' like precious stones, pearls, silks and all kinds of spices from India and other regions.[5] There were obviously wonderful possibilities for trade and accumulating wealth. The challenge was simply how to get there. The best route was surely a northern one through the Arctic oceans, which, according to the experts, were perfectly navigable. From the beginning, English navigators, buoyed up by patriotic self-congratulation, believed it would be easy – certainly far easier than the long sea journey around the Cape of Good Hope that Portuguese ships had to make to Portugal's outposts in the East Indies.

Early English efforts to find a sea route to Asia had taken navigators and their crews across the north Atlantic towards America – and Sebastian Cabot and his father John had led the way. After living for some time in Valencia, the Cabots, a family of Genoese origins, came to England at some point in the 1490s, where their first base was the port town of Bristol. When and where they sailed is impossible to determine for sure; around 1497 they perhaps reached Labrador or Novia Scotia, and ten or eleven years later Sebastian might have explored the Arctic waters of the northern coast of North America, possibly reaching the entrance to Hudson Bay.[6]

In 1512 Sebastian left England for Spain. Six years later he was appointed pilot major at the Casa de la Contratación, where he worked for the better part of thirty years, following in the footsteps of pilots as distinguished as Amerigo Vespucci and Juan Díaz de Solís. His job was to train and license Spain's navigators; he was, in other words, at the cutting edge of navigational technique and theory, which gave him unrivalled experience.

Sebastian Cabot's return to England in 1547 or 1548 is one of the pivotal events of this book: it is hard to imagine London's global ambitions getting quite the start that they did without his energy and vision. He was an accomplished cartographer: between 1544 and 1549 he produced a world map, manuscript copies of which he sent to Seville and to England. It was a map that a later adventurer, Sir Humphrey Gilbert, saw in the Queen's Gallery at Whitehall Palace in the 1560s, and engraved copies hung in the houses of many London merchants as well.[7] Cabot's knowledge was priceless. He knew all about Spanish efforts in the Americas and Portuguese encounters with the southern coast of Ming China, seeing the limitations as well as the achievements of the Iberian powers.[8] Actively recruited by Edward VI's government, Cabot's move from Spain was orchestrated by the king's Privy Council, which paid £100 – a huge sum of money then – to bring him over 'to serve and inhabit in England'. Thereafter he was paid a very generous yearly pension of £166.[9] In 1549 and 1550, after King Edward was pointedly informed by Charles V that Cabot was drawing an imperial salary, there were some months of diplomatic frostiness over his refusal to return to Spain, with Cabot himself admitting that he had 'knowledge of certain things very necessary for the emperor's knowledge'.[10] One of the things that infuriated Charles was that Cabot's world map incorporated many of the secret details from that used by the Casa de la Contratación. In many ways, Sebastian's departure for England was practically a defection.[11]

In London Cabot put together an embryonic trading company he called 'The mystery and company of the merchants adventurers for the discovery of regions, dominions, islands and places unknown'. If the title was unwieldy, the idea behind the company was strikingly new, at least in London. Here Cabot was at his most effective, putting in place the structures of an organization that owed a debt to the advanced business practices of Italy and the Mediterranean. What Sebastian did with his 'mystery' was to build a company whose focus was on a single venture and expedition to make the first, definitive breakthrough to Cathay, and whose funding came not just from merchants but from other investors too. How much of this was planned by Cabot in the earliest stages is not clear. But the speed with which his new company was transformed into a formidable corporate entity shows that Cabot and those London merchants who backed him were thinking a long way beyond the conventional.

Cabot captured the moment perfectly. London's mercantile elite were feeling the pinch. The years between 1550 and 1553 were painful for merchants and deeply unsettling for Edward VI's government. With the king's Privy Council spectacularly mishandling economic policy, and Thomas Gresham trying to get Crown debt under control at the New Bourse, London's merchants found themselves squeezed on all sides. In 1550 the price of the cloth they were taking across the English Channel had fallen sharply on the Antwerp market, rising only to fall again: the problem was one of over-production of cloth for a market already saturated with it. Sterling, too, seemed precarious. The security of the Antwerp–London axis of trade, which for decades had served English merchants so well, suddenly looked fragile. The Cathay project offered hope.

Cabot was able to secure political backing. The most powerful man in the boy king's council, the Duke of Northumberland, was a supporter, and it was no accident that he was the dedicatee of Richard Eden's translation of one of the greatest contemporary works of world geography, Sebastian Münster's formidable *Cosmographia* (1544). Eden knew exactly the point to make. Playing on English sensitivities about the global reach and power of Spain and Portugal, Eden wrote to Northumberland of Spanish treasure then in Seville that might instead have been sitting in the Tower of London.[12] Whether or not Cabot briefed Eden on this, the suggestion was provocative, tantalizing and patriotic: what the Spanish are doing, we might do bétter – and should have done sooner. At a time of unpredictable markets and shaky trade, surely there was so much wealth to be gathered in from Asia. The model of Spain's global reach was a compelling one for Eden, who in another of his translations (from 1555) published Pietro Martire d'Anghiera's multi-volume compilation *The decades of the newe worlde or west India conteynyng the navigations and conquestes of the Spanyardes, with the particular description of the moste ryche and large landes and Ilandes lately founde in the west Ocean perteynyng to the inheritaunce of the kinges of Spayne.*[13] In 1553 Eden saw in his mind's eye great fleets returning to England loaded with treasure. Cathay would be to England what the Americas were to Spain.

And so Cabot's expedition had a political complexion. It was all at once a mercantile venture and an effort on behalf of the

English kingdom to find new riches. Eden, celebrating the Duke of Northumberland as 'a great furtherer' of the voyage, commended efforts at commercial exploration to the 'glory of God and commodity of our country'.[14] And many were convinced. One further striking feature of Sebastian Cabot's 'mystery' is that it spoke to a waiting constituency of persuadable wealthy investors outside London's mercantile community – men and women with the means and the inclination to put their money into this kind of venture. This opened up huge possibilities not only for Cabot's project, but for future expeditions also. Experienced and astute men invested, including Sir William Cecil, King Edward's secretary and Northumberland's right-hand man, who had worked with Thomas Gresham on that ambitious plan in 1552 to pay off the king's debts. Cecil was a supporter of Cabot's enterprise, buying a share in the new company in March 1553.[15] Another was Sir Henry Sidney, a friend to the young king and a gentleman of his Privy Chamber. Both Cecil and Sidney were highly intelligent and experienced men who entertained the hope of a good return on their money.

If London's merchants and other investors believed Cabot's venture had substance, the geographers and navigators felt they knew what they were doing. Cabot was as sure of success as Richard Eden. Eden was convinced that it was perfectly possible to sail from London to Cathay by a north-eastern route, up the coast of Norway and into what he called the 'frozen sea'. He had little time for those who doubted the navigability of those northern regions: many faint-hearted men, he wrote, were discouraged when they looked at globes and maps and saw land extending all the way up to the North Pole, but he put that down to the old and mistaken geography of Ptolemy. As Eden pointed out to his readers, Ptolemy knew nothing about the existence of America. With all the certainty of a scholar sitting comfortably in his study, Eden was convinced that the expedition was worth the effort, even in the face of failure: 'if no good can be done this way, it were worthy the adventure to attempt'.[16] For the sailors who months later found themselves in wooden sailing ships of between 90 and 160 tons in freezing and stormy seas, it was quite a different matter.

Cabot raised from his investors about £6,000, a huge sum of money that was quickly spent on the cost of the ships and their crews and everything they would take with them to the far side of Asia. Essential were food and drink, weapons and ammunition, special company liveries for the sailors and navigational equipment like astrolabes, maps and charts. There were well over a hundred men to provide for, from the captain general and pilot general of the expedition, other gentlemen, a minister of religion, merchants and ships' masters to the crewmen, gunners, cooks, carpenters and coopers.[17] Cabot insisted that no corner should be cut in preparing for an expedition he believed could change the history of a kingdom. Where Eden had written about Spain's American riches lying in Seville, Sebastian Cabot's hope for the voyage was nothing short of equalling in achievement Portugal's opening up of the riches of 'the Orient and Occidental Indies'. World history was just about to be changed.[18]

One thing, however, is startlingly clear. In 1553, for all of Cabot's ambition and Eden's self-confidence, the expedition had no proper idea of what or whom it would encounter on the way to Cathay. Like Eden, Cabot dismissed the warnings of writers who had said that a sea passage so close to the North Pole was impossible because of 'such dangers of the seas, perils of ice, intolerable colds, and other impediments'.[19] And this was one of the wonders of the new company: the adventurers knew so little about the world. They believed they had some geographical knowledge; they had their investors' money; they had confidence. And they took such a big step, feeling as they went the shape of a world known only from maps and the pronouncements of the cosmographical authorities. Within a single reflex were contained both formidable ambition and startling ignorance.

In a calculating, pragmatic and essentially conservative world, it was a bold and imaginative leap into the unknown. And it would have huge consequences for England. The ancestry of what later became Britain's mature mercantile empire needs to be traced back to this root – a single, ambitious and (from one perspective at least) hare-brained project that grew up in and around London in the early 1550s. So much that characterized that later empire – driven initially by trade and always by money, private and corporate – was reflected in Cabot's venture. But what was imagined in 1552 and 1553 was not an acquisitive grab for land and people in the far reaches of the globe. The hope, in fact, was for peaceful trade between far distant parts of the world, the aspiration a noble one: contact, trade, peace and friendship. It was on every level a fantasy.

The expedition that went out from London to Cathay in 1553 carried with it a letter from King Edward VI. It was a letter of introduction, addressed 'to the kings, princes, and other potentates, inhabiting the northeast parts of the world, toward the mighty empire of Cathay', in which Edward spoke to his brother monarchs of peace and friendship. Here was trade as the work of God in bringing peoples together, sharing the 'commodities' of the world. This 'universal amity' – a global friendship – was brought about by commerce:

> Merchants, who wandering about the world, search both the land and the sea, to carry such goods and profitable things as are found in their countries to remote regions and kingdoms, and again to bring from the same such things as they find there commodious for their own countries . . .

Edward promised the princes of the north and east, 'by the God of all things that are contained in heaven, earth, and the sea', that their subjects would be warmly welcomed into England. The letter, written out in Latin, in Greek and in other languages, reached out across the world to unfamiliar peoples and powers. It ended with an effort at finding common ground with others, being dated from London in 'the year from the creation of the world 5515'.[20]

Sebastian Cabot signed and sealed the instructions for the expedition on Tuesday, 9 May 1553. They were to be read out weekly on board all three ships, the *Bona Speranza*, *Edward Bonaventure* and *Bona Confidentia* (hope, good fortune and confidence).[21] Order, discipline and a sense of common purpose were essential.[22]

Cabot left nothing to chance. In charge of the fleet was its captain general, Sir Hugh Willoughby. Eleven other councillors would offer Willoughby their advice, including Richard Chancellor (who was the expedition's pilot general), two of the London merchants and the ships' masters and mates. The unity and agreement of this council governed everything: navigation, where to land and how to search new territory, meetings with foreign potentates, any trade with other countries. The common interest and benefit of the company outweighed any private profit. Sealed up before the journey home, goods and merchandise brought back to London would be unpacked and inspected on arrival by senior officials of the company. Here the newness of the venture, its sense of being a corporate enterprise, trumped the business interests of any single merchant: 'the whole company . . . to have that which by right unto them appertaineth, and no embezzlement shall be used, but the truth of the whole voyage to be opened to the common wealth and benefit of the whole company'.

There were sure to be encounters with strange peoples. With only books to go on, Cabot prepared his crews for meetings with men in bear and lion skins carrying longbows, and for raiding parties of cannibals who might swim naked up to the ships and take their victims unawares. He wrote about dinners with foreign princes and the dangers of ambush. Caution was the watchword. The crews were to observe and listen; not to give away anything about their religious practices; to be courteous and friendly; to be careful not to be tempted by gold, silver or riches into parting with their own goods; not to stay too long in one place; and generally to exercise 'prudent circumspection'. No violence was to be used against any stranger, but low cunning was permitted. A local could be invited on board ship, entertained, given clothes and put back on shore to attract the attention of others. Alcohol might be used 'to learn the secrets of his heart'. On how the crews and the locals would communicate, Cabot was silent: he wrote not one word about foreign languages. A wonderful clause of the instructions for the fleet suggests a fantastical encounter that would not be out of place in Shakespeare's *The Tempest*:

> . . . if people shall appear gathering of stones, gold, metal or other like on the sand, your pinnaces* may draw nigh, marking what things they gather, using or playing upon the drum or such other instruments, as may allure them to harkening to fantasy or desire to see and hear your instruments and voices; but keep you out of danger and show to them no point or sign or rigour or hostility.

On paper Cabot and his company made the first, tentative steps towards new and strange encounters.

The expedition set off from Deptford, a little way down the Thames from London, on 10 May 1553. It sailed past Greenwich Palace on the

* A pinnace was a small sailing boat that could be towed by a larger ship.

following day and fired a salute with the ships' cannon. King Edward was too ill to watch the three ships go by: two months later he was dead. It so happened that Willoughby's fleet became in those northern seas the last, floating outpost of Edward's Protestant England, its men dutifully reading their prayer book services and keeping to the laws passed by Edward's parliaments, as Cabot's regulations had instructed them to do, insulated from the kingdom's return – after 1553 – to the Catholic Church.

On the day Edward died – 6 July – the ships were sailing out towards Scandinavia. On the day he was buried in Westminster Abbey – 8 August – *Bona Speranza*, Willoughby's flagship, beset by strong west-northwesterly winds, was adrift, having lost sight of *Edward Bonaventure* because of fog. Separated once and for all from the other ships, in September *Bona Speranza* found shelter in a haven on the northernmost coast of Scandinavia. Willoughby recorded in a logbook later recovered that at sea they saw seals 'and other great fishes', and on land bears, deer, foxes and 'divers great beasts . . . and such other which were to us unknown and also wonderful'. But the fact was that they were trapped. They had no idea of where they were, and the weather was appalling, 'as frost, snow and hail as though it had been the deep of winter'. Choosing to dig in, Willoughby sent out scouts to find human settlement. The final entry in the logbook sends a chill down the spine:

> Wherefore we sent out three men south-south-west, to search if they could find people, who went three days' journey, but could find none: after that, we sent other three westward four days' journey, which also returned without finding any people. Then sent we three men southeast three days' journey, who in like sort returned without finding of people, or any similitude of habitation.[23]

For Sir Hugh Willoughby and the crew of *Bona Speranza* it was almost the end of the adventure. All of them perished. Among them were six merchants of Cabot's company: William Gittons, Charles Barret, Gabriel Willoughby, John Andrewes, Alexander Woodford and Ralfe Chatterton.

The two other ships of the expedition also endured horrible weather, but they were so much more fortunate than the men of *Bona*

Speranza, finding shelter in the White Sea on the north-west coast of Russia. They discovered land near the end of August 1553 and some people that the survivors' leader, Richard Chancellor, called barbarians. It was the kind of human contact that had eluded Sir Hugh and his men, but it offered some hope.

And so it was that about seventy Englishmen in search of the riches of Cathay, with really no idea of where they were, separated from their flagship, carrying the letters of a dead king and feeling the bitter cold of the far north, encountered a country they had at best read about in books of cosmography. Out of what was in so many ways a disaster, a connection was made that helped to some degree to make Elizabethan London a city of mercantile empire. When Chancellor and his men landed, they had no idea of the significance of those few steps from boat to shore. In fact they were the first Englishmen to set foot in Russia. They had reached a country new to them and their countrymen – and they had done so entirely by accident.

For Chancellor, his crew, the merchants back in London, the investors in the Cathay venture and pretty much everyone else, Russia was terra incognita. Few western Europeans knew anything about it, though the diplomats of the Holy Roman Empire had been filing reports on their encounters with Muscovy since the fifteenth century, and some northern Italian merchants had also travelled there. The acknowledged contemporary authority was an imperial diplomat called Sigismund von Herberstein, the account of whose embassy of 1517 was printed in Vienna in 1549 and became something of a bestseller: reprinted in Latin three times between 1551 and 1557 and translated into German, Polish, Italian and English (in 1555), it revolutionized European knowledge of the Russian state. But it seems highly unlikely that, when he arrived at the port of St Nicholas, Richard Chancellor was acquainted with Herberstein's work in any great detail (though Cabot and Richard Eden may have known the book), and he and later English diplomats and merchants tended to rely upon their own observations of what they saw.[24] Certainly they found Muscovy strange and alien; they recognized its vastness, felt its deep winter chill in their bones, and made their own appraisals of its tsar, Ivan IV ('The Terrible'), who appeared to exercise absolute (even tyrannical) power.

The voyage to Cathay, 1553, and Richard Chancellor's discovery of Russia instead.

Given all this, two things are especially striking about what Elizabethans were not embarrassed to describe as their 'discovery' of Russia. The first is that it was so very unexpected and accidental, though not of course beyond the imaginative possibilities of Edward VI's polyglot letter to any or all of the kings, princes and potentates 'inhabiting the northeast parts of the world'. The second is that Cabot's merchant-investors in London were so brilliantly effective at taking full advantage of an instance of navigational happenstance. The cumbersome 'Mystery and company of the merchants adventurers for the discovery of regions, dominions, islands and places unknown' was, on Chancellor's return, now simply the Muscovy Company, with its headquarters in the parish of St Dunstan in the East, close to the quays and wharves of the port of London. There was already an enviable dynamism to the venture. In February 1555 the company received a founding royal charter from Queen Mary I and her husband King Philip, the result of two or three months of hard lobbying by London's Muscovy investors.[25]

It was Chancellor and the merchants with him who had done the really tough work a few months earlier. They were kept for a long time at St Nicholas, but at last, when permission arrived for them to travel on to Moscow, they set off on an extraordinary journey 'which was very long and most troublesome, wherein he [Chancellor] had the use of certain sleds, which in that country are very common . . . the cause whereof is the exceeding hardness of the ground, congealed in the winter time by the force of the cold, which in those places is very extreme and horrible'.[26]

In the Kremlin, Chancellor and his men met the tsar, who entertained them lavishly with a show of gold and grandeur and feasts of quite epic proportions. While Chancellor's party wanted to trade, Ivan, fighting wars to expand his territories, was after support and weapons from the West. How they communicated is impossible to say for sure: probably they, their hosts and translators muddled through in Polish, Italian or even Greek.[27] They came pragmatically and quickly to an understanding that gave exclusive trading privileges to Cabot's company. At first the agreement was broadly defined: the tsar permitted them to come and go to Russia and to move freely, 'to frequent free marts, with all sorts of merchandizes, and upon the same to have wares for their return'. Really precise agreements would take another few years to perfect. But this was enough of a beginning to make viable Anglo-Russian trade with and through London.[28]

For the moment Cathay, the merchants' fantasy, was put to one side. Once Chancellor was back in London, it was clear that there were valuable raw materials to import from Russia: furs, train oil from seals (used for heat and light), tallow, wax, cordage (the ropes for rigging a ship) and 'ickary' or 'cavery' – caviar – which, if Elizabethans themselves seem to have had no great taste for it, the food markets of France and Italy later did.[29] In 1557 the mathematician Robert Recorde promised the Muscovy Company's governors a clear route of navigation to what he called 'the northeast Indies', though he suggested that this journey to Cathay was as yet some way off.[30] With the company in London beginning to build up Anglo-Russian trade, there now seemed to be no great hurry.

The Muscovy Company was a venture with huge possibilities. It offered a powerful model for international mercantile endeavour. A company with a royal charter, it had investors (many of whom were powerful men in the queen's government), its own staff and bureaucracy and its own common seal, showing a merchant ship flying the flag of St George. From the beginning it was woven into the already complex mercantile fabric of London. Sebastian Cabot was its governor, assisted by four consuls (of whom two were city aldermen) and twenty-four other charter assistants. The first named of these assistants was Thomas Gresham's uncle Sir John, then an alderman and a former sheriff and only a few years earlier London's lord mayor. Thomas himself was a charter member and investor in the company.

To look at the names of the other company members is to see straight away the density of connection and financial and family interest within the city establishment. A single example of the relationships between four families suggests a common pattern. The two alderman consuls of the company in 1555 were the London grandees Sir George Barne and Sir William Garrard; Garrard indeed was elected lord mayor in 1555. Two other original charter members were Alexander Carleill, a London importer of wine, and John Rivers, a generation younger than Barne and Garrard, and a member of the Grocers' Company. Barne's son George married Garrard's daughter Anne, while Barne's daughter Elizabeth married John Rivers. Alexander Carleill married Barne's other daughter Anne who, after Carleill died, married Francis Walsingham, a young man from a political family with London mercantile connections, and later an ambassador and powerful adviser to Queen Elizabeth I. For the Carleills and the Garrards, a second generation inherited their families' Russian interests. Here was the tight weave of the threads of elite city life.

The Muscovy Company was a corporate entity, formally independent of the English Crown. But the Crown had given the company its charter and the company's agents had the privilege of flying royal banners and ensigns over any city, town, village, castle, island or piece of land they discovered and claimed. Here was the promise of a kind of mercantile operation that was driven by aggressive trading, funded by investors' money and backed up by the political clout of government. This was the method and the mentality that fifty years later was taken out to America by the colonists of the Virginia Company of London, and eventually to Asia by the London East India Company.

Edward VI's letter had spoken to foreign princes of universal friendship and the necessity of trade to humanity, evoking a happy picture of merchants bravely travelling the globe in search of reciprocal and mutual benefit between peoples. But the opportunity of Anglo-Russian trade was seized so decisively and completely by the Muscovy Company that its charter left no space at all for the openness of a free and competitive market. Carefully and deliberately, the charter closed out all other claims on its discovery. It meant, for example, that no merchant outside the company could trade with Russia. The company even claimed exclusive charter rights over any navigation and discovery made by 'sailing [from England] northwards, northeastwards, and northwestwards, or any parts thereof', and it defended those rights vigorously.[31]

Present once again were those tensions that together, out of a peculiar alchemy, made for something strikingly creative. First, there were the conservative and protectionist instincts of the city elite, which embedded themselves in the Muscovy Company's determination to protect its hard-won achievements. But secondly, there was something ambitious at work in the encounter between city and government. After this, for better or worse, it was very difficult to prise apart merchants, investors and royal government. This was a working model for the future.

The Tudor search for Cathay, the empire of the Great Khan, was never quite given up. But in 1555 it could wait. Russia, alien and unfamiliar, was the opportunity of the moment, to be seized and exploited.

CHAPTER SEVEN
A Russian Embassy

Sebastian Cabot was governor of the Muscovy Company for perhaps two years. He probably died in 1557, though from the sources, such as they are, it is hard to tell. He seems to have drawn his royal pension at the end of September 1557, but not at Christmas of the same year. Richard Eden was apparently with him at the end, many years later describing Cabot as 'the good old man, in that extreme age, somewhat doted'. Cabot's papers, 'his own maps and discourses, drawn and written by himself', were still in private hands in the early 1580s. A proposal to publish them came to nothing. It is an odd anticlimax. Visionary and dynamic, then within a very few years elderly and confused: with fantastic understatement, Sebastian Cabot shuffles quietly out of the story.[1]

Yet even without Cabot's energy, the Muscovy Company thrived and flourished. Within a few years it was impressively successful. Its base after 1564 was a large tenement on Seething Lane in the parish of St Olave, Hart Street, abutting the garden of the old Crutched Friars and close to the Tower of London and the gallows and scaffold of Tower Hill. The whole parish spoke of mercantile prosperity and comfort, and Muscovy House was one of the grandest places on a city lane of 'divers fair and large houses'.[2] The company's tenement had once belonged to Sir Richard Haddon, one of the grandees of the Mercers' Company in the early sixteenth century, and it was still described as Haddon's 'great place'. When he died in 1517, he left it to his widow Katherine, for life. Katherine's first husband was

Thomas Wyndout, the mercer we met in the first chapter of this book. When Katherine herself died in 1525, Sir Richard's palatial townhouse passed (as he had specified in his will) to the Mercers' Company, and some of the money the company made in renting it out paid for Haddon's commemorative prayers in the mercers' chapel of St Thomas of Acon.[3]

What had been Haddon's 'great place' gave the Muscovy Company just the cachet it needed, for once it had found its feet, this experimental trading company deserved an impressive second headquarters. Its first, in the parish of St Dunstan in the East, was no more than a stone's throw from the wharves and quays of the city's port and customs house, probably in one of the 'many fair houses large for stowage' that stood to the north and south of Thames Street.[4] If Cabot did not live long enough to know Muscovy House on Seething Lane, he was certainly familiar with the company's first home, where it all began – with trade and hard graft. In 1555 the founding members knew that they were building a corporation from the ground up, a working endeavour.

And busy the company certainly was in 1555 and 1556. In November 1555 George Killingworth, the first resident agent the company sent to Russia, reported from Moscow on the initial full negotiations over its privileges. Richard Chancellor was in the city too, the company's premier Russia expert by virtue of the months he had already spent in the country, as well as Robert Best, a talented linguist and the company's first English translator.[5] Killingworth was optimistic. Sweetened by a present of sugar from London, Ivan IV and his officials seemed receptive; certainly his secretary met them 'with a cheerful countenance and cheerful words', and they were dined in grand style. All this time the merchants were making sense of the new country, its geography, the distances between its towns and cities, its natural resources and commodities, its markets and traders, its weights and measures, and its currency of roubles and altines. The company's agents and servants had a pragmatic eye for detail: they observed and they learned, and all for the purpose of trade and business.[6]

The scale of the venture was huge. Russia, with its often brutal climate and perilous autumn and winter journeys by sled, was a world away from the familiar bustle of St Dunstan's in the East. Letters in theory passed between London and Moscow through English merchants resident in Danzig on Poland's Baltic coast, speeding up communication by avoiding the entire journey from St Nicholas on the White Sea back to Muscovy House, a route impassable anyway for part of the year. Even within Russia the company's officials had to deal with one another over hundreds of miles. London's Russia operation was from its beginning a triumph of mercantile grit over some formidable obstacles.[7]

In 1557 the company entertained in London the first ambassador Ivan IV sent to England. He was the elusive Osip Nepea (or Osip Nepeya Grigor'ev) for whom this single embassy is the only reconstructable incident of an otherwise inscrutably obscure career. He may have been a senior official in the service of the tsar's chancellory of foreign affairs, and probably he was a prosperous merchant from the city of Kholmogory, one of the Muscovy Company's bases in Russia. But whoever or whatever he was, Nepea played his part to perfection. Received in London (in the understanding of at least one observer) as a 'duke of Moscovia', his embassy was treated in the city and at court as deserving of fantastic and lavish spectacle.[8]

It was no easy assignment for Nepea and a delicate business for the company. Nepea's job was to represent in person the emperor whose long string of titles had to be set out in full in order not to bruise his imperial dignity. There was tricky diplomatic protocol to navigate, along with the challenge of communication, though, thanks to George Killingworth's companion Robert Best, the company was quickly building up its expertise in Anglo-Russian translation.

Where Killingworth had sat down with officials in Moscow to negotiate on behalf of Cabot's new company in London, Nepea had likewise to agree with Queen Mary's Privy Council the terms for trade between Muscovy and England, doubtless with an emphasis on reciprocity: for all of the privileges granted to the Muscovy Company (which it needed to defend and nurture), Russian merchants had to be given a fair share of the trade passing between the two countries. If Nepea was indeed both an official of the chancellory of foreign affairs and a successful merchant, then he was the ideal man of experience to send to London. It seems likely in fact that in 1555 Nepea had led the negotiations with Killingworth and the Muscovy merchants in Moscow.[9]

For Nepea and the Muscovy Company men that left Russia with him, it turned out to be a perilous and appalling journey. They sailed for England in the summer of 1556 and arrived in London on horseback in February 1557. Four of the company's ships left the port of St Nicholas on the White Sea, but only one returned to England – the *Philip and Mary* – which took months to limp its way back, arriving in the Thames in April 1557. Of the others, one was smashed to pieces on rocks on the coast of Norway, and another disappeared and was never seen again.[10] The fourth ship was the *Edward Bonaventure*, carrying Richard Chancellor. At anchor in the bay of Pitsligo in Aberdeenshire on 10 November 1556, having successfully negotiated Arctic waters with Ivan's ambassador, the ship faced a great storm that blew up and pushed it dangerously onto the rocks. When it began to break into pieces, Chancellor ordered Nepea and his men into a boat that was itself quickly overwhelmed by the sea. At night, in tempestuous waves, Nepea nearly drowned. Chancellor lost his life, along with seven of Nepea's party and a number of his own crew.

In their efforts to establish Anglo-Russian trade, the Muscovy Company of London took very heavy losses: the lives of Sir Hugh Willoughby, Richard Chancellor and some London merchants, as well as many ships and their crews. The serious cost in men and money of global mercantile endeavour was viscerally clear from the beginning.

To add further pain and grievance to this latest disaster, most of the goods that Nepea had brought with him from Russia were looted from the wreck by what the company's account of the journey called 'the rude and ravenous people of the country thereunto adjoining'. The cargo of the *Edward Bonaventure* was worth a fortune, estimated by the Muscovy Company at a sum of £26,000, of which £6,000 worth of goods may have belonged to Nepea himself. As well as the loss of train oil, tallow, furs, felts and yarns, the looters pulled the ship itself to pieces and made away with almost everything on it.[11]

Nepea was stranded in the north of Scotland, but with deft diplomacy the government of Queen Mary and King Philip was able to negotiate his safety and accommodate him there. Men from the company were sent up to Edinburgh with money and a translator. Hoping to recover some of the goods (but discovering instead the loss of 'jewels, rich apparel, presents, gold, silver, costly furs and such like'), their most important job was to conduct Nepea to London.[12] Instead of a grand reception for the ambassador on the River Thames, he and the survivors of his party had an impromptu journey through Scotland and England. They arrived in Berwick-upon-Tweed on 18 February 1557. Moving down the Great North Road as briskly as ambassadorial dignity would allow, nine days later Nepea and his escort were a few miles away from London.[13]

The first encounters between Nepea and the Muscovy Company lodged themselves firmly in the memory of Henry Machyn, a citizen of London and merchant taylor who kept a journal of life in his city. Machyn's keen mercantile eye was able to appreciate fully the sumptuousness of Nepea's reception by the city's grandees. Another eyewitness was the Muscovy Company's official representative who, though his name is not recorded, was in all likelihood Robert Best, the 'talmach or speechman' (translator) the company had sent up to Edinburgh in December.[14]

Just outside the village of Shoreditch were waiting eighty of London's merchants dressed in all their finery, in 'coats of velvet and coats of fine cloth guarded with velvet, and with fringe of silk and chains of gold'. Attending them were servants in the full blue livery of the Muscovy Company. Greeting the ambassador, they led the party to within four miles of the city. Presented 'with a quantity of gold, velvet and silk, with all furniture thereunto requisite', Nepea was made welcome for the night at a merchant's country house.[15]

The following day, 140 members of the Muscovy Company, with at least as many servants dressed in the blue livery, came out to meet Nepea and his party and lead them into the city proper. On the way he was shown 'the hunting of the fox and such like sport'. To everything there was a purposeful choreography. Nepea's movement towards the city was like a moving tableau – all at once an entertainment and an education in the life of England and London. Nothing was spared in making him welcome. Received and embraced on behalf of the queen by Viscount Montague, Nepea was given an escort of 300 mounted knights, esquires, gentlemen and yeomen. Four 'notable merchants richly apparelled' presented him with the gift of a large gelding 'richly trapped', the footcloth of which was a fine eastern crimson velvet sewn with gold lace. Mounting the horse, Nepea rode to Smithfield, where he entered London proper with Montague on one side and the lord mayor, Sir Thomas Offley, on the other. With the mayor were the aldermen in their scarlet gowns and great numbers of London's merchants, followed by servants and apprentices. The streets were packed with people trying to keep up with the procession.[16]

Henry Machyn saw it all for himself. Lapsing into a kind of historical present tense, there is a breathless immediacy to Machyn's account of Nepea and his embassy passing by:

> And after comes my Lord Montague and divers lords and knights and gentlemen in gorgeous apparel; and after comes my lord mayor and aldermen in scarlet, and the ambassador, his garment of tissue broidered with pearls and stones; and his men in coarse cloth of gold down to the calf of the leg, like gowns, and high coping capes, and so to Master Dymoke's place in Fenchurch Street, the merchant; and his cape and his night cap set with pearls and stones.[17]

Nepea and his men were dazzling. Here was an ambassador dressed in the fashion of a Russian nobleman, as described by a later writer:

> First a *Tassia* or little night cap on his head, that covereth little more than his crown, commonly very rich wrought of silk and gold thread, and set with pearl and precious stone . . . Over the *Tassia* he weareth a wide cap of black fox . . . with a *tiara* or long bonnet put within it, standing up like a Persian or Babilonian hat.[18]

Machyn was gripped by the colour and exoticism of the spectacle. Osip Nepeya Grigor'ev would have looked to Londoners on that February day like the model of a fantastic eastern potentate – the nearest it was possible to come to meeting the tsar himself.

John Dymoke of Fenchurch Street was one of London's mercantile greybeards, at the age of about sixty; he was a member of the Drapers' Company. Nepea and his men were offered Dymoke's townhouse at their own convenience. It was grand enough to serve the same purpose a few years later for ambassadors from the Holy Roman emperor and the regent of Flanders.[19] For Nepea, two chambers had been beautifully furnished and hung with sumptuous tapestries, while he and his embassy dined off valuable plate, every day visited by city aldermen and prominent members of the Muscovy Company. It was at Dymoke's house that Nepea was presented with the most powerfully symbolic of all the gifts, those of Queen Mary: 'one rich piece of cloth of tissue, a piece of cloth of gold, another piece of cloth of gold raised with crimson velvet, a piece of crimson velvet in grain, a piece of purple velvet, a piece of damask purpled, a piece of crimson damask'.[20]

Osip Nepea's long stay in London was a masterpiece of stage-managed munificence. The timing was fortunate: Mary's court was at an elevated pitch of anticipation at the return to England of the queen's only occasionally present husband, King Philip of Spain. Four days after Philip's arrival in Westminster, Nepea went to Whitehall Palace; it was Lady Day, 25 March, the feast of the Annunciation, the first day of the new calendar year. With no context against which to judge what he saw, Nepea experienced London as a Catholic city in a kingdom now part of a composite Habsburg monarchy that stretched from England and the Spanish Netherlands to the Iberian and Italian peninsulas. Nepea may have been entirely unaware of Henry VIII's break with Rome, or the scouring Reformation of Edward VI, the young king who had once given his blessing to Sebastian Cabot's efforts to find the riches of Cathay.

Nepea went to Whitehall on 25 March dressed in cloth of tissue (interwoven with gold and silver thread), with a hat and cape set with pearls and other precious stones. Those with him, merchants like Feofan Makarov and Mikhail Grigor'ev Kosityn, were resplendent in cloth of gold and red damask. The whole party was accompanied to the palace by city aldermen and London's Muscovy merchants, Nepea taking a barge at the Three Cranes stairs, a busy wharf of warehouses and lifting gear a little way down the Thames from Queenhithe: this was exactly the journey that a new lord mayor made to the landing stage at Whitehall. When Nepea arrived at court he gave to Mary and Philip his letters from Ivan IV, made an oration, and presented a gift (less impressive than it would have been before his shipwreck) of eighty sable furs which had been salvaged from the *Edward Bonaventure*. Everything he said was translated into English and, for the benefit of King Philip and his entourage, also into Spanish.[21]

Behind the impeccable protocol were negotiations on the terms of Anglo-Russian trade. That, bluntly, was Nepea's job, however much his visit to London was on the surface an exercise in public relations. On the English side, Mary's government and the Muscovy Company worked powerfully together on the terms of the agreement: Mary had given the company its charter, and the company and its investors possessed financial clout – many of those investors being, of course, courtiers and government officials.

Nepea and his team negotiated with Mary's advisers to produce a 'league and articles of amity', a grand document in Latin authenticated by the great seal of England.[22] These articles reciprocated to Nepea's satisfaction (or at least to the full limits of his negotiating hand) the Muscovy Company's privileges in Russia. They gave trading rights and protection to Russian merchants in England, including the right to establish a base in London, or indeed in any other English city – potentially a headquarters like the Steelyard of the Hanse, matching to some degree the Muscovy Company's warehouses in Kholmogory, Vologda and Moscow.

Diplomats and merchants were pragmatic men with an eye for the possible. But the language of the league with Russia addressed more generally – even aspirationally – the benefits of international trade: 'So do we trust that this good foundation of mutual friendship thus well laid and agreed upon shall bring forth plentiful fruits both of brotherly love and assured amity between us and our successors and perpetual traffic between our subjects.'[23]

However, the Anglo-Russian agreement was much more than this. Of huge significance was the fact that, together, a chartered trading company and the English Crown had used the instruments of diplomacy to negotiate with a foreign power a mercantile treaty. An agreement of international weight and meaning had been drawn up to facilitate privileged trade between two nations. More than this, even, was the fact that the political priorities of Mary I's government fitted hand in glove with the business interests of London's mercantile elite.

The negotiations were opened and concluded within two days of Nepea's audience at Whitehall. He may have been a difficult man to negotiate with, though. One later source says that 'The English merchants found that he was not so conformable to reason, as at first they thought he should have been; being very mistrustful, and thinking every man would beguile him.'[24] But the city's easy hospitality never faltered, and it was doubtless in anticipation of full counting houses that Nepea was dined in grand style by the lord mayor, five of London's leading knights, its aldermen and many of the Muscovy merchants.[25] He was taken on a tour of London to see its sights: 'as the king's palace and house, the churches of Westminster and Paul's, the Tower and Guildhall of London, and suchlike memorable spectacles'. And on 23 April Nepea was an honoured guest at the great feast at Whitehall of the Order of the Garter, England's premier order of chivalry.[26]

The greatest event the Muscovy Company put on for the ambassador was a dinner held in his honour in the hall of the Drapers' Company on 29 April. His embassy was nearly over. So far as the company was concerned, its most important business had been settled weeks before in the trade agreement. But in trade, as in diplomacy, great symbolic gestures were essential. As the Russians well understood – and as the Muscovy Company's men knew from their weeks and months in the Moscow Kremlin – there was nothing like a feast of epic proportions, well lubricated with alcohol, to show all at once generosity, magnificence and friendship.

The choice of the Drapers' Hall was no accident. The Muscovy Company's own base in the port of London was a working headquarters, and probably lacking in space and glamour. Senior and wealthy drapers like John Dymoke and Sir William Chester were investors in the Muscovy trade, and certainly both men were busy in preparing for what the company's accounts called (with a sense of great ceremony) the 'coming of the Moscovian to the hall'.[27]

The hall was on Throgmorton Street, and it was one of the grandest in London. Quick to spot an opportunity, the drapers had bought it four years after the execution of the man who built it, Thomas Cromwell. The great complex of buildings reflected Cromwell's anticipation of the political muscle he would come to exercise during the 1530s. It was a very impressive house for a very important man, with a great gate and a paved courtyard, a winding staircase lit by bay windows and clerestories that led into the hall, a parlour, butteries, kitchens, a cellar, a jewel house, and a beautiful and extensive garden. This garden was an acre and a half, and the drapers nurtured it as much as Cromwell had done, planting it with lilies, roses, columbines, fruit and herbs. With garden borders and hedges of privet and whitethorn, the company had added in 1546 two bowling alleys and a sundial. On a late afternoon in spring, there would have been few more peaceful or pleasurable retreats in London.[28]

But peaceful the meal was not. In Nepea's honour, the city and the Muscovy Company laid on 'a notable supper garnished with music, interludes and banquets', with a heavy emphasis on friendship and good will. They drank toasts, and as a mark of their generosity the company gave Nepea gifts to compensate for his costs in travelling from Scotland to England.[29] Any pain felt by merchants and investors of London at the loss of four ships from its fledgling fleet and of the looting of *Edward Bonaventure* had to be forgotten for the evening: doubtless the company men put their minds to further investments of capital, dazzled by a formidable display over months of canny public relations.

It was certainly not a supper over which to count costs. Instead, there was a trading relationship to be further embraced, a new and exclusive commercial pact between two very different powers. The Muscovy Company had pulled off something remarkable: it now had privileges in importing and exporting goods that other merchants and countries in Europe would envy for decades. The future rewards would be immense.

Dining in the Drapers' Hall that Thursday was most probably Sir William Cecil, perhaps wearing a cap newly bought and the black velvet gown trimmed with fur that had been repaired only a few days before the feast. Cecil was a confident investor in the Muscovy venture, so confident in fact, that he had sent one of his servants along to Muscovy House with the handsome sum of £30 for further shares a fortnight before Nepea and Mary's councillors agreed the new treaty.[30] But there again Cecil had impeccable sources. The chief English negotiator in March 1557 was Sir William Petre, a former colleague and a close friend of the Cecil family. During these months Cecil took boats up, down and across the Thames from his house on Cannon Row near Whitehall Palace to visit friends in Westminster, Lambeth and London. He passed his time at Whitehall playing cards with Queen

Mary's advisers and courtiers. Doubtless the few pennies he lost in the games – usually about 4 pence and never more than 12 pence – were well worth the gossip and information he was able to absorb.[31]

At this time Sir William Cecil was temporarily out of high office. One day he would be secretary again, and after that – as Lord Burghley – lord high treasurer of England. In the reign of Queen Elizabeth I, there would be no commercial venture in which William Cecil did not have a stake or on which he did not have an opinion.

Osip Nepea left London for Gravesend on 3 May 1557. Any later in the year and the voyage back to Russia would have been too dangerous. He was sent off with gifts from Queen Mary and King Philip: beautiful fabrics, a lion and a lioness, as well as plate and tableware and a chain of gold. For his part, Nepea could only describe the gifts sent by Ivan that had been looted out of Pitsligo Bay: furs and skins, a hawk and other birds, with drums and hoops and a lure to call the gyr falcon. The account of the whole embassy, along with an inventory of gifts, was held to be of such significance that it was written up and sworn to by city aldermen and other leading members of the Muscovy Company. With the help of Robert Best, his interpreter, Nepea agreed that it was a wholly accurate narrative. It was a record for posterity – and evidence for both parties of the company's generosity.[32]

A number of things stand out from the visit of Osip Nepea to London in 1557. One is the energy and dynamism of the Muscovy Company, the city elite and the queen's government. The interplay of money and political power was obvious from the beginning. No expense was spared by a company that in the first two years of its existence had lost many men, thousands of pounds in merchandise and equipment, and most of its fleet – in fact, the whole of its £6,000 initial capital investment.[33] Nothing was spared to put on the grandest possible show for Nepea. Its stage management was superb. Everything that London had to offer – its sights, its riches, its impressive livery companies, its people and of course the court of the king and queen – was thrown at the hope of building Anglo-Russian relations. It was very different from what future English ambassadors often experienced in the Kremlin, where, rather than being honoured as guests, they felt more like prisoners.

Who knows what Osip Nepea made of his months in London. Elizabethans who went to Russia often struggled to make sense of people they believed to be little better than barbarians. Even the high nobility and officials were difficult to read: brusque and uncommunicative, they survived (or not) in an imperial court that even by Tudor standards was stark and brutal. Perhaps Nepea's assessment of his English hosts was as unflattering.

In London the effort was believed to be worth it, the potential of Anglo-Russian trade immense. Dedicating a book to the governors of the Muscovy Company six months after Nepea left the city, Robert Recorde wrote: 'if you continue with courage, as you have well begun, you shall not only win great riches to yourselves and bring wonderful commodities to your country, but you shall purchase therewith immortal fame and be praised for ever'.[34] Recorde, like Richard Eden and many others, was overstating the reality. Versed in the arts of persuasive rhetoric, they knew how to talk up a project. But their optimism was infectious: what the investments of men like William Cecil and work of London's Muscovy merchants show very clearly is that what Cecil called 'The society of adventurers of Russia' was breaking through into a new world full of unknown but surely enormous possibilities. 'Adventure', or simply 'venture', soon became fixed in the vocabulary of world ambition, fusing together exploration, trade, investment and, in the future, colonial plantation.

CHAPTER EIGHT

The Brothers Isham

A star in the London mercantile firmament like Thomas Gresham was a very long way from being a typical city merchant. He, like his father Richard, was a grandee, set apart from others by wealth, power, reach and influence. The same was true of the great merchants like John Dymoke of Fenchurch Street, who put their capital into the Muscovy Company and entertained Osip Nepea so lavishly in 1557. Masters of the livery companies, holders of high office in city government, connected by marriage to other influential families, and, of course, possessors of vast fortunes – these were the elite of London, its super rich, the men the city's workaday merchants could only hope to emulate.

One of those workaday merchants was John Isham. He was, on the face of it, the model of ordinariness: prosperous and comfortable, conservative in outlook, always preferring the known to the unknown, averse to risk, but shrewd all the same. The modest office he held in the Mercers' Company for a year in the 1560s speaks eloquently of a man who was never in danger of outpacing himself by overweening ambition. After a long effort at seeking election, Isham became the company's renter warden, supervising the rental income that came in from the mercers' property portfolio. It was a job that called for steady application and a talent for the routine, and John Isham was perfectly suited to it. Solid and dependable, he could never be called a high-flyer.

From a later family history, for which his son was an important source, we know something of Isham's character and personality.

Heavy with platitudes and conventionalities, the account tells us that Isham was generous and upright, a loving but strict father to his children (rarely did he show them 'a familiar countenance, as some fond fathers do'), companionable, and a recounter of stories and table talk, fond of sayings and proverbs. An intellectual polymath he most certainly was not: 'Worthily it might be reported of him, he was a wise man, though altogether unlearned, writing and reading English only excepted.' And he loved his food, on which subject the biography is disarmingly blunt: 'Of body he was corpulent, big-boned and reasonably tall of stature, a man of very good stomach to his victuals.' When his term as renter warden came to an end, he gave a feast for the company of almost embarrassing magnificence, so proud was he of having held the job. Just to prove a point, he had made sure before the meal that the carcasses of the thirty-three 'fat and large' bucks for the kitchen were put on display, leaving his fellow mercers goggle-eyed.[1]

A portrait of John Isham from this time shows him in all his mercantile bulk. Given that his only exercise was in the saddle, riding on business between London and the cloth country of the West Riding of Yorkshire, by his early forties he was heavy and thickset, with dark cropped hair and a greying beard. Put this together with the family biography, and we might assume that Isham was merely a sedentary bore with a stock of tedious stories and trite proverbs. But actually his portrait quickly brings us up sharp. Though not a brilliant picture, the artist managed nevertheless to capture the alertness and resolution of Isham's eyes. A prominent nose and high cheekbones suggest that before he encountered the bulk of middle age, Isham had been physically imposing as a young man. Even in this modest portrait, he looks perceptive and appraising. In business he was no man's fool. His were not the exceptional talents of a Gresham or any other merchant prince, to be sure: they were instead the solid achievements and comforts of a man who knew his trade and operated according to principles of business he had tested over a quarter of a century.

The man himself looks, not surprisingly, conventional enough. Isham's heavy black gown is edged with brown fur, and he wears a merchant's black cap. He has an eye for fine things, of course, and in his left hand he holds brown leather gloves so delicately patterned that set beside the bulky merchant they look a little incongruous. The artist offers all the usual reminders of mortality, the standard kit of the standard portrait. The rich material evidence of Isham's success in life sits alongside emblems of the inevitability of his death. Sometimes they are one and the same thing. Above the table in the picture is a wall clock in black, red and gold, a neat way of showing Isham's taste for a beautiful and functional object, while at the same time reminding the viewer of the passing of time and the futility of worldly goods. Isham's index finger of the same hand points to a human skull, the familiar memento mori of portraits.

The portrait tells us even more, though. John Isham had ambitions that lay outside the city. As a younger son of minor gentry with very little money, he wanted an estate of his own, and for twenty years or more Isham dreamed of the life of the country gentleman. Standing out boldly in his portrait is Isham's coat of arms, that defining badge of gentility and landed belonging. In Tudor society, true gentlemen kept estates, not warehouses – indeed, true gentlemen were often socially contemptuous of the very merchants who kept afloat with loans their pretensions to gentility. But Isham, born a gentleman, was not shy about how he made his money. In the picture, his account books and ledgers sit prominently on a plain and handsome wooden cabinet.[2] We can imagine Isham sitting for the portrait in the counting house of his house on St Sithe's Lane in the parish of St Antholin's. If the coat of arms and the folds of the background curtains were the standard contrivances of the portrait of any man of substance, the account books, as well as paper and a quill, were the immovable fixtures of Isham's mercantile life, and he was proud of them.

It had all begun a quarter of a century earlier on a summer's day in the last half decade of Henry VIII's reign. On 19 June, St Peter's Day, in 1542, sixteen-year-old John Isham arrived in London from his father's estates at Pytchley in Northamptonshire, a quiet rural backwater. John had no schooling to boast of and no rounded education to prepare him for the wider world. He was thrown into a city that must have left him utterly stunned.

John's new master was Otwell Hill, a native of Rochdale in Lancashire, a young man probably still in his middle twenties, and a rising star of the Mercers' Company, to which he had been admitted as a freeman only two years earlier. Hill had married into the great mercantile dynasty of Lok, as prominent in London in the 1520s and 1530s as the Greshams (and a family to be followed a little later in this book), having served his apprenticeship with William Gresham, Sir Richard Gresham's brother and Thomas Gresham's uncle. Young John Isham had fallen on his feet, working for a master who was young, dynamic and successful.

But John's time with Otwell Hill was all too brief. Within months Hill was dead, and Isham worked out his apprenticeship with another mercer, Thomas Gigges, who ran a successful business between London and Antwerp. From Gigges, Isham learned his trade from the ground up, doing menial chores like carrying water to and from the Thames, a fact that Isham's titled successors later tried to expunge from the family biography.[3]

John Isham always knew that he would have to make his own living. In a landed society that privileged eldest boys as the heirs to estates, John was the fourth youngest of five sons of Euseby and Ann Isham. Euseby's ancestors had owned their land since about 1300, but the fantastic size of his family (he and Ann had twenty children in the space of twenty-one years) stretched an at best modest income, and the Isham boys had to make their own way in the world. The older boys, Giles and Robert, were able: Giles, the eldest, went off to London to study law in the Middle Temple; Robert to Cambridge with an eye on the priesthood. The three youngest sons, Gregory, John and Henry, whether by inclination, choice or circumstance, became merchants. Each one steadily worked his way from apprenticeship to the freedom of the Mercers' Company.

In the case of Gregory Isham the fit was perfect: he was an instinctive merchant, astute and intelligent, with the keenest eye for business of all his brothers. Gregory, we can guess, was our John's hero: five or six years older, the young man who, by the time John went to London, was impressively settled in the life of the city. Giles and Robert were men of different spheres; their talents and accomplishments in London and Cambridge were so many strides ahead of John's very limited education. Taught by his father in order to save money, John's written English was at best passable.

So much of John Isham's story is bound up with Gregory's, a little of whose energy and talent is captured by the family history: 'bred up likewise in his youth at learning', Gregory 'afterwards being of sufficient years was sent to London, and there bound prentice to one free of the company of the mercers, to which trade he diligently applying himself did in short time grow to such great wealth . . .'⁴ Needless to say, he was a great success.

Gregory Isham got his freedom of the Mercers' Company in 1546, and it is likely that from the beginning he had an excellent feel for mercantile strategy. He almost certainly kept a close and protective eye on his brother. John worked hard. As Thomas Gigges's apprentice he saw at first hand his master's operation in Antwerp, buying and selling real estate in the city, but principally trading in luxury textiles, importing into England through Antwerp fine silks and satins. This was the foundation for the Ishams' own businesses as mercers.⁵

Gigges himself died in 1551, the ninth and final year of John's apprenticeship. With his freedom of the Mercers' Company granted that same year, Isham was now a merchant in his own right. Like any young man setting himself up in the city, he needed capital, but there was no family fortune for him to call on. When Euseby Isham died in 1546, he had left to John a little over £3: it was not a sum of money to sniff at, but it was a long way short of what John needed to establish his business.⁶

John Isham knew how to seize the moment, though, and that is exactly what he did – surely with Gregory's advice – in October 1552, when he married Elizabeth Barker, the widow of Leonard, a fellow mercer, who had died a few months earlier. Elizabeth had been Leonard's second wife; his first, next to whom he was to be buried, lay in the mercers' chapel of St Thomas of Acon. The Barkers were well provided for in Leonard's will. Elizabeth would have the lease of the family home on Ironmonger Lane, and if she remarried (which Leonard's will rather assumed that she would), their eldest son Thomas would inherit a tenement on White Hart Street, as well as other property. The Barkers' daughter Anne, set up as well as a daughter could be, was her father's executrix. As a business arrangement, Elizabeth's marriage to John Isham was perfect. She opened up for her new husband further contacts in the city. Most importantly of all, she was the source of capital. This fact was recounted by the family history with some delicacy, which recorded that the 'convenient sum' Elizabeth brought to the marriage was increased by John's 'careful heed'.[7] This 'convenient sum' was in fact a fortune. It was the classic pattern of life in the very small world of the city. There seems little doubt that John Isham would have known the Barker family very well, and probably soon after Barker's death he had been among those enjoying the mercers' dinner for which Leonard had left the generous sum of £8.[8]

In the years that followed, John worked with his brothers Gregory and Henry to build up a business that concentrated on the familiar trading axis of London–Antwerp. They did not involve themselves in ventures like the Muscovy Company, though they knew merchants who did: Gregory's brother-in-law Walter Marler, a London haberdasher and merchant adventurer, was one of that company's charter members in 1555.[9] The brothers' business was a success, and Gregory, John and Henry worked well together. With their base in London and factors handling most of the Ishams' business in Antwerp, they exported fine plain-woven black cloth (broadcloth) from Suffolk, Somerset and Wiltshire and light kerseys from Yorkshire, and bought and imported luxury textiles. To find the best cloth John was a frequent visitor to Halifax and the precipitous Pennine hill country of Yorkshire. His London house in the 1550s was on Bow Lane, not far from Cheapside, the showcase of London's riches.[10]

Mortality was as real to Isham as it was to any other Londoner of his generation. The first death in London that shaped his life was Otwell Hill's. The second, Leonard Barker's, helped him to trade as a merchant in his own right. The third was the most shocking and challenging of all: his brother Gregory's in September 1558. Gregory was thirty-eight years of age, a talented and rich man, the father of Euseby and Mary and the husband of Elizabeth, who was pregnant with their third child. Gregory, seriously ill, had made his will at his manor house at Braunston in Northamptonshire on 3 September. John was there to witness it.[11]

Something of Gregory's plainness manages to sidestep all the conventional phrasings and formulae of a standard will. He chose not to preface the disposition of his worldly goods with elaborate declarations of faith and intercession. What little he said by way of preamble was earnestly to the point. He wanted to settle his affairs 'to the intent I may be the more at quiet to give myself wholly to godly meditations'. Leaving ten shillings to the curate of his London parish, Sir Draper (the 'sir' was an old-fashioned honorific title for a priest), the work of burying him would fall to the priests of Braunston: Gregory Isham wanted to lie in his own soil. He gave money to the poor of the parishes of the Isham family's estates, with no direction (as would have commonly been the case decades earlier) that they should pray for him. He made bequests for his family and servants: to his 'loving mother', to large numbers of cousins, and to nephews and nieces. He wanted his many friends to have mourning rings. He left £20 to give his fellow mercers two commemorative feasts, knowing very well the form of the company's dinners and suppers, with their sumptuous courses of venison, sturgeon, pike, salmon and quails. Perhaps he too had attended Leonard Barker's dinner a few years earlier.[12]

Most important to Gregory was the future security of his children – Euseby, Mary and Elizabeth, the unborn little girl he never knew. He sought the help of powerful men in the city, one a former master of the Mercers' Company, two others city aldermen, asking them 'to be good to my wife and children and that they will be a means that my children's portions may be distributed according to my will', all for the reward of £5 each: it was a token sum of money for men worth thousands of pounds, a modestly significant mark of friendship and obligation. Gregory, it was clear, was a young man with friends in high places.

What is striking about Gregory's will is how far he also fell back on the help and support of all his brothers. There were years between them, and yet together they would keep an eye on Elizabeth and their children. They would even, in the event of Elizabeth's remarriage, step in to take the custody of Euseby, Mary and little Elizabeth. Though it looks today a peculiar and even cruel arrangement, this was simply a further device to protect the children's inheritance and future.

Lying sick in his Northamptonshire manor house, Gregory knew that tying up the business of his estate would be tricky. He took no chances, naming all four of his brothers as his executors and appointing six others to oversee the whole process, one of whom, Sir Edward Griffin, was a Northamptonshire neighbour as well as the queen's attorney general. Another was Gregory's brother-in-law and partner in business, Walter Marler: no one would have been better acquainted with Gregory's financial dealings.

Time was short for Gregory Isham. London and the English countryside were being ravaged by fever and influenza. Whatever killed Gregory, it did its work quickly. He was dead within a couple of weeks at most.

Death invites the inevitable processes of officialdom and administration. Three weeks after Gregory Isham settled his affairs and made his peace with God, a post mortem inventory was made of his London house, and less than a fortnight after that, the same was done for the manor house in Braunston. The searching eyes of the appraisers missed nothing. Everything was reduced down to sums of money in pounds, shillings and pence, even the rites of parting. At Braunston, precisely £100 was spent on 'meat and drink, black gowns, priests' wages and other things' for Gregory's funeral.[13]

From the bare bones of these documents, we can make at least a bit of sense of Gregory's life in London: we can visualize what a merchant's house looked like in the middle of the sixteenth century – we can imagine the colours and the textures.

Gregory's London house was in the parish of St Michael Paternoster, a stone's throw from the Vintry wharf and the Three Cranes stairs, a busy place for boats and passengers into the city. The bustle of the Thames was very much part of Gregory's life. Not far away was an almshouse founded by Richard Whytyngdone (the 'Dick Whittington' of the popular story) in the early fourteenth century and still supported over 200 years later by the Mercers' Company. Gregory left in his will the handsome sum of £20 'towards the maintenance of the poor children' there.[14]

The large townhouse had plenty of room for family and servants to live and work in comfortably. It had a kitchen, a hall, a parlour, a buttery, nurseries, a great chamber and attics. One chamber was put aside for Elizabeth Isham's confinement in the final weeks of her pregnancy. The Ishams' possessions were, not surprisingly for a family in the business of importing fine materials, sumptuous. Their parlour was furnished with tapestries, a Turkey carpet, cushions, chairs and stools. The colour scheme of their great chamber was red and green, and in it were featherbeds and bolsters, a table, a money chest and blankets and rugs. Cushions were of crimson velvet, the carpets of hard-wearing fustian (a coarse cloth woven out of cotton and flax), which Gregory imported through Antwerp from Italy. The curtains were strikingly colourful: crimson sarsenet (this was a very fine material of silk) with vallances of taffeta (a type of plainly woven silk with a flecked surface) and sarsenet and gold fringes.

Gregory had looked every inch the successful merchant. About town he had cut a dash in gowns faced with damask and satin, cloaks of velvet and damask, coats of satin and taffeta, his russet satin doublets, and others of black satin and taffeta with satin sleeves. He had a cape and carried a sword, that essential accessory for any gentleman.[15]

What the Ishams did to relax is harder to ascertain, though the appraisers noted two virginals in the family's London parlour. Familiarity with the virginal was, like learning to dance, part of the repertoire of gentility and refinement. Did Gregory himself play, or was it a pastime for the whole family? Tuition on the virginal was cheap enough in London for a man of Gregory's fortune. Just over a year before he made his will, for example, one Master Ellys had been paid nine shillings and fourpence for seven weeks' teaching of the virginal to the young gentlemen in Sir William Cecil's household, and to tune the instruments themselves cost two shillings – the combined cost of a gallon of strong beer, four short boat trips on the Thames and two loins of veal for the kitchen table.[16]

Gregory's intellectual interests are much harder to make out. Probably he sat somewhere in the middle range between his brothers: at one extreme there was Giles and Robert, barrister and priest, and at the other John. The appraisers in 1558 noted only two books or manuscripts in the London house. One was 'a story of Mary Magdalene', the other 'a story of Jonas'. Both were biblical and probably devotional. But the second title offers an intriguing possibility, for it might refer to 'The Storie of the prophete Jonas' by William Tyndale. This had been printed around 1531 in Antwerp, the town

Gregory knew so well, and it was a risky book to be found reading in Mary I's Catholic England. Tyndale was a banned author, and
Protestants in 1558 were being burned at the stake, or in exile. It was
common enough for English merchants to pick up Protestant beliefs
in the trading cities of mainland Europe; Tyndale himself had sought
refuge in Antwerp. This might explain the plainness of Gregory's will
when it came to expressions of faith. With no reference to the intercession of the Virgin Mary or the holy company of heaven, Gregory
was businesslike to the end: 'I commit myself wholly both body and
soul into the hands of Almighty God . . . believing perfectly through
Christ's death and passion that it [his own body] shall be raised up
again at the latter day and joined to my soul to live there everlast-
ingly.' This is a very long way from being conclusive evidence that
Gregory was a Protestant. But if he was, one of his elder brothers – a
brother whom he trusted with the welfare of his family – was a chap-
lain to a combatively orthodox Catholic queen.[17]

Gregory's townhouse was a business headquarters as well as a family
home. It was self-contained and self-sufficient, with its own courtyard
and well, a counting house and warehouses. And those warehouses
in September 1558 were full of valuable goods: a fortune's worth, in
fact, of Dutch worsteds and English kerseys, along with a great stock
of the finest Italian fabrics, like fustian, satin, silk canvas, sarsenet and
mockado, the latter an imitation velvet of wool and silk. All of this
was valued at the eye-watering sum of over £1,200.[18]

What is clear is that Gregory Isham's business was in full play.
'Neither a borrower nor a lender be' is the famous line from
Shakespeare's *Hamlet* (I. iii. 75), but no London merchant – especially not the entrepreneurial Gregory Isham – could take Polonius's
advice very seriously. Gregory's accounts show how complex and
extensive his interests were: he imported and exported textiles, and he
both owed and was owed great sums of money. Many of his cloths –
and his debts – were in Antwerp. It was business on a grand scale.
Well over £7,000 was owing to him, and he had debts not far short
of £9,000 in England and Flanders. The cloths sitting in his warehouses in St Michael Paternoster had come, through Antwerp, from
some of the greatest Italian merchant houses in Genoa and Lucca.
He had warehoused in Antwerp £3,000 worth of English cloths, and

he was beginning to store wool at his country house in Braunston. His landed estates had a capital value of about £8,000. Just for comparison, in the 1550s the yearly income of Eton College, a prestigious royal school foundation of about 100 boys and men, was something around £1,000.[19]

Gregory was a moneylender: he used his capital to make loans for which he charged interest, something long condemned by the Church and actually illegal in England. As we will discover later in this book, Elizabethan preachers and moralists were caught up in a moral panic about usury. But merchants were not theologians. To a man like Gregory, money was a commodity, to be lent out for a reasonable price.

A single example neatly illustrates Gregory's financial and social reach as a moneylender. In 1553 he and his brother-in-law Walter Marler and a fellow mercer called Thomas Revett lent £3,700 to the earls of Westmorland and Rutland, a loan secured on some of the earls' properties in Northamptonshire and Devon. Careful to keep within the letter of the law, no payment of interest was stated, though concealed it was probably in fact the sum of £700 – that is 23 per cent of the loan amount of £3,000. Their contract stated that the full amount of money was to be repaid on 30 November 1554, St Andrew's Day, 'at the font stone . . . in the cathedral church of St Paul in London . . . betwixt the hours of nine and twelve o'clock in the forenoon . . . in gold or in new fine silver money current in England'. This was common and established practice: before the building of the Royal Exchange (the subject of the next chapter), the font of St Paul's was well known as the place in London where debtors settled with their creditors.[20]

We have to make the imaginative leap for ourselves: Gregory, Walter and Thomas pacing St Paul's on a morning in late autumn, waiting for the earls' stewards to bring the bags of gold and silver coins. It would have been one transaction among many – the practice of usury right under the nose of the Church. And the Church knew it. One Elizabethan bishop was furious at how openly the cathedral was routinely abused for worldly purposes: 'The south alley for popery and usury, the north for simony, and the horse fair in the midst for all kinds of bargains, meetings, brawlings, murders, conspiracies, and the font for ordinary payment of money, as well known to all men as the beggar knows his bush.'[21] How Gregory Isham reconciled all this with the 'godly meditations' of his will, we will never know. But there again he did not become a rich young man through naive passivity; his eye for business was a shrewd one.

Steady, perceptive, careful, solid, a taker of few risks: the John Isham of the portrait is very much the man we find at work in London after Gregory's death. John had only a little of Gregory's mercantile panache, and there is no way to tell how, had Gregory lived for a decade or two more, the brothers would have done business. Perhaps they would have invested in the new opportunities beyond Europe; perhaps Muscovy might have beckoned. Already London ships like the *Swallow* and *Charity* were coming in from Russia with their cargoes of wax, tallow, cordage, silk, calf skins, cinnamon and rhubarb, yarn, wolf skins, seal skins, wolverines, minks, ermines and beavers. New markets beyond Antwerp called.[22]

Yet John Isham was content to follow the old path. In the 1560s, ships came into the port of London carrying Isham's cargoes of fustian from Genoa and Naples, boultel (a very fine cloth that could be used for sieving), worsted and frizado, velvet and mockado, and madder for dyeing cloth. But some of the old certainties were changing. By 1567, when John Isham gave that great carnivorous banquet for his fellow mercers, London's trade with Antwerp was a long way from its days of mercantile glory decades before. There were political pressures and fears of revolt, with religious civil war in the Low Countries, as well as diplomatic wrangling with England. An especially harsh winter in 1564 and 1565 had frozen the Scheldt river and precipitated famine in Brabant, and there was reported to be 'great anxiety and lack of business' in Antwerp. All of these realities shook some of the old faith in Antwerp's greatness.[23]

John Isham typified London at its most conservative. He was not a man built for new markets, opportunities and challenges. He knew his trade, and he was canny with money and, like Gregory, understood the technique of lending money while staying within the law and was himself a prolific moneylender. For years he had had an eye on the country of his Pytchley ancestors, and in 1560 he once again seized a life-defining opportunity. In that year he borrowed £250 from three fellow mercers to buy the manor of Lamport Hall in Northamptonshire. The seller was none other than Sir William Cecil, friend of Sir Thomas Gresham, Muscovy investor, and now, after a few years out of office in Mary's reign, secretary to Queen Elizabeth I. In 1572 John Isham retired from London and went off to live at Lamport as a country gentleman.

When John Isham made his will, in 1594 or 1595, he saluted his former life in London. Just as his merchant's account books had been props in his portrait, he was not embarrassed about how he had made his money. A gentleman with a manor house and estates, as well as a merchant, he wanted 'a fair plain stone' to lie on his grave showing

> such other arms, superscriptions, verses and posies . . . to testify to posterity of what house I descend both of my father and of my mother's side, that I was a merchant adventurer of the city of London and free of the company of mercers and by that means, with the blessing of God, received of my preferment, and was enabled to purchase the manor of Lamport and patronage and the church thereof.[24]

CHAPTER NINE

'So fair a bourse in London'

Right at the heart of Elizabethan London was a building that John Isham would have visited only in the few years before his retirement from the city – and one that Gregory Isham would not have known at all. It became the centrepiece of London's mercantile world, a mark of the city's ambition, exercising a magnetic pull on all Londoners. It was just as much a stage for London as the city's theatres. Every day a drama was played out there that never changed or altered: London's double triumph of riches and poverty. The building was Sir Thomas Gresham's Royal Exchange.

There is something neatly symmetrical about the story of the Exchange – like the building itself, a late Renaissance masterpiece so startlingly different from the old Gothic crevices of St Paul's Cathedral and Guildhall. In the 1530s London's ruling corporation tried and failed to build the kind of bourse of which other towns and cities could boast. As lord mayor, Sir Richard Gresham had nudged along Thomas Cromwell and Henry VIII. All the obstacles were overcome, but, for reasons that are not at all clear or obvious, nothing happened. A generation later, Sir Richard's son Thomas took it up as his own project. As the royal agent in Antwerp he knew that town's New Bourse as well as anyone else alive, monitoring every nuance of its business. And so the story's symmetry lies in the completion by Thomas Gresham of a project more than thirty years in gestation in which his father had played a part.

There was always something a little different about Thomas Gresham's career. Unlike his father, he never quite took the conventional path. Where a city man of Gresham's standing might set out in middle age to pursue civic office, Sir Thomas showed no particular inclination to stand for election as a sheriff, alderman or lord mayor. He was the queen's man in Antwerp as well as a London merchant of formidable reach. And he was enormously wealthy. The furnishings of just one of his country houses, Mayfield in Sussex, were valued at an astonishing £7,550, though grander still was his great palace at Osterley Park in Middlesex, and Gresham House on Bishopsgate, a few minutes' walk from the Exchange, was furnished at a cost of £1,128. Sir Thomas Gresham was a tycoon *sans pareil*, more than simply a merchant (even a startlingly rich one) and different from the normal kind of royal courtier. He was ever the elusive hybrid, as he had been since his twenties and thirties. We can look back to that early Antwerp portrait of Gresham in his twenty-sixth year – on the surface unadorned and unostentatious, but in style and message audaciously ambitious – and compare it to Sir Thomas two decades later in a picture by the Dutch artist Anthonis Mor. This time seated, turned at an angle to the viewer, Gresham looks as plain as ever in an impeccable black doublet of a glossy sheen, with a high white ruff and a black cap. The face is one, not so much of power or the need to command, but of experience, patience and control: spare, lean and a little lined around the cheeks and eyes, with a greying beard and steady eyes of hazel. Above all, it is Gresham's eyes, which in their time had observed and made sense of so many people and situations, that hold and penetrate. The quiet shrewdness of the man is impossible to miss.

The Royal Exchange was Sir Thomas Gresham's greatest legacy, his gift to his native city. It was a bourse for the merchants of Europe; for Gresham, a home from home. But more than this it was a place where Londoners could meet, rivalling St Paul's and Paul's Cross churchyard. It represented 'exchange' in the broadest sense: of conversation, of news and opinions, of entertainment, of goods and services, standing magnificently between Cornhill and Lombard Street. The words the poet Daniel Rogers used to describe the New Bourse in Antwerp applied just as well to Gresham's Exchange in London: 'A confused sound of all languages was heard there, and one saw a parti-coloured medley of all possible styles of dress; in short . . . a small world wherein all parts of the great world were united.'[1]

No one understood the fact that an exchange for London was long overdue better than Richard Clough, Sir Thomas Gresham's man in Antwerp. Clough was every inch the gentleman, elegant in a dark and fashionably slashed doublet, pale-coloured hose and high ruff, with fine brown gloves and a decorated rapier. Doing business with some of the most powerful and elusive men in Europe, he dressed the part. But Clough was very much more than a man of style. His face was one obviously beaten into shape by experience and hard work, with the pale forehead of a man who spends too long at a desk, and the wrinkles and greying beard of a tough negotiator who put in long hours at the bourse and on the Antwerp quayside. And he valued plain words. About London's city fathers he was blunt. They refused to do anything for the benefit of London, he wrote to Gresham in 1561, 'as for example considering what a city London is, and that in so many years they have not found the means to make a bourse, but must walk in the rain when it raineth, more like pedlars than merchants'. Clough himself was itching to get on with the job: 'I will not doubt but to make so fair a bourse in London as the great bourse is in Antwerp.'[2]

The key year was 1563. In May, London's ruling corporation asked Gresham to build a bourse for the city – that was the formal approach, but Sir Thomas and the corporation had probably been in informal talks for a few months beforehand. Perhaps the negotiations would have rumbled on for months or years. What changed the dynamic completely and terribly was the shock for Gresham of the death of his son Richard at sixteen years old. Richard had fallen ill in Antwerp on 1 May with what was described as pleurisy. He was bled, but the treatment achieved nothing and he died the following day. One of Gresham's servants wrote, with characteristic Tudor understatement: 'it was no small grief unto my master and to my lady for that they had no more children'. Bereft of a son and heir, Gresham threw both his grief and his considerable fortune at the Exchange project.[3]

The deal was done in January 1564: Gresham would build an Exchange for London out of his own fortune, on condition that the city government would provide the necessary land. A small committee of aldermen quickly found a suitable site on the north side of Cornhill. The negotiations for clearing the site of tenements, storehouses and gardens (not to say the tenants themselves) were as delicate as they were expensive, and in the demolition work a number of people were seriously injured, two of whom were nearly killed. But by May 1566 the site was ready, and on Friday, 7 June, between four and five o'clock in the afternoon, Gresham himself laid the first brick. The bricklayers who continued the work were most probably Flemings, which led to a howl of protest by the Bricklayers' Company of London, the picketing of the building site and intimations of violence, all of which were negotiated with authority by London's corporation and by Gresham. Gresham's choice of master mason was Hendryck van Paesschen of Antwerp. John Stow described in his *Survey* the completion of the Exchange: 'by the month of November, in the year 1567, the same was covered with slate, and shortly after fully finished'.[4]

From the start it was an ambitious project. An early scale drawing shows a rectangular court with columned arcades. There would be two doorways, one out to Lombard Street, the other to Cornhill, as well as two towers, each with a spiral staircase and (shown prominently on the plans) a double privy on the ground floor. Early copperplate engravings by Frans Hogenberg show just what Paesschen was able to do, for Gresham's Exchange was to become an achievement of architectural grandeur unrivalled anywhere in London, not even by the Guildhall. It was one of the few buildings in the city to be entirely new, rising up from a site cleared of its past. The work of a Londoner whose money came from Antwerp and whose master mason was a Fleming, it was a powerful statement of cosmopolitan ambition.

This is really the key to understanding Gresham's intentions. Building the Exchange was a conflation of private and public ambitions: Sir Thomas, a great benefactor of his city, was offering to London's citizens a bourse that was the equal of Antwerp's. Perhaps it was a mark, too, of Gresham's objective of recalibrating the relationship between Antwerp and London; certainly the Exchange was out of all proportion to London's status in the early sixteenth century as a modest satellite of western European trade and finance. But the Exchange was more even than this. It was Gresham's personal

1. A village just outside the city: an Elizabethan fete at Bermondsey on the south bank of the River Thames, attributed to Marcus Gheeraerts the elder, c. 1569.

2. Members of the City elite: the lord mayor (*left*), an alderman (*centre*) and a senior merchant of a livery company (*right*) in their robes of office.

3. Commemorative death's head rings were commonly bequeathed in the wills of wealthy Londoners as memento mori.

4. Paul's Cross, the most important preaching pulpit in London, in the shadow of St Paul's Cathedral, and close to the stalls and shops of the city's printers and booksellers.

5. Detail from Anthonis van den Wyngaerde's panorama of London in the 1540s, looking north from Southwark showing London Bridge. The tall, narrow, decorated spire whose point is between the two distant settlements (Holywell Priory in Shoreditch is on the right) is that of Austin Friars.

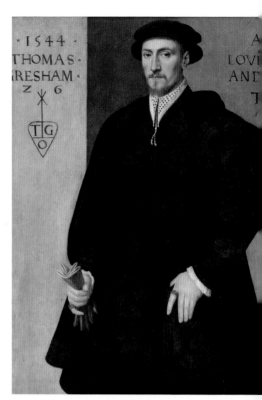

6. A family motif: the grasshopper of the influential Greshams, engraved on the underside of a ring.

7. Thomas Gresham in 1544: the young merchant as aspiring courtier.

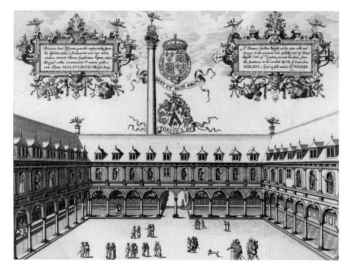

8. Sir Thomas Gresham's greatest legacy, the Royal Exchange, c. 1600, modelled on Antwerp's bourse, a meeting place for Londoners to rival St Paul's Cathedral.

9. The model merchant: John Isham in his middle forties, well-fed and prosperous, but conscious, too, of his own mortality.

10. Sir Thomas Gresham in his prime by Anthonis Mor: wealth, power and taste all in a single portrait.

legacy. Where most city grandees were content to hold high office for short periods of time, Gresham wanted to make a permanent, physical mark upon London, something for future generations to wonder at. 'I will not doubt but to make so fair a bourse in London as the great bourse is in Antwerp': Richard Clough's words might have been Gresham's. And Clough's language is significant: more than simply a place of business, the Exchange stood for beauty, culture and consumption, a meeting place for Londoners to rival St Paul's Cathedral and Paul's Churchyard. By nature a workaholic, Sir Thomas Gresham had spent a fortune on his own houses; and as a lover of fine things, the Exchange offered just a sample of his tastes as a connoisseur.

The scale of the building was correspondingly impressive, a quadrangle eighty paces long and sixty wide, estimated by one visitor to be large enough to hold 4,000 merchants. Engravings show a courtyard paved and cobbled in a style reminiscent of the patterning of a knot garden. Marble columns set ten feet apart formed a sheltered colonnade on two levels. Similar columns helped to form the two doorways, above each of which was a bas-relief of the royal arms of England. There were three galleries. The first, known as New Venice (a nod to the most formidable European mercantile city in the Mediterranean), was a kind of undercroft used by drapers and cloth merchants. In the upper gallery there were perhaps as many as 150 stalls selling expensive merchandise. The southern gallery on Cornhill was known 'the Pawn'. This name, like the building itself, had its origins in the Low Countries: 'pawn' derived from *pand*, the kind of cloister or arcade where merchants and retailers set up their stalls during the great Antwerp marts. Set just to the east of the southern doorway out onto Cornhill was a tower with a bell, which rang to indicate the end of trading as well as to tell the time. A clock with face and hands was added in 1599.

It was emphatically the *Royal* Exchange, enhanced in reputation and status by the queen's personal approval. The message projected by those bas-reliefs of the royal arms of England was unambiguous. Elizabeth herself made a visit in January 1571. Attended by her nobility, she came from Somerset House on the Strand to Temple Bar, along Fleet Street and Cheapside to Threadneedle Street. After dining with Sir Thomas at Gresham House, she and her courtiers entered the Exchange from Cornhill: 'and after that she had viewed every part thereof above the ground, especially the pawn, which was richly furnished with all sorts of the finest wares in the city: she caused the same bourse by an herald and a trumpet, to be proclaimed the Royal Exchange, and so to be called from thenceforth, and not otherwise.'[5]

For merchants, the working day at the Exchange (or at least the formal bit of it) was very short. There were two sessions: one before dinner (between eleven o'clock and twelve noon), the second before supper (between five and six o'clock in the afternoon). Hundreds of merchants and moneylenders met to put together deals and to gossip. Instead of meeting in the jostle of Lombard Street in all weathers, separate 'nations' of merchants had – in theory – their own allotted portions of the Exchange. In practice, however, movement throughout the courtyard and colonnades was free, and one would have bumped into all kinds of men from France, the Low Countries, Germany, Italy and Spain. Activity and busyness were the keynotes, with the arrival and departures of the merchants' 'posts' (couriers) bringing news and bills of exchange.

One essential thing to emphasize is that the Exchange was a public and not a private space. It was more like a shopping mall that happened also to be the beating heart of a city's mercantile life. All sorts of Londoners went there – to buy and consume, to pose, to talk, to gossip and to beg. This was no more incongruous than the way Londoners had long used St Paul's Cathedral: 'It is . . . the whole world's map, which you may here discern in its perfect'st motion jostling and turning. It is a heap of stones and men, with a vast confusion of languages . . . The noise in it is like that of bees, a strange humming or buzz, mixed of walking, tongues, and feet.'[6] St Paul's was still busy with Londoners. But the Exchange was quickly its equal – noisy, lively and polyglot. As Thomas Dekker put it: 'They talk in several languages, and (like the murmuring fall of waters) in the hum of several businesses: insomuch as the place seems a Babel (a confusion of tongues).'[7]

One Elizabethan moralist worked up a whole parade of characters who walked in the Exchange, finding in that place eighty paces by sixty a microcosm of society: merchants, retailers, strangers (that is foreigners), 'sadducees and libertines', worshipful gentlemen, the poor, printers and stationers, sailors, sea captains and gentlemen soldiers, musers upon God, as well as husbands and wives 'who likewise have their pleasurable walking there at convenient times'.[8] For those with full purses, it offered things to appeal to all the senses: shopping at the Pawn, listening to music played in the galleries on the long afternoons of spring and summer, and eating and drinking next door at the Castle tavern, where gentlemen frequently entertained their friends.[9]

The shops were kept only by retailers who could afford Gresham's hefty rents. Wealthy Londoners bought all kinds of things there. Thomas Deane, a haberdasher, sold parchment, writing tablets, silk purses, pomanders, linen and silk threads, tapes and ribbons, fastenings for clothes and shoes, decorative laces and ties, and handkerchiefs. Deane, with a house in the city furnished in modest affluence, did well for himself. Other shops in the Pawn sold mousetraps, birdcages, shoe-horns, lanthorns and jew's harps, and in the upper gallery there were the shops of apothecaries, booksellers, goldsmiths, glass-sellers and armourers.[10]

Fashionable consumption coexisted with poverty. London's poor were rarely out of sight of the rich, and the Exchange was a magnet for vagrants and beggars hoping for a few pennies out of the purses of merchants and gentlemen. These beggars were an irritation, and the perennial Elizabethan anxiety about poverty and crime meant that the city fathers were always trying to clear out of the Exchange the rogues, thieves, beggars and children who were upsetting the dealings of honest citizens. 'The poor . . . pass to and fro through the Exchange,' John Payne wrote in 1597, 'both the godly poor and profane poor, the one under God's blessing and favour, the other under his frowns and displeasure.'[11] The deserving poor, genuinely in need of help, like a woman who gave birth in the Exchange in 1573 or a little boy abandoned there by his mother in 1601, were supported by local parishes.[12] But stalking wealthy Elizabethans in particular was the fear of being duped by organized criminals – a character like the 'cheater' or 'fingerer', who on the surface looked like a well-dressed gentleman, but was in fact an idle vagabond. Such men, so John Awdeley wrote in 1575, 'go so gorgeously, sometime with waiting men and sometime without. Their trade is to walk in such places where as gentlemen and other worshipful citizens do resort, as at Paul's, or at Christ's Hospital, and sometime at the Royal Exchange.' Feigning friendship, the fingerer preyed on rich and naive young gentlemen with an eye to spending their fortunes.[13]

Bookshops quickly became a feature of the Pawn. Clever London booksellers like Thomas Hacket saw the possibilities for selling books from the most glamorous meeting place in the city, and in about 1572, having run shops in Paul's Churchyard and on Lombard Street, he opened a new one in the Exchange at the sign of the green dragon. Hacket, as we will see later, was an entrepreneur with a keen feel for the kinds of books Londoners liked. He specialized in books on practical subjects like seamanship and navigation, and he came to the Exchange with a reputation for translating the latest accounts of global discovery. Hacket also knew the secret of an eye-catching title, and he had a talent for courting the interest of powerful patrons: the first book that advertised his shop in the Exchange begins with a letter of dedication printed for Sir Thomas Gresham himself, with a self-confident flourish: 'From London, by yours for ever, Thomas Hacket.'[14]

At the Exchange, information was a living currency all of its own. Merchants relied upon private letters, reports and fuller newsletters that gave digests of intelligence from all over Europe. A busy and crowded exchange was the perfect place for some Londoners to advertise themselves and their wares; for others it was an easy spot to merge in with the crowd and hide in plain sight. Noticed there in 1574 was the English agent of the feared Spanish general, the Duke of Alba, one Philippes, 'seen at London [at] the Royal Exchange, all in black apparel, after the manner of a merchant'.[15] Plastered all around were bills and posters, just as they were outside St Paul's Cathedral.[16] One of Gresham's own doctors advertised in the Exchange, and Sir Thomas himself complained when a 'testimonial upon the Royal Exchange of the cures he hath done' was pulled down by a rival physician.[17] The seriously aggrieved Clement Draper, a merchant whose business was ruined by a long-running feud with the Earl of Huntingdon, made his case directly to fellow merchants at the Exchange: 'I protested publicly unto my creditors and spread the same protests upon the Royal Exchange and gates of the city, to manifest my wrongs and to crave liberty.'[18]

The Royal Exchange was not surprisingly a gift for London's Elizabethan and Jacobean dramatists. It was a place of meeting and of movement, of (sometimes dubious) business, of retail and fashion and all the promenading vanities moralists and preachers loved to denounce. It was itself a kind of stage that opened up the imaginative worlds of the city and its many kinds of people, capturing something of the range of human life and society: as Thomas Dekker wrote, 'This world is a Royal Exchange, where all sorts of men are merchants: kings hold commerce with kings, and their voyages are upon high negotiations.'[19]

Later Elizabethan dramatists looked to the city around them, one their audiences knew as well as they did. The first to do this was William Haughton in *Englishmen for My Money* (1598), a play about merchants, gentlemen, money and thwarted love. A key part of the action takes place at the Royal Exchange, during the first session of business between eleven o'clock and noon. When the Exchange bell rings to end business for the morning, it marks also the end of the scene. Haughton's merchants come together to do business – in part the principal character's selling off of his daughters in marriage. There is news of a ship with a valuable cargo lost to pirates, and the arrival of the post carrying a highly suspicious and potentially ruinous bill of exchange that turns out in the end to be genuine – a portrayal of that ever-fine balance between a merchant's success and the failure of his business. Money is everything. 'Go to th'Exchange,' one character says, 'crave gold as you intend.'[20]

Naturally the Royal Exchange was deeply imprinted with associations of mercantile money, retail and display, while news and information were very important too. In the revised version of Ben Jonson's *Every Man In His Humour* (c. 1610), reputations are made and lost at the Exchange. The merchant Kitely, fearing his ruin, says, 'Lost i' my fame for ever, talk for th'Exchange', a position quite opposite to that of the real Clement Draper who, out of desperation, went publicly to the Exchange to recover his name and his liberty.[21]

For dramatists, the Exchange offered a superlative vehicle for the scrutiny of riches and consumption. In Thomas Middleton's *A Chaste Maid in Cheapside* (1613) we encounter the heavily pregnant Mistress Allwit, who in the final stages of her pregnancy (longing for nothing but pickled cucumbers) is surrounded by all her trinkets. Her husband says:

> When she lies in,
> As now, she's even upon the point of grunting,
> A lady lies not in like her; there's her embossings,
> Embroid'rings, spanglings, and I know not what,
> As if she lay with all the gaudy-shops
> In Gresham's Burse about her . . . (I. ii. 30–35)

If this kind of consumption touches on the vulgar, there was the further vanity of public display in the city's fashionable places. In Jonson's *Bartholomew Fair* (1614), Master Littlewit says of his promenading wife:

> I challenge all Cheapside, to show such another – Moorfields, Pimlico path, or the Exchange, in a summer evening with a lace to boot as this has. (I. ii. 5–6]

And there was satire even sharper than this, exposing some of the tensions and contradictions of a society frankly ambivalent about the social and moral consequences of vast wealth. The Exchange existed for the purposes of making and spending money: no statement of the power and reach that came from material riches could be more obvious. Of two kinds of Londoner who worked in the Exchange – the first a merchant and moneylender, the second a boy who stole out of poverty – who, a poet asked, was the greater criminal?

> 'Mongst the monopolists on London's burse,
> Priscus was ta'en for cutting a purse,
> And being reviled, made this bold question, 'Why
> Are these monopolists excused, since I
> Did cut but one man's purse, while they cut all?'
> But thus we see, the weakest goes to th' wall.[22]

The bold innovation of writers like Dekker, Haughton, Jonson and Middleton was to use in their drama the city they and their audiences knew. London was their stage: it was familiar and tangible; they saw it all around them in stone, brick, wood, plaster and slate. Layered upon this were the people and their manners. London, huge and still growing, was ripe for dramatic action, and somewhere like the Royal Exchange made it possible to explore the inevitable strains of a city where tens and then hundreds of thousands of people were living, working, playing and dying so closely together. Audiences in the theatres of Southwark must have loved the familiar types and stereotypes of London, for they wrestled constantly in their own lives with money, power, social rank and the pretensions and ostentatious display of the elite, as well as with poverty and crime. Types were easy to spot and, in the safety of the theatre, to laugh at. In *Every Man Out of His Humour* (1599), Ben Jonson set out with sharp satirical wit the characters of his play. Fastidious Briske is the 'neat, spruce, affecting courtier', the fashionable dresser who practises his salutations in a mirror, and can 'post himself into credit with his merchant only with the jingle of his spur and the jerk of his wand'. Deliro is that merchant, rich and dull, the 'good doting citizen of London'. Macilente is 'a sufficient scholar, and travelled', embittered by the world's reluctance to reward his talents, and Puntarvolo a 'vainglorious knight' with a talent for self-flattery. In the play Deliro reflects upon his financial hold over Briske. All of Briske's lands are mortgaged and now forfeit to Deliro, who imagines Briske's arrest for debt. But the courtier has a plan: Malicente tells Deliro that Briske has gone off to meet Puntarvolo at a notary's office at the Royal Exchange (IV. i. 77–84).

For the audience watching *Every Man Out of His Humour*, all of this was tangible and immediate. It was there in London, a boat ride or walk from the theatre – across London Bridge to New Fish Street and Gracechurch Street, left on Lombard Street and in at the southern door of the Exchange. Jonson's audiences would have been familiar with all the social microclimates of London, of which the Exchange was one of the most intense. They would have known that merchants attracted specialists like notaries, whose job it was to draw up and witness legal documents. They would have seen for themselves the parading of glamorous gentlemen in slashed doublets and hose, shopping at the Pawn and dining at the Castle tavern. They would have recognized, too, that the real power lay with the merchants and moneylenders in their discreet but expensive black suits. Here was a world crammed with different kinds of people – noisy, raucous, polyglot and complex, always shifting and fluid – and shown for all to see on the stage of Sir Thomas Gresham's Exchange.

CHAPTER TEN

Aliens and Strangers

Elizabethans loved to poke fun at foreigners, and they had a taste for easy stereotypes. The boorish Dutch were heavy drinkers and the Italians conspiring Machiavels, while the over-courteous and amorous French looked down their noses at everyone else. The Muscovy trade helped to popularize the image of ordinary Russians as fat, drunk, slow-witted, servile and superstitious, and their rulers as cruel tyrants.

Some of this was patriotic self-congratulation; at the best of times there was a feeling that odd and often bad things happened abroad. And who, after all, could offer a better measure of normality than the English and their ways? A strand of it was prejudice: the categories of 'savage' and 'barbarian' came easily to Elizabethans. But much was simply born of fear in a difficult and confusing century, when faith and religious identity got tangled up in all sorts of ways with old friendships and especially old rivalries with nations and peoples. Some foreigners shared the same faith; others were condemned as idolaters, persecutors and enemies. Who, in a far from straightforward world, was to be repulsed and who embraced? With France divided by civil war and the armies of King Philip II of Spain rumbling through the Netherlands, thousands of Protestant men, women and children from those countries sought refuge in England. Many, unsurprisingly, were drawn to London.

Safety from religious persecution was a straightforward enough justification for migration. But what if there was a different reason? What

116

if some of them wanted to come to London to work, with religion as a secondary consideration? Elizabethan Londoners found their loyalties and prejudices pulled in two opposite directions. For foreigners who came to London the challenge was as great. Very many émigrés must have asked themselves, were they wanted, and would they ever be welcomed?

Tudor Londoners were long used to rich strangers who lived and worked in their city. Old family firms such as the Cavalcanti and the Bonvisi were deeply embedded in city trade and finance – without them Henry VIII would have been unable to raise his first Antwerp loan in the 1540s. Money bought privilege and political contacts. The fully Anglo-Italian Antonio Bonvisi (he was born in England) was in 1535 the fifth richest man in London, a great friend of Thomas More, and saluted by Sir Richard Gresham when he made his will in 1549: Bonvisi, along with practically the whole governing establishment of England, was bequeathed one of Sir Richard's mourning rings. For merchant-bankers like Antonio Bonvisi and Antione Vivaldi (Vivaldi was in 1535 jointly the fourth wealthiest man in London), life was easy. They were diplomats of the banking houses, intermediaries and brokers of power.[1]

Resident aliens living in London – or elsewhere in England – were called 'strangers'. Many merchants were happy to live in London on these terms, just as London's merchants had long lived and worked in Antwerp, yet remained subjects of the English Crown. But some aliens who came to London and wanted to stay permanently preferred to give up their status as aliens and become naturalized. This could be done in one of two ways: the first was to secure a private Act of Parliament, the second to obtain a grant from the Crown. Both processes were cumbersome and expensive, and well beyond the means of those without money and time to spare or influential friends to call on. For the vast majority of aliens living in London – at least for those who worked in modest trades – to become naturalized citizens was impossible. They remained 'strangers', whether they liked it or not.

The lives of most strangers in Elizabethan London were hugely different from merchant princes like the Bonvisi or Vivaldi. Without the cushioning of wealth or contacts, they were set apart from those with native rights. This meant that, for ordinary men and women working to earn a living, their lives were hedged in by restrictions. They could not own property or take a case to the law courts. A stranger paid a higher rate of tax and could not practise his trade in any parts of the city under the authority of the corporation of the lord mayor and aldermen: all over London was a patchwork of old precincts and liberties (many of them remnants of the old dissolved monastic houses) just out of reach of London's elite. For outsiders, the path to citizenship was blocked: every citizen of London had to swear an oath that he would not employ as an apprentice a stranger's son.[2]

Thus strangers, native non-citizens and citizens occupied the same city, but lived parallel and exclusive lives. Status was everything: to have it meant possessing an identity and a voice; not to have it meant difference and marginalization.

Especially prominent in London from the 1550s were émigrés from the Low Countries. Their reason for settlement in the city and elsewhere in England was clear enough: Dutch Protestants, persecuted and in danger, needed help. The first émigrés of the early 1550s were joined in the 1560s by many more. When Spanish forces took Antwerp in 1567, thousands of people fled the town, along with many others from Brabant, Dutch Flanders and the French-speaking Walloon provinces of the southern Netherlands. Given London's historic trading connections with the Low Countries, the city was a natural refuge.[3]

In 1549 King Edward VI gave the fledgling Dutch community a place in which to worship, founded as the 'Temple of Jesus' in London's abandoned Augustinian priory near the city wall at Bishopsgate.[4] This was the Austin Friars, where in the 1520s Thomas Cromwell had lived in a smart house at the priory's gate. In its heyday Austin Friars was a great complex of beautiful buildings, with a spectacular church spire described by John Stow in his *Survey of London*: 'a most fine spired steeple, small, high, and straight, I have not seen the like'.[5] By Edward's reign, however, that was the only reminder of the priory's pre-Reformation grandeur. Gutted of everything valuable, the choir of the priory church was being used to store coal and corn, and the lead from the roof and even gravestones and monuments were sold off for cash. The Dutch community occupied the church's old preaching nave, a plain building of rag-stone and chalk, decorated with flint – a nod, perhaps, to a cleansed Calvinist austerity. In 1553 the congregation stood at about a thousand strong.[6]

The Dutch Church in London kept a close eye on members of its community living and working in the city. Like Calvinist congregations throughout Europe, church ministers and elders enforced strict moral discipline, and it is thanks to the records they kept that we have some insight into strangers' lives in Elizabethan London. The ideal was quiet godliness, exemplified by the description of one émigré as 'a good, honest, modest woman', safely and properly married.[7] But month after month and year after year, the church elders at Jesus Temple heard confessions for sexual indiscretions, drunkenness, fighting and what they called 'irregular' lives. There was, for example, the case of a woman called Corbeels who assaulted another woman near London Bridge because of a debt. Wouter Shoemans was disciplined for entertaining a married woman in his house overnight. The illicit relationship of Jan Bones and Naantgen Marten fell apart after Naantgen refused to marry him. Jan, it seems, was trouble from the start, imprisoned at least once in London 'on account of his bad language and tumultuous conduct'. War back in the home country upset new lives being made. Mayken Vanden Wortele, all alone in the city, was told that her husband, Joos, had died in fighting near Haarlem. In London she had fallen in love with another man, Gillis Jacobs, and went to the consistory for permission to marry him. With no sure evidence of Joos Vanden Wortele's death, the consistory refused, and the elders asked her to wait for firm news. But she and Gillis married anyway, 'secretly, and outside the community'.[8]

Only a small number of Dutch strangers were hauled before the consistory at Austin Friars, and of those a portion were repeat offenders. Most émigrés behaved themselves and simply got on with the business of putting food on the table, trying to fit in with their surroundings, living in small stranger households of husbands, wives, children and servants. Many of the men were skilled craftsmen and tradesmen, and a good number of them managed to build up thriving businesses.

Most strangers of whatever nationality kept to the edges of London; but the fact that they so often lived and worked in liberties just beyond the reach of the city government was for the mayor and corporation as infuriating as it was threatening. These were the nooks and corners of the city: Southwark, East Smithfield, around the Tower of London, at St Martin's and near the city ditch between Bishopsgate and Bedlam.

Dutch, French and other strangers worked as button-makers, hat-makers, starchers and tailors, silk-spinners, silk-weavers, brewers, leatherworkers, joiners and glass-makers. A good number worked in the workshops of London's printers. With many skilled typeset-ters and bookbinders coming from Antwerp, whose book trade had been large and highly sophisticated before the troubles, it was no sur-prise that the printers of the Elizabethan city readily used stranger workmen, even if it meant they had to circumvent the regulations of the printers' and booksellers' trade body, the Stationers' Company. Some established and expert printers from Antwerp set themselves up in London. Wouter van Lin (anglicized to Walter Lynne) lived and worked in 1549 on Somar's quay at Billingsgate and had a shop next door to St Paul's School in Paul's churchyard at the sign of the eagle.[9] Another Antwerpian successful in London was Steven Mierdman, who sometimes printed books for Lynne to sell. Reyner Wolfe, born in Gelderland, was King Edward VI's official typographer and book-seller of works in Latin, Greek and Hebrew.[10] The technical virtuosity of men like these gave London a profile in European print culture that the city had never before enjoyed.

How did Londoners feel about the strangers? And how did the stran-gers settle themselves into a city that so obviously discriminated against outsiders? The topic of immigration touched off all kinds of mixed responses and emotions – practically every point on the scale between tolerant humour and outright aggression. But two big themes emerge.

The first is that most Londoners were just about able to contain their most violent impulses. And those impulses were powerful. Fear and dislike of strangers united poor and rich, though for different reasons: the poor, because they felt their charity being squeezed and their at best precarious existence in the city threatened, and the rich because they saw the hard-won privileges of citizens under attack.

The second theme is just how deftly many strangers were able to work themselves into the fabric of London society, while keeping a sense of separateness and community. And the context of the city is important too. In spite of the restrictions on strangers' lives, they were probably no worse off than the tens of thousands of unskilled English migrants who flooded into the city in the 1580s and 1590s. Most Londoners struggled to live and work, but the strangers had the advantage of their skills, their tenacity and their sense of group identity.

Any outsider is likely to be the butt of jokes and humour, and that was certainly true of the Dutch in Elizabethan London. This verse was composed in the fifteenth century:

> Ye have herde that twoo Flemmynges togedere
> Wol undertake, or they goo ony whethere,
> Or they rise onys, to drinke a barelle fulle
> Of gode berkyne; so sore they hale and pulle,
> Undre the borde they pissen as they sitte.[11]

There is nothing so resilient as a national stereotype, and lines like these would not have been out of place in Thomas Dekker's comedy historical romance *The Shoemaker's Holiday* (1600). Dekker gives us a good idea of how laughing at foreigners allowed Elizabethan Londoners both to mark them as outsiders and to tolerate their difference.

In the play, a young man named Rowland Lacy, nephew to the Earl of Lincoln, falls in love with the daughter of the lord mayor of London. To drive the couple apart, the earl sends Lacy to France to fight in the wars. But Lacy deserts his commission and secretly returns to England. Using skills he has picked up on his travels, he disguises himself as a Dutch shoemaker. A master shoemaker considers giving him a job. His journeyman is the mischievous Firk.

Lacy makes his entrance onto the stage singing a ridiculous song about an intoxicated 'bore van Gelderland': 'There was a boor from Gelderland, merry they be. He was so drunk he could not stand; pissed they all be.' (I. iv. 39–44)[12] Firk thinks the singing Dutchman

looks like a shoemaker, and asks him 'Are you of the gentle craft?'
'Yes, yes, I am a shoemaker', Lacy replies:

LACY: *Yaw, yaw, ik bin den skomawker.*

FIRK: *Den skomaker,* quoth 'a! And hark you, skomaker, have you all
your tools – a good rubbing-pin, a good stopper, a good dresser,
your four sorts of awls, and your two balls of wax, your paring
knife, your hand- and thumb-leathers, and good St Hugh's Bones
to smooth up your work?

LACY: *Yaw, yaw, be neit vorveard. Ik hab al de dingen voour mack
skoes groot end klene.* [Yes, yes, never fear. I have everything for
making shoes large and small.]

FIRK: Ha, ha! Good master, hire him. He'll make me laugh so that I
shall work more in mirth than I can in earnest.

Firk sees at once the chance for heavy drinking with strong beer.
Making fun of his foreign accent, he says that Lacy's 'yes, yeses'
sounds like a pet jackdaw: '*Yaw, yaw!* He speaks yawing like a jackdaw that gapes to be fed with cheese-curds. Oh, he'll give a villainous
pull at a can of double beer.' (I. iv.75–95)[13]

Dekker plays here with all kinds of jokes. We find the social order
turned upside down (the nephew of an earl becomes a humble shoemaker), the familiarity of the drunken Dutchman, and of course
Rowland Lacy's comedy patois. We can assume that Lacy's mock
Dutch was understandable enough to be funny for Dekker's audience.
This was exactly the kind of humour that must have gone down a
storm with London's theatre audiences: sharply observed, irreverent,
subversive and satirical.

Of course the contrived fantasy of Rowland Lacy's assumed life
on stage – the lovelorn gentleman playing a part with a funny accent
to get close to his master's daughter – was a long way from the
more common experiences of London's Elizabethan strangers. They
were probably laughed at (at least on the stages of Southwark) and
more often than not tolerated, but sometimes resented and hated.
While Thomas Dekker made fun of Rowland Lacy's 'Yaw, yawing', the
residual grievances of London's dispossessed, especially of its apprentices and apprentice drop-outs, boiled over on occasion into riots
and violence. In 1606 the lord mayor accused the strangers, working

outside the city's jurisdiction, of having 'devised and practised by all sinister and subtle means how to defraud and defeat' London's charters.[14] These were strong words to use. If the wealthy and comfortably established of London felt under assault by the strangers, then it is no surprise that the city's disenfranchised underclass took to the streets against those they considered aliens and outsiders.

In a conservative and protectionist society, resentments and accusations bubbled away under a surface tolerance. There were worries about secret corruption, with foreigners up to no good. Early in Elizabeth's reign, for example, there were allegations that a cabal of thirty-seven Italian merchants working in England had together tried to subvert the English cloth trade in Antwerp and used sharp practice by making bogus entries in the London customs books.[15]

More potent a decade later was the worry about economic migration. Seeking a new life in London to follow one's faith free from persecution was one thing, but coming to the city just to work was quite another. The data that London's government and stranger churches (by Elizabeth's reign there were French and Italian congregations as well as the Dutch community at Austin Friars) sent on to the queen's Privy Council gave cause for concern – for the churches as well as for the London corporation. In 1573, returns showed that 7,143 resident aliens were living in the city and suburbs. Of these, 2,561 (nearly 36 per cent) admitted that they had come to London only to find work. A high number of strangers belonged to no church at all, but even of those who attended the stranger congregations, 1,828 said that they were in London primarily for work and not for religion.[16] With these numbers in mind, all the systems that the corporation, the stranger churches and the Bishop of London had in place to monitor foreigners in the city, including certificates of church attendance and formal letters of introduction from congregations in mainland Europe, seem to mean very little. Effectively under the radar of discipline and supervision, large numbers of strangers wanted to live their own lives and work to keep themselves in the city.

A worry for natives was that the strangers were more skilled than they were: the fear was that a stranger employed meant an unemployed Londoner. Those at the lower end of London's social hierarchy believed that strangers threatened their fragile livelihoods. For those at the top of the city hierarchy, the fear was, oddly, a similar one. The privileges of citizenship seemed to be under attack, and if strangers were allowed to compete on equal terms with citizens, disaster would follow. When in 1587 the Privy Council suggested opening up the city's cloth market fully to foreigners and strangers, the mayor and aldermen reacted in horror: such a change, they protested, would break apart the Company of Merchant Adventurers and bring violence to the streets of the city.[17] Hackles were quick to rise, sharp accusations easy to make. In 1595 London's English silk-weavers wrote directly to the pastors of the French and Dutch Churches, alleging that strangers sought 'their own private lucre without any Christian regard of the native born of our country and without respect of the liberties of this honourable city'.[18]

With worry and anxiety bubbling away for decades, it was no surprise that London's strangers lived with threats and intimidation and sometimes open violence. Trouble never seemed far away. In 1567 the city's watch was put on alert because posters were pasted up around London that showed Flemings strung up on gallows. Conditions in the city inflamed native prejudices and grievances. London had a sizeable underclass of young apprentices, masterless men, vagrants and demobilized soldiers. By the 1590s there were high levels of unemployment in the city, some vicious outbreaks of plague and sickness, successive crop failures, rising prices and military conscription. It was easy to blame the strangers for problems not of their making. Resentments built and built, to be released either by riot or the threat of it.

At about the time of the performance of *The Shoemaker's Holiday*, in 1600, Thomas Dekker collaborated with other playwrights, including William Shakespeare, on a play about the life and career of Sir Thomas More. A part of the play went back to the events of 'Ill May Day' in 1517, when the houses of merchant strangers in London had been attacked. In *Sir Thomas More*, More himself, as a city under-sheriff, confronts the rioters. At the end of the sixteenth century, such a dramatic moment acted out on stage was something much more than a remote historical reference. The play dealt here with an issue so delicate and potentially inflammatory that it was censored by Edmund Tilney, an official of Queen Elizabeth's court. Tilney insisted upon a sleight of word: any reference to 'stranger' had to be replaced by the much less problematic (but still to some extent loaded) 'Lombard', a reference to the powerful bankers who had lived and worked in London a century or two earlier.[19]

In the surviving manuscript of the play, the scene written by Shakespeare does not have this concession to Tilney. In it, citizens and apprentices come on to the stage armed and looking for trouble. Using language that Shakespeare would have heard for himself on London's streets and in its alehouses and taverns, they complain about the price of food, claiming that butter would rise to an astronomical eleven pence a pound (in 1600 this was easily more than the daily wage of a London labourer), meal at nine shillings a bushel and beef at four nobles a stone. One of them says, 'It will come to that pass if strangers be suffered'. They get angrier, talking about the infections brought into the country by foreign vegetables. 'Strange roots' undo poor apprentices; they are trash, breeding sore eyes, infecting London with a palsy that will make the city shake; the unfortunate vegetables are 'bastards of dung' (II. iii.1–20).

Thomas More speaks to their humanity. He speaks also to the worries, fears and anger of Londoners at the turn of a new century:

> MORE: . . . what is it you have got
>   Although we grant you get the thing you seek?
> BETTS: Marry, the removing of the strangers,
>   which cannot choose but much advantage the poor
>   handicrafts of the city.
> MORE: Grant them removed, and grant that this your noise
>   Hath chid down all the majesty of England;
>   Imagine that you see the wretched strangers,
>   Their babies at their backs, with their poor luggage,
>   Plodding to the th' ports and coasts for transportation,
>   And that you sit as kings in your desires,
>   Authority quite silenced by your brawl,
>   And you in ruff of your opinions clothed:
>   What had you got? I'll tell you: you had taught
>   How insolence and strong hand should prevail,
>   How order should be quelled . . . (II. iii. 78–93)

The message, powerfully written, was plain: in persecuting poor refugees seeking shelter, the rioting men of London were persecuting humanity itself – insolent power would break down already wretched men, women and children. It was a brave and provocative piece of theatre: *Sir Thomas More* confronted a Southwark audience with its own prejudices and discontents, the rumblings and moanings of a city on the edge, picking on the outsiders out of fear or hatred or both. The words of More in the play are Shakespeare's, and so too is that unerring sense of the human condition. And Shakespeare himself knew some of the strangers of London at close hand: on Silver Street, tucked away in the north-west corner of the walled city, he lodged from 1603 with a family of French émigrés called the Mountjoys.[20]

To make a home in a city is to make in turn all kinds of adjustments to life, work and worldview. Given that London was the kind of city it was, there were tens of thousands of new Londoners, most of them not strangers, who had to adapt themselves to its sheer scale. It must have been a big enough shock for natives, but for strangers the challenge was immense, especially given the restrictions on where they could live and how they could (or could not) work. Not surprisingly, the strangers tended to coalesce in their own communities. To break out of those created further difficulties; to live and talk like a native while holding on to one's family and community was the greatest feat of all, and we can be sure that many second- and third-generation strangers achieved it, though not without a struggle.

An illustration of all this can be found in the lives of two Cornelis Spierincks, father and son, who lived in Elizabethan London. The elder Cornelis, born in Antwerp, was a prominent Calvinist there, and brought his family and servants to the city soon after Antwerp's short-lived 'Wonderyear', when Calvinists experienced freedom of worship – until King Philip of Spain sent the Duke of Alba into the the Low Countries with an army of 10,000 crack Spanish troops and, in the Conseil des Troubles (nicknamed by Calvinists the 'Blood Council'), established a mechanism to root out heresy. The Spierincks, like so many Protestants in the Low Countries, found in London safety for both body and conscience.

They rented first in the parish of St Benet Sherehog, but then settled in Ironmonger Lane close to Guildhall, where Dr Spierinck practised as a physician. He was an elder of the Italian Church in London and a pillar of his community. He died in 1578, leaving a rather terse will that he dictated in Dutch. It was witnessed by two notaries, of whom one, Paul Typootes, was a fellow elder of the Italian Church. To his son Cornelis, Dr Spierinck bequeathed his estate, his six best shirts, a piece of fine black cloth, and his summer and winter clothes. As for his daughter Mary, he expected from her no complaints about what she received from the will: she and her husband Francis still owed him 500 guilders from the 1,000 they had borrowed.[21]

The younger Cornelis was training to be a notary public with Paul Typootes. To read the wills Typootes and Cornelis drew up in the 1580s and 1590s is to be taken to the bedsides of stranger merchants living in London, and to see something of the weave of community life. What stands out from these wills are double obligations of charity to the stranger churches and London parishes and the complexities of having far-flung families, businesses and real estate in the Netherlands.

On a July day in 1582, Cornelis and Typootes went to a house on St Nicholas Lane, close to the Royal Exchange, where they witnessed the will of a Dutch merchant stranger called Melchior van Asse. Cornelis must have known Melchior for the whole of his life in London: he was a man of substance from the old country, a native of Gelderland in the central Netherlands, and for years a stalwart of the Dutch congregation in London, living in the city probably before Cornelis was born. In 1550 he had been one of the first deacons at Austin Friars. Responsible for supporting the members of the congregation, Melchior would have seen at close hand men and women making new lives for themselves in the city, as well as keeping in touch with friends and family in the Low Countries. Melchior van Asse was one of the foundation stones of a proud community.[22]

He was married twice, first to Anna, the mother of their four children, and then to Maijken (or Mary) Obrijs. Melchior and Maijken had married at Austin Friars in April 1575. Maijken was the widow of a Dutch church elder called Thomas Soenen, and probably Melchior had known her since she and Thomas had first come to England about ten years before. The stranger community of London, especially at its elite end, neatly paralleled the patterns of citizen marriages and remarriages – theirs was a very small world.[23]

And so, on that summer's day in 1582, Paul Typootes and Cornelis Spierinck helped Melchior van Asse tie up his affairs in London and the Netherlands, overseen by at least one of Melchior's very old friends, another merchant stranger called Geleyn de Beste, with whom he had once served as deacon at Austin Friars. Melchior van Asse had known London for over three decades – easily the entire lifespan of an Elizabethan Londoner. Yet he was bound by the deep ties of the Dutch community whose focus, for van Asse and others like him, was the Jesus Temple at the Austin Friars.[24]

With the wills and testaments of London's strangers, Cornelis Spierinck learned his trade. The kind of work he did meant that he knew the most private business of many families just like his. And he did well for himself. By 1585 he was a notary in his own right. Eight years later he was living in St Christopher's parish with his wife Katherine, their boys of seven and five, and their two servants, both strangers, one born in London, the other in Brabant. A few years after that, in 1599, he moved to the neighbouring parish of St Bartholomew's near the Exchange, a place we will return to later.[25]

This very short account of the two Cornelis Spierincks could be replicated many hundreds of times over. It is the classic émigré story: a father who spoke his own native language to the end – conservative, wary, comfortable in his community; and a son who was able to push further out into the stronger currents of city life. Where Dr Spierinck was a man who had preserved his separateness, young Cornelis was of a different generation and experience. His memories of Antwerp, if indeed he had any, must have been fragmentary. Though rooted in the émigré community, his world was London and its people. In the 1590s his life was settled in a part of the city that was busy and international, five minutes' walk from Austin Friars and the French strangers' congregation on Threadneedle Street, and just across the road from the Royal Exchange. He and his family heard the bells of St Bartholomew's ring to celebrate the queen's birthday in September and the anniversary of her coronation each November. They were Londoners by adoption – but so too were many thousands of others.

Cornelis Spierinck takes us back, just for a moment, to Sir Thomas Gresham's Royal Exchange. The Exchange was a notary's paradise of merchants' business, with news brought daily from the Low Countries by the posts and couriers. Its very architecture conjured a memory of Antwerp. For those in the shadow of its bell tower, natives as well as strangers, it spoke to a cosmopolitan reality – a difference and otherness accepted or challenged – that a growing and complex city was trying to make sense of.

CHAPER ELEVEN

'Travails, pains, and dangers'

When Ivan the Terrible's ambassador, Osip Nepea, had left London for Russia in 1557, the young man who went with him as the Muscovy Company's captain was already one of the most precocious mercantile adventurers of his day. His name was Anthony Jenkinson. Four years earlier, when he was twenty-four, Jenkinson had seen the Ottoman sultan ride into Aleppo at the head of a vast army. It was a memory to last a lifetime: Suleiman the Magnificent in cloth of gold and precious stones, his crown topped by white ostrich feathers, a monarch resplendent and commanding. Jenkinson stands out from his contemporaries, almost a prototype for the hero of a John Buchan thriller: a man of the world, tenacious and imperturbable, endlessly inventive, a born diplomat equally at ease in royal courts and hostile wildernesses.

The Muscovy Company in 1557 was ambitious for success. Its losses in men, ships and cargo in only three years would have broken any other mercantile venture. But behind the company was the combined financial and political heft of the city of London, its charter members and its investors. Those investors were some of the most powerful figures in England: law officers, royal councillors and leading courtiers. In its trade negotiations with Nepea in 1557, the full power of international diplomacy had been directed at a single corporate operation that, by its charter, commanded a monopoly of trade and exploration, not only with and beyond Russia, but throughout the whole northern ocean. No mercantile company could have been more enmeshed in city and government.

Much of the company's attention was given to building up its knowledge and expertise: it was, after all, trying to make sense of an empire that it had bumped into by accident on the way to Cathay. They possessed fragments of knowledge, from old books of cosmography to tentative maps of Asia. Richard Chancellor and others had written accounts of their months in Russia; the company's agents continued to measure and map the tsar's territories; every fleet that went out to the White Sea refined by practice the hard business of sailing in northern waters. In London there were experts, prominent among them Richard Eden and Robert Recorde, and probably also the elder Richard Hakluyt, a barrister of the Middle Temple, a keen geographer. Another was John Dee, the son of a London mercer, a brilliant and eccentric polymath whose mind was never at rest. A graduate of Cambridge who had travelled into the Low Countries for further study, Dee was introduced at Edward VI's court by the king's own tutor. On Richard Chancellor's return to London from Russia in 1554, Dee and Chancellor had worked closely together. Dee could not praise the Muscovy Company's leading Russian expert highly enough, later celebrating him as 'the incomparable Master Richard Chancellor'. After Chancellor's death, Dee gave tuition to the company's chief pilots, the brothers Stephen and William Borough.[1]

Dee's time in the Low Countries meant that he knew some of the greatest geographical talents in Europe. He was a voracious collector of books and instruments, the owner of two great globes made by Gerardus Mercator and an astronomer's staff and ring made to the designs of the famous Gemma Frisius. He also devised his own instruments for those going on the Muscovy voyages, such as hour, half-hour and three-hour sandglasses, sea-compasses and a water clock that was supposedly able to measure the seconds of an hour. Even to measure a minute accurately in the sixteenth century was a huge step forward in timekeeping.[2]

And so it was that with these resources – political and diplomatic support as well as intellectual firepower – the merchants and investors

of Muscovy House pushed and pressed themselves to dominate
Europe's Russian trade.

John Dee was always and emphatically at the centre of his life's narrative. Anthony Jenkinson was not. Like many merchants, he was a clear,
precise and observant writer. But he wrote very little about himself, and
the early years of his life especially are obscure. Born in 1529, the son of
an innkeeper in rural Leicestershire, Jenkinson made his way – perhaps
through London, perhaps through another English port – out to the
empire of the sultan he and others called the Great Turk, where, in his
early twenties, he had his own ship, men and cargo and Suleiman's safe
conduct. In the 1540s he must have served some kind of apprenticeship,
just as he must have served some kind of master: but neither is docu-
mented. He really appears out of nowhere. Jenkinson's one slip from
his habitual modesty was later to allow the younger Richard Hakluyt
to print the accounts of his travels in *The principal navigations*. Even
then, Jenkinson never indulged in self-heroic hyperbole.

His talent was for the unknown, the alien and the unfamiliar. He
was all at once a merchant, an adventurer and a frontiersman – tough
and fearless, with a keen observer's eye and a talent for supple diplomacy. All of these qualities would help him to pursue the Muscovy
Company's double objective in 1557: to consolidate its operations
in Russia after the treaty negotiated with Nepea, and to push on to
Cathay and the empire of the Great Khan. What helped with the first
of these was Jenkinson's easy relationship with Ivan the Terrible. The
second was as much on his agenda as it was on the company's.

The *Primrose*, *John the Evangelist*, *Anne* and *Trinity*, all four ships
under Jenkinson's overall command, sailed out to Russia by the now
familiar route around Scandinavia. On 6 July 1557 the fleet passed
by the place where Sir Hugh Willoughby and his men had perished
on that first expedition to Cathay, near the River Varzina, at the latitude of 68 degrees north. They arrived safely a few weeks later at
St Nicholas on the White Sea. Nepea and his entourage left Jenkinson
and the company's men to make their own way south to Moscow. It
was a journey with few comforts: 'All the way I never came in house,'
Jenkinson wrote, 'but lodged in the wilderness, by the river's side, and
carried provision for the way.' They foraged and camped: 'And he that

will travel those ways, must carry with him an hatchet, a tinder box, and a kettle, to make fire and seethe meat, when he hath it: for there is small succour in those parts, unless it be in towns.'[3]

In December they reached Vologda, one of Russia's major cities and an established base for the Muscovy Company. From Vologda, Jenkinson and his men took post-sledges of the kind that Sigismund von Herberstein, an ambassador for the Holy Roman emperor, had used in Russia decades earlier. Herberstein's account of his embassy, first printed in Latin in Vienna in 1549, was something of a European bestseller (it was translated early on into German, Italian and English), and for Jenkinson – if indeed he had a copy – it was the only serviceable handbook on a country that in 1557 was entirely new to him. A woodcut illustration in Herberstein's book shows the sledges drawn by horses, their passengers wrapped up heavily in furs. This was by far the quickest way to travel during a Russian winter, and in only six days Jenkinson and his men were in Moscow.

Jenkinson's first audience with Ivan the Terrible was on Christmas Day. Received into the emperor's presence, he kissed Ivan's hand. He would have found in the tsar reflections of the magnificence of the Ottoman sultan. Ivan sat on a great throne, wearing a crown and holding a staff of gold in his hand; he was covered all over in gold and precious stones. It was all much as Richard Chancellor had experienced a few years earlier. And like Chancellor, Jenkinson was invited as a special guest to a feast of epic proportions: 600 guests, with Jenkinson placed at a small table directly in front of the emperor. In a mark of great favour, Ivan himself sent Jenkinson cups of wine and mead and dishes of meat. The tableware was staggeringly expensive: out of all the silver, gold and precious stones, Jenkinson estimated a single cup to be worth £400. Indeed, he appraised everything he saw with a sharp eye. He described Moscow and its Kremlin, where 2,000 Tatar warriors had gathered to offer their service to Ivan. Jenkinson recognized at once the unquestioned authority of the emperor: 'He keepeth his people in great subjection: all matters pass his judgement, be they never so small. The law is sharp for all offenders.'[4]

For four months Jenkinson successfully consolidated relations between the Muscovy Company and the emperor and his officials. He was in favour; it was indeed the high point of Anglo-Russian diplomatic relations in the sixteenth and early seventeenth centuries. But Jenkinson knew that his task was to press on into Asia, and so, with Ivan's safe conduct, in April 1558 he set off from Moscow with Richard and Robert Johnson of the Muscovy Company, their Tatar translator (and presumably other servants too) and a consignment of English cloths. If they took with them a European map, it was most likely Herberstein's, which showed in rough detail the countries, provinces, peoples, rivers, forests and mountains of Russia, extending as far as Astrakhan and the northernmost waters of the Caspian Sea. It was at best the vaguest of guides.[5]

They saw within weeks the savage realities of the tsar's wars against the nomadic tribes of the east. In May they reached Kazan on the river Volga, a month later encountering the Nogai Tatars in a country ravaged by war and disease. In his description of the nomadic Nogai, Jenkinson was a precise and compelling observer, making sense of words far from familiar to English ears. He described, for example, the 'hordes' of the Nogai, a word doubtless used by his translator, though it had appeared in English in the works of Richard Eden. A few years earlier Eden had written: 'The Tatars are divided by companies which they call hordes, which word in their tongue signifieth a consenting company of people gathered together in form of a city.'[6] We might imagine Jenkinson before his voyage to Russia doing his homework at Muscovy House with books like Eden's.

Jenkinson missed nothing. He saw fishing for sturgeon on the Volga, and his professional interest was engaged by the kinds of cloths and silks brought by the Tatars out of Persia. In Astrakhan he saw the bodies of thousands of the Nogai who had starved to death, 'which lay all the island through in heaps dead, and like to beasts, unburied, very pitiful to behold'.[7]

All this time Jenkinson and his party kept moving with their packs of London cloth, negotiating raids by bandits and a particularly ferocious storm on the Caspian Sea. They joined a caravan of a thousand camels. In October they met the local potentate, Hadjim Khan, who gave them a feast of wild horse and mare's milk. Jenkinson produced his safe conduct from Ivan the Terrible and presented a gift to the prince. The next day Hadjim Khan sent for Jenkinson. He 'asked of me divers questions,' Jenkinson later wrote, 'as well touching the affairs of the emperor of Russia, as of our country and laws, to which I answered as I thought good'. Thanks to his tact and supple diplomacy, Jenkinson was given further letters of safe conduct. Nevertheless it was a dangerous journey and the caravan had to fight off bandits all the way to Bukhara. It was there, surely with sighs of relief, that Jenkinson and his men arrived on 23 December.[8]

This was as far as they could go. It was in Bukhara, in what is today Uzbekistan, that Anthony Jenkinson found himself well on the silk road to Cathay, which, by his calculations, it would take a further hundred days' journey to reach. But the route was blocked, he was told, cut off by war for the last three years. So Jenkinson and his party stayed in Bukhara, trying to sell the Muscovy Company's cloths to merchants who had travelled from India with their spun silks, red hides, slaves and horses. Jenkinson wrote that these merchants 'made little account' of the English kerseys they had been carrying with them across seas, through forests and over mountains for twenty months.[9]

Bukhara was a very long way from London; but of course for Jenkinson it was not as far as he had wanted to go. Doubtless he had imagined himself in the palace of the Great Khan, a prince by reputation more magnificent even than the Great Turk or the emperor of Russia. Instead, setting out from Bukhara in the spring of 1559, Jenkinson returned to Moscow, still optimistic about the mercantile possibilities of opening up Asia to the Muscovy Company's monopoly. He wrote to the company's agent in Vologda:

> And although our journey hath been so miserable, dangerous, and chargeable with losses, charges and expenses, as my pen is not able to express the same: yet shall we be able to satisfy the worshipful company's minds, as touching the discovery of the Caspian Sea, with the trade of merchandise to be had in such lands and countries as be thereabout adjacent, and have brought of the wares and commodities of those countries able to answer the principal with profit.[10]

He was convinced that they were close to a mercantile coup in Asia that only a decade before would have seemed fantastically remote.

When Jenkinson returned to London, he was feted by the Mercers' Company, which, in recognition of the fact that he had 'been as far . . . in all parts as ever any Englishman', gave him its freedom.[11] In that same year – 1561 – Richard Eden was just as effusive, praising Jenkinson to the skies for the 'travails, pains, and dangers he hath sustained, and hardly escaped, and what diligence and art he hath used in the searching of strange countries, and in the description of those his voyages'. Eden celebrated the Muscovy Company's employment of Jenkinson, 'more like an ambassador sent from any prince or emperor, than from a company of merchant men'.[12] And Eden was right. Jenkinson's skills were those of an accomplished diplomat, vital when the operation of a chartered company of merchants was becoming more or less a branch of government. Muscovy men were quick to point out to Elizabeth I's advisers how important the company was to England's prestige in Europe (Denmark and Sweden, for example, were furious that the Muscovy merchants had a monopoly on Europe's trade with Russia) and in the kingdom's defence: great quantities of cordage – the ropes used for rigging the ships of Elizabeth's navy – came to the port of London from Russia, as well as necessary supplies of pitch and tar and the materials to make sails, masts and cables.[13]

As soon as he returned home, Jenkinson's report of what he had seen and experienced on the long journeys to and from Bukhara was being read in London. The governors of the Muscovy Company, experts like Eden and the mercantile community more broadly would have been gripped by Jenkinson's account of his travels, especially his estimate of the potential for trade with Asia.

But Jenkinson's greatest achievement was visual, not literary. It was a map, which was printed in London in 1562 and which he dedicated to Sir Henry Sidney, a courtier and Muscovy investor. On one level, Jenkinson's map was a bravura piece of cartography, put together from his own notes and measurements and the work of others in the Muscovy Company. On another, it did more than this: in pictures and cartouches it told the story of Jenkinson's journey into Russia and on to Asia. The scenes shown on the map are wonderful. Amongst the rivers and forests of northern Russia, sledges make their way through the snow. There are caravans of camels pulling carts loaded high with wares. Cossack and Tatar warriors fire their short bows, and the hordes of the Nogai make camp near their resting camels, horses and covered wagons. Potentates sit cross-legged, most strikingly Hadjim Khan and his advisers. The map is full of activity and busyness. Only at its edges are there sensations of the violence and brutality Jenkinson saw on his journey. But stability wins over everything. In one scene, even heavy waves do not disturb a beautifully detailed if unlikely Elizabethan galleon under full sail on the Caspian. And so the map brings to life the east as Anthony Jenkinson was keen to communicate it: it populates it and makes it real, showing places and people and landscapes; and it points the way to the glories of Cathay.

In London, thanks to the cartographer and engraver Nicholas Reynolds and the naturalized stranger printer Reyner Wolfe, Jenkinson offered an account of his fantastic journey and a prospectus for future mercantile endeavour. Londoners who went to Wolfe's shop at the sign of the brazen serpent in Paul's Churchyard could begin to make sense of Russia and Asia for themselves, stripped of the medieval fantasy of Sir John Mandeville's *Travels*, but exotic nevertheless, and leaps and bounds beyond Herberstein. Not surprisingly, the significance of Jenkinson's map was understood straight away. Abraham Ortelius, the greatest European cartographer of his day, was in communication about it with Nicholas Reynolds in 1562, and less than a decade later it was the template Ortelius used for Russia in his revolutionary world atlas – the most important volume of maps of the age, and one that Sir William Cecil, the powerful Muscovy investor, himself owned and annotated.[14]

If the expedition out to Bukhara had been the last of Anthony Jenkinson's great adventures, it would have been by itself groundbreaking. But between 1562 and 1564 he went once again to Russia and on to Persia, with the ambition of putting down the foundations for reliable Anglo-Persian trade. The *Swallow*, a Muscovy Company ship, was packed with 400 kerseys that Jenkinson would take with him to Moscow and Persia. He travelled to the Persian court at Quazvin by way of Shemakha, where he was received by the ruler of Shirvan, Abdul-khan. Jenkinson carried with him a letter from Queen Elizabeth I to the Shah of Persia, the 'Great Sophy'. On 20

November 1562, Jenkinson and his interpreter were admitted to the shah's presence:

> Thus coming before his majesty with such reverence as I thought meet to be used, I delivered the queen's majesty's letters with my present, which he accepted, demanded of me of what country of Franks I was, and what affairs I had there to do: unto whom I answered that I was of the famous city of London within the noble realm of England, and that I was sent thither from the most excellent and gracious sovereign lady Elizabeth, queen of the said realm, for to treat of friendship, and free passage of our merchants and people, to repair and traffic within his dominions, for to bring in our commodities, and to carry away theirs, to the honour of both princes, the mutual commodity of both realms, and wealth of the subjects.[15]

It was an ambitious pitch and, given the shah's hostility at Jenkinson's profession of Christianity, it looked unlikely to get very far. But Jenkinson's skills of patient negotiation and his careful diplomacy helped in fact to pull off just the kind of mercantile coup he was hoping for. On his return journey to Moscow he was able to negotiate exclusive trading privileges for the Muscovy Company in the territories ruled by the king of Shirvan and Hircan, helped (against all the indications) by a letter of support from the shah himself.[16] 'The silks of the Medes to come by way of Muscovia into England is a strange hearing': so wrote Sir Thomas Smith, Elizabeth's ambassador to the French court and many years earlier Richard Eden's tutor in Cambridge, hoping that this breakthrough into Asia would put England on an equal footing with Spain and Portugal.[17]

Yet, in spite of his success in Persia, Jenkinson's ambitions for Cathay were undimmed: its wealth and potential as a market for English cloth were as clear to him as they had been in 1558. And so, when he was back in England in 1564, he put his mind to a petition to the queen for Cathay's discovery. Knowing from his journey to Bukhara that the land route was impassable because of war and banditry, he wanted to go by sea. In this, like Sebastian Cabot and Richard Eden before him, he made the two typical assumptions of his age: first, that there was an easily navigable sea route from England to Cathay; and secondly, that this northern voyage was shorter than the route the

Portuguese used to get to the eastern seas of Asia.[18] Even the tireless Anthony Jenkinson had now leapt a number of steps beyond what was possible.

The response to Jenkinson's petition at Elizabeth's court was a resounding silence. And by 1566 he had a competitor just as keen to unlock the riches of Asian trade. This was Sir Humphrey Gilbert, a Devonshire gentleman whose later military posting to Ireland gave him a deserved reputation for brutality. Where Jenkinson favoured a passage to Cathay by sailing around Scandinavia and northern Russia, Gilbert suggested instead a route by the north-west, past and beyond the continent of America. Sir Humphrey went full tilt at the project, petitioning the queen that in return for discovering Cathay 'and all the other east parts of the world' – at his own cost – he and his heirs might be given exclusive rights of navigation to get there and back, and a portion of what he imagined would be very healthy customs revenue.[19]

Both men wildly overestimated their chances of getting what they wanted. At first competitors, making cases for their separate projects, they fairly quickly joined forces. Still there was silence at court. Sir William Cecil, as the queen's secretary, simply sat on his hands and did nothing. The Muscovy Company was up in arms at Gilbert's proposal in particular, which they saw as a flagrant challenge to their own inviolable charter rights over any navigation of the northern seas. Sir Humphrey had further annoyed its grandees by suggesting that he was a Muscovy Company man, when plainly he was not. The company's governors appealed, successfully, to Cecil.[20] When by 1568 there was the germ of an idea at Muscovy House for an expedition to find a north-western passage to Cathay, it was most likely touted to emphasize and protect the company's monopoly.[21]

Here, beautifully encapsulated in a single episode, were all the possibilities and problems of mercantile London in Elizabeth's reign: energy, enterprise, tenacity and talent, all counterbalanced by a determination to protect hard-won charter rights. Even Anthony Jenkinson, who had ridden, sailed and fought his way to Bukhara and carried himself with poise and dignity in Persia, could do nothing to shake the masterly inactivity of the queen's secretary or the conservatism of the city's establishment. Their interests had to be protected. But, as we will see, men like Sir Humphrey Gilbert did not go away. More projects and proposals appeared, setting out to claim portions of an always expanding world. And so a powerful mercantile and political establishment – merchants and royal government broadly working together for profit and policy – adapted and reinvented themselves to changing circumstances.

For all this, Anthony Jenkinson was not a kind of excluded outsider whose petition for the voyage to Cathay, if the queen had granted it, would have made London's greater fortune in the empire of the Great Khan. His project for Cathay was as flawed as Sir Humphrey Gilbert's: both would have encountered seas of impassable ice. And Jenkinson was a Muscovy Company man, as well as the queen's also. In the 1570s he would serve as a successful ambassador to the court of Ivan the Terrible. In an arrangement that suited Elizabeth I very well, the company paid for royal embassies whose job, after all, was to keep Anglo-Russian trade afloat. Throughout his career he was part a diplomat, part a merchant – and as skilled as he had been on those first journeys into Russia and Asia.

In January 1568 Jenkinson married into the elite set of family and business interests that made up the sinews of London's body mercantile. His wife was Judith, the daughter of John and Alice Marshe. Judith's maternal grandfather was William Gresham, a cousin of Sir Thomas Gresham. John Marshe was a mercer, six times a governor of the Merchant Adventurers' Company and one of the founding members of the Muscovy Company. Anthony and Judith married in the church of St Michael on Wood Street, close to Cheapside and the company halls of the haberdashers, wax chandlers, embroiderers and goldsmiths. It was a London church like so many others, packed with the memorial stones and brasses of two centuries' worth of city merchants and craftsmen. In such a setting, the range and breadth of Anthony Jenkinson's experiences stood out. He knew with some confidence that he had seen more of the world than anyone in that church, living or dead, could have imagined.

A year later, Jenkinson was granted a coat of arms. He was a man who knew the significance of documents, and so the royal heralds read for themselves the portfolio of papers from his travels that Richard Hakluyt the younger later printed in his magnificent

Principal navigations. The letters of recommendation from Ivan the Terrible to the Shah of Persia and other potentates, a safe conduct from Suleiman the Magnificent, papers from Hadjim Khan, testimonials of Jenkinson's being in Jerusalem – all were, in the eyes of the heralds, 'evident tokens of his virtue, honesty and wisdom'. But they were proof above all of the journeys on which he had travelled beyond Europe to Asia, risking his life and putting his body under strain. The heralds captured the drama of it all:

> Northwards [he] hath also sailed on the frozen seas many days within the Arctic Circle, and travelled throughout the ample dominions of the emperor of Russia and Muscovia and the confines of Norway and Lappia over to the Caspian Sea, and into divers countries thereabouts, to the old cosmographers utterly unknown.

Jenkinson's new coat of arms was highly appropriate for a sea captain and adventurer: waves of sea in blue and silver and three golden stars, with the crest of a sea horse.[22]

His impressive public reputation was as tenacious as the man himself, and more so with the publication in 1589 of Hakluyt's *Principal navigations* and its second edition at the end of the century. Man of adventure, a fearless traveller, merchant and a diplomat, servant of queen and country, Jenkinson was also celebrated in 1596 in a verse history of England:

> Yet longer . . . let us dwell
> Of Jenkinson. But where shall we begin his lauds to tell?
> In Europe, Asia, Affrick? For these all he saw, in all
> Employed for England's common good.[23]

But above all Anthony Jenkinson was the man who pushed the Muscovy merchants' interests out into Asia. Convinced still by Cathay, he took London's name to parts of the world that earlier generations would have considered fantastically remote. And it was there that Elizabethans wanted to go and London's merchants needed to trade – into countries utterly unknown.

CHAPTER TWELVE
Flourishing Lands

In the same year that Anthony Jenkinson married Judith Marshe, a teenage schoolboy made his way across London to the chambers of his cousin, a lawyer, in the Middle Temple. His school – Westminster – was a short boat ride down the Thames to the Temple stairs, or a walk of half an hour or so past the queen's palace of Whitehall, up to the Charing Cross and then along the Strand to Temple Bar and into the privileged warren of lawyers' London. But this visit was different to any other he had made before or would make again. It was (as he remembered it thirty years later) a dramatic moment of realization and revelation, the instantaneous understanding and unfolding of a life's purpose: to make sense of countries and peoples as yet undiscovered – an ambition that from the very beginning was fuelled by the energy of mercantile London. The career and especially the writings of Richard Hakluyt will run as a connecting thread through everything that follows: Hakluyt is a name to remember.

Both the lawyer and the young man shared the name of Richard Hakluyt. The younger Richard was the son of a London citizen and freeman of the Skinners' Company who had died in March 1557, a month after Osip Nepea had paraded through the city. Young Richard Hakluyt was then about five years old. Soon afterwards he and his brothers lost their mother, and they were left in the care of the lawyer, to whom the boys' father (the lawyer's uncle) had on his deathbed entrusted his whole family.[1] Richard was a bright boy, and he was clever enough to be chosen as one of the queen's scholars at

Westminster School. There, from 1564, he and forty other boys lived in the precincts of the ancient abbey, following the rigorous daily routine of boarding school life and receiving in return a robust education in the Greek and Roman classics.

The elder Richard had been admitted to the Middle Temple back in 1555. Over the following decade he did well for himself as a London lawyer. He would have known Giles Isham, a fellow Temple barrister, who was elder brother to John and Gregory, the merchants and moneylenders. Richard Hakluyt's chambers were near the lane that led down from the Temple Bar on Fleet Street, somewhere just to the north-west of the Temple church, famous for its funeral monuments of medieval knights templar. Hakluyt shared an upper chamber with another lawyer, Fabian Phillips, but below that was another for which Richard alone paid a yearly rent of six shillings and eight pence.[2]

As a successful barrister, Richard Hakluyt's chambers must have overflowed with law papers and files. But his passion was the science Elizabethans called cosmography, and we can be pretty certain that he owned a substantial collection of books about geography, navigation and astronomy. It was these, not the lawyer's papers, that gripped the younger Richard, who remembered entering his cousin's chamber to find 'certain books of cosmography' lying open on a table, as well as a map of the world. The elder Hakluyt pounced straight away on his cousin's interest and, using the map, gave him an impromptu tutorial on the physical and political geography of the world. Hakluyt pointed out for Richard all the known seas, gulfs, bays, straits, capes, rivers, empires, kingdoms, dukedoms and territories. He talked, too, about the world's various resources and how they were traded: those 'special commodities, and particular wants, which by the benefit of traffic, and intercourse of merchants, are plentifully supplied'.

Probably Hakluyt loved the captive audience of one, while he pointed with his wand to what was probably a pretty large map. Which map it was is hard to know for certain, though one possibility is that it was Sebastian Cabot's world map of 1544–8, engraved in London in 1549. The world Cabot showed was one broadly familiar to us, a projection centred on the Atlantic Ocean, and around and beyond it the familiar shapes of Africa, South America, Europe and India. Cabot exaggerated the size of the Caribbean at the expense of a rather flattened

North America, while furthest Asia was wrapped around the map's edges – literally the Far East becoming also the far west. Australia had no existence at all. The continents are shown full of rivers and mountains and peoples, and ships sail all the seas and oceans. This was a world all at once bustling with life, activity and adventure, a world that extended far beyond the chambers of the Middle Temple in London – exotic and distant, but somehow from the map real and tangible.[3]

The elder Richard Hakluyt shared with his young cousin his deep sense of God's providence, explaining to the boy that when people set out to explore the world they did so from divine impulse. Discovery and navigation represented the unfolding of God's purpose for the world. Hakluyt took young Richard to a copy of the Bible and, in a moment full of significance, they read the twenty-third and twenty-fourth verses of Psalm 107 in the Old Testament: 'that they which go down to the sea in ships, and occupy by the great waters, they see the works of the Lord, and his wonders in the deep'. The younger Richard Hakluyt later wrote that he resolved there and then that he would 'by God's assistance prosecute that knowledge and kind of literature, the doors whereof (after a sort) were so happily opened before me'.

Two years later he went off to study at Christ Church, Oxford, and there he read everything he could on discoveries and voyages around the world. A talented and voracious linguist, he gathered up all sorts of works written in Greek, Latin, Italian, Spanish, Portuguese, French and English, and, when at last he began to teach, introduced his students to the latest maps, globes, spheres and navigational instruments. Never a man troubled by modesty, he later wrote how much his pupils had loved his teaching. Over time he got to know the men who actually went out to see the world, 'the chiefest captains at sea, the greatest merchants, and the best mariners of our nation'. To collect together and make sense of everything the travellers encountered became for Richard Hakluyt the life's work that stretched his intellect.[4]

But this is to jump too far ahead. In London in 1568 – in that chamber of the Middle Temple, a stone's throw from the Thames, close to the merchants' halls and houses, the quays and wharves of the river – Richard Hakluyt the younger achieved a moment of understanding.

In those Old Testament verses he felt an act of God's providence. He became, in a sense, the recording angel of English discovery across the globe.

Certainly it was at the very least lucky happenstance that a boy brilliantly attuned to cosmography was able to learn from his cousin and to read his books. We can guess that it was the size of the elder Richard Hakluyt's library that explains why he rented a second chamber in the Middle Temple. On any cosmographer's shelves was a magpie collection of works on geography, cartography, history, anthropology, navigation, mathematics and astronomy, insofar as those separate disciplines existed then as they do today. Some of the great cosmographical authorities, like the Greek scholar Ptolemy, were very old. Others, like Sebastian Münster or Pietro Martire d'Anghiera, were more or less contemporary. What united them all was the scholarly discipline John Dee called the 'peculiar art', one that, by studying the heavens and the earth, sought to come to 'the description of the whole and universal frame of the world'.[5] Cosmography was the great explanatory science and art of its day, able to reveal the operations of the whole planet. Its exponents delighted in showing how important it was. There was no one 'so mean witted', one Elizabethan cosmographer wrote, 'but will confess her [cosmography's] ample use, nor yet so simply learned but must acknowledge her manifold benefit'.[6]

The elder Richard Hakluyt loved maps, but thought that most of them were far too big and unwieldy to be of real use. At about the time of the visit of his cousin to the Middle Temple, Hakluyt wrote to Abraham Ortelius with a description of what he believed the ideal map would look like. In size it would be twelve by three or four feet set up on revolving rods. The cartography would, of course, have to be exact. Hakluyt's description of what the map would show gives us a sense of his eye for detail, as well as the breadth of his geographical knowledge that so gripped young Richard:

In the middle is to be placed the meridian line or first degree of longitude running from north to south . . . so that eastwards on the six feet of the map to the right of this line will be found Europe, Africa, and Asia as far as the river Ganges . . . And just where you stop in East India or the kingdom of Cathay you will start again at the edge of the six feet to the left of the meridian . . . and continue the degrees of longitude, inserting Cathay, America, Florida and Baccalaos . . . Now let there be placed on either side of the equinoctial line the two Tropics, the Arctic and Antarctic Circles.[7]

The elder Hakluyt was one of a European network of like-minded cosmographical enthusiasts, familiar enough with Ortelius to be able to write to him such a robustly self-confident and knowledgeable letter. In fact it is quite possible that Hakluyt knew Ortelius's sister Elisabeth, for she and her husband Jacob Cool came from Antwerp to live as strangers in London some time in the middle 1560s.[8]

Like most English cosmographers of his time, the elder Richard Hakluyt exercised his brain by trying to discern a navigable sea route to Asia. It was on his mind when he wrote to Abraham Ortelius, and we can guess with a very high degree of certainty that it formed part of the extempore lesson for his cousin. Sebastian Cabot, Richard Chancellor, John Dee, Anthony Jenkinson, the grandees of the Muscovy Company, Sir Humphrey Gilbert: each and every one of these men believed that there was some way to sail to the empire of Cathay, even if they disagreed on precisely how to get there – by going north-east or by going north-west. Hakluyt was at the very least indirectly involved in what at times became a heated debate at court: when Sir Humphrey Gilbert wrote a treatise in 1566 in support of his ambitious Cathay project, some of the evidence he deployed came probably from Hakluyt's own researches.[9]

The two Richard Hakluyts knew what was at stake by the middle 1560s: England's trade, investors' money, riches, mercantile ambition, political patronage, reputation and ego. Here were merchants, courtiers and adventurers who wanted to explore the world and make their fortunes. Coming into focus already were some insistent themes of the younger Richard Hakluyt's life's work: the essential need for England to trade globally; the patriotic and providential impulse of the kingdom to put its stamp on the world; and the great task of collecting and understanding every possible piece of written material on exploration and navigation.

The Hakluyts were specialists: self-taught men who, through their own efforts, knew the leading cosmographical minds of their day. The elder Hakluyt would have been used to that from his years as a young barrister in London, learning the law in the Middle Temple, not from a syllabus or curriculum – there was none – but from those who practised it. His cousin did the same, at Oxford and in London. They were practitioners as well as theorists; they rolled up their sleeves and got on with the job of making themselves experts. They read books and absorbed the work of fellow specialists. Surely sitting on the shelves of Hakluyt's chambers were Richard Eden's English translations of Münster's *Cosmographia* (*Universal Cosmography*, 1553) and *The decades of the newe worlde* . . . by Pietro Martire d'Anghiera (1555), the Milanese scholar who had chronicled the voyages of Christopher Columbus. These were books printed in London when the younger Richard was a baby and toddler.

And of course the Hakluyts lived in the city, on the doorstep of news and discovery. The elder Richard arrived in the Middle Temple in the year of the Muscovy Company's royal charter. In London, a short, triumphant account was printed of Richard Chancellor's discovery of Russia, complete, in elegant Latin, with a great speech by Chancellor in the style of high Roman oratory (sixteenth-century humanists generally preferred to write what *should* have been said rather than what *was* said by the speaker). Hakluyt could not have missed Robert Recorde's dedication of his books to the grandees of the Muscovy Company, and we can imagine how he devoured every detail of Anthony Jenkinson's map of Russia and Asia.

The latest news came in from the wharves and quays on the Thames. It is easy today to forget the uncertainty of life and exploration in the Hakluyts' lifetimes. Navigators and merchants like Chancellor and Jenkinson sailed off to far distant places. They were often gone for two or three years at a time. Getting a letter successfully back to London was in itself a minor miracle. The probability was always of failure; it was no wonder that crews and companies put their trust in providence. But when these voyages did succeed, the reports they brought home with them must have had London buzzing with news and speculation. Step by step new discoveries were made, and every year small fragments of the great puzzle of the globe gradually assimilated into the bigger picture: step by step all kinds of Londoners began to make sense of lands hundreds and thousands of miles away.

* * *

One of the secrets of the younger Richard Hakluyt's later brilliance as a compiler of accounts of exploration and discovery was his skill as an editor. Though always in charge of the travel accounts he printed, he was able to slip far enough into the background to allow the accounts to speak for themselves – for the narratives to be fresh and arresting. He believed that the old cosmographers had done little more than stitch together ancient authorities that had been endlessly retold and reprinted – stories that, when they were put to the test, simply did not tell the truth. Hakluyt valued veracity above everything else. His gold standard was the eyewitness account. This was why he and Anthony Jenkinson were later able to collaborate so beautifully, for what suited Hakluyt in *Principal navigations* was Jenkinson's keen eye, the unaffected precision of his writing and the supreme balance of his temperament and judgement.

Hakluyt became the pre-eminent editor and navigational expert of the 1580s and 1590s. Instinctively able, he learned his trade in London and Oxford. In London, when he was growing up, he would have read what other Londoners read also: tales of expeditions and voyages to remote and foreign places set out in lively English, in pamphlets and short books that sold in and around Paul's Churchyard for only a few pennies. These, as the young Richard may have realized, were the future: vivid eyewitness accounts unlike the great clunking works of old cosmography whose authors got themselves tangled up in labyrinths of self-referencing scholarly debate. The booksellers who sold these new pamphlets saw that they had a readership, recognizing also that they had to compete in a busy marketplace dominated by the printing of cheap popular ballads, comedies, almanacs and prognostications, sensational accounts of murders or monstrous births, sermons, songs and sonnets. Weighty volumes of earnest scholarship were all very well, but what most Londoners in Paul's Churchyard and the Royal Exchange wanted were lively and vivid books they could read, share and talk about.

One bookseller who knew this instinctively was Thomas Hacket, with his shop at the sign of the green dragon in the Royal Exchange. Hacket was a canny publisher and a good translator. Before opening his shop at the Exchange, he had sold books in the 1560s from the sign of the key in Paul's Churchyard, another on Lombard Street, right in the heart of the mercantile city. There is every reason to think that the two Richard Hakluyts browsed in Hacket's shops, especially given the kinds of books he commissioned and sold. In the 1560s Hacket published two books on the mysterious continent of North America.

The first, in 1563, was Hacket's own translation of an expedition to America led by a French pilot called Jean Ribault. When the book appeared in Hacket's London bookshops, the voyage was only months old and it seemed full of possibilities. Ribault and his crews had set out from France in February 1562. In April they had arrived off the east coast of the Florida peninsula and then sailed north, going ashore at a river Ribault called 'May' because it was discovered on the first day of that month. Sailing along the coast for two weeks, they found a place to establish a colony, at Port Royal in present-day South Carolina. Naming it Charlesfort, Ribault garrisoned the encampment with thirty men under the command of one Captain Nicholas Barré.[10]

The colony came to nothing. Charlesfort was abandoned in the summer of 1563, by which time Ribault had set sail, first for France and then for England. Finding France convulsed by religious civil war, Ribault, a Protestant, travelled to England, where he arrived in March 1563. It says something for Hacket's speed in picking up Ribault's story that its English translation was printed, from Ribault's French manuscript, in London only a few weeks later. As quick to spot an opportunity was a Devonshire soldier and adventurer called Thomas Stucley. By the summer of 1563 Stucley was proposing a joint expedition with Ribault out to 'Terra Florida' – 'the flourishing land'. Stucley's abilities were praised to the skies, and in a pamphlet recommending the forthcoming 'adventurous voyage' he was likened – improbably – to 'A young Aeneas bold / With heart and courage stout', though it seems most likely that this latter-day Aeneas was really intending to use the putative expedition as a cover for attacks on Spanish shipping.[11]

Everything about Hacket's account of Ribault's expedition was meant to catch the eye and capture the imagination. Hacket understood the skill of selling a book by its title page: *Terra Florida: Englished, the Flourishing Land*, 'the wonderful strange natures and manners of the people, with the marvellous commodities and treasures of the country'. For Ribault there had been both a sense of patriotic mission as well as a colonizing agenda:

> That France might one day through new discoveries have knowledge of strange countries and also thereof to receive (by means of continual traffic) rich and inestimable commodities, as other nations have done, by taking in hand such far navigations . . .[12]

All a reader had to do was to substitute 'England' for 'France' and this might very well be Richard Eden writing about the great empire of Cathay – or indeed either of the Richard Hakluyts later writing about the northernmost parts of the American continent.

Rich, visual and arresting, Hacket's translation of Ribault evoked for Elizabethan Londoners a first encounter with places and people far beyond the reaches of their imagination. Away from the jostling bustle of Paul's Churchyard, in the shadows of a huge Gothic cathedral, Hacket's readers were transported off to the pristine forests of an as yet uncharted continent. Ribault and his men had wondered at the beauty of an immense coastline marked out by 'an infinite number of fair and high trees'. Hacket's translation stimulated his readers' senses, recording 'unspeakable pleasure' at colour and smell.[13] There was something here of the essence of human society as unspoiled as the continent itself: of the native people – naked, beautiful, gentle and courteous – and of earth unbroken by plough irons.[14] Ribault gave a great catalogue of all kinds of trees, birds and animals they had seen.[15] Significantly, he suggested possibilities for plantation and cultivation in a fruitful land. Terra Florida was about as different from London as it was possible to comprehend. With and for the natives of this flourishing land there was no hostility. Only their difference was noted: 'They be of tawney colour, hawk-nosed and of a pleasant countenance.'[16] But the hope was for religious conversion, giving the gift of civilization by bringing the true faith to 'brutish people' ignorant of Jesus Christ.[17]

Hacket sold the book at no more than twopence a copy. He priced it to sell: in 1563 the daily wage of a London labourer was ninepence. But Hacket's eye was also on London's mercantile elite, and he produced a special edition of his translation, which he dedicated to

Sir Martin Bowes, a leading city figure. Hacket's address to Sir Martin began with all the familiar notions of a generation: the 'forwardness in these late years of Englishmen' in making great voyages and navigations, the propagation of Christianity and the enriching of kingdoms.[18]

In bringing to life these flourishing lands of potential, Hacket wrote for all Londoners, the humble and the grand. He was able to introduce them to navigators like Ribault, and to leading European talents such as the French traveller and writer André Thevet. In 1563 it was Florida and South Carolina. Five years later, Hacket was selling in Paul's Churchyard his translation of Thevet's account of America, which he presented to Sir Henry Sidney, the same dedicatee back in 1562 of Anthony Jenkinson's map of Russia. In choosing first Bowes and then Sidney (and later, for another book, Sir Thomas Gresham), Hacket knew exactly how to speak to the two constituencies that made possible the voyages, expeditions and mercantile ventures of Elizabeth's reign: the merchants themselves and their powerful courtier investors. And he understood, too, how to capture the excitement of new and exotic places, something shown to perfection in his title for Thevet's book on America: *The new found worlde, or Antarctike, wherin is contained wonderful and strange things, as well of humaine creatures, as Beastes, Fishes, Foules, and Serpents, Trees, Plants, Mines of Golde and Silver: garnished with many learned authorities.*[19]

Striking in Thevet's book is Hacket's own sense of English mission – of the urge to discover and to shake up comfortable lives and attitudes, all with a sense of patriotic purpose: 'How much are they to be praised, that for their country's sake refuse no imminent peril . . . to abandon themselves and their sweetest lives to the favour of the boisterous seas . . . only to increase the same and good renown of their country.' They worked both for God's glory and the benefit of England.[20] If this was Thomas Hacket writing in 1568, it might also have been Richard Eden fifteen years earlier, urging on Sebastian Cabot's London expedition to Cathay. It was a powerful theme in this kind of Elizabethan writing: the insistent desire to emulate and then surpass the achievements of Spain and Portugal.

Thomas Hacket wanted readers of Thevet to embrace the strangeness of the new world they would soon be reading about. Like Ribault,

Thevet was fresh, vivid, odd and challenging, avoiding the mistakes and slips made by cosmographers who had merely pasted together second- or third-hand tales and descriptions:

> Also let it not seem to thee strange the setting forth of many strange trees, as palm trees and others, with beasts of the field and fowls of the air, the which are clean contrary to the setting forth of our cosmographers and ancient writers, who for because that they have not seen the places, and for the small experience and knowledge that they had, did greatly err.[21]

Here was a fantastic possibility that must have struck at least some of the browsers and buyers in Paul's Churchyard: that readers of books like Ribault's or Thevet's had at their fingertips descriptions more accurate than old scholarly cosmographies. So fresh and contemporary were Hacket's translations that he asked his readers to excuse the rough edges of any rude or ill-placed words. Here was a kind of democratization of the globe – a discovery of far distant continents for the price of a meal in a London tavern.

The younger Richard Hakluyt absorbed the method. Not satisfied with tired old sources, he wanted the kind of reports fresh from the pens of captains, merchants and sailors just off the ships that came into the port of London – accounts that had about them the sharp tang of the sea. Hakluyt and Hacket and others shared common aims: as well as wanting to sell their books, they sought to set out and to celebrate the voyages and expeditions of their day (especially if they were English), as well as to encourage others to push further into new worlds and flourishing lands.

It was the impulse to discover: to find, to describe, to trade, to map, and eventually to dominate. And Elizabethans wanted to do all these things for a number of reasons: for riches, for the preaching of the true (Protestant) faith, for patriotic reputation, and later on for plantation and colonization. For Thomas Hacket, introducing his translation of André Thevet, it was almost a physical urge – the abandonment of self and home and wives and children for an even greater enterprise. It was a mission bigger than the city of London: it was for the whole kingdom. This was why it was so easy to think about investments in the Muscovy Company and later Elizabethan ventures as representing much more than profits for a few: London, England and indeed the whole world all began to blur together.

By the time of young Richard Hakluyt's visit to his cousin's chamber in the Middle Temple, London's mercantile interests were becoming ever more difficult to disentangle from the fractious politics of European diplomacy. The Muscovy Company's breakthrough into Persia was a triumph, squeezing out all competition. As two senior company men wrote from Russia: 'It is a great honour unto our country to have such a trade privately to ourselves, where no other nations hath any entrance.' They recognized that merchants from the Baltic down to France and Italy had done their best to subvert the company's business. Market dominance was national dominance, and this was why the company wanted the power of Elizabeth's government four-square behind it.[22]

More obvious diplomatically was Elizabethan England's early frostiness with King Philip II of Spain. Here, in a further blurring of politics and mercantile adventure, Elizabeth's government began early in the reign to turn a blind eye to privateering. The most effective exponent of this sort of licensed piracy was John Hawkins, a Plymouth sea captain who by the early 1560s had a house in Deptford and another in London in the parish of St Dunstan in the East, near to the first Muscovy House. Between 1562 and 1569 Hawkins and his crews sailed out into seas dominated by Spain. One purpose of Hawkins's expeditions was to disrupt the Spanish silver fleets sailing between Spain and Mexico. The other was slaving, with Hawkins seizing Africans and selling them in the Caribbean, a trade in human beings in which Queen Elizabeth and her courtiers cheerfully invested. This was celebrated in the granting of a coat of arms to Hawkins in 1565, topped by a crest of an African, bound and captive.

Just as Londoners in the 1560s could read Ribault and Thevet, so Hawkins's voyages were brought to life for them in compact narratives full of action and adventure, where there were encounters with Spanish treasure fleets, great winds and storms. The most exciting moments were picked out by spare and pointed notes in the margins of these popular pamphlets: 'North winds perilous'; 'Sharp wars'; 'A hard case'; 'Fire'; 'Small hope of life'; 'Hard choice'; 'Many miseries'.[23]

All of these things – the discipline of cosmography, the chance to discover new worlds, mercantile ambition, patriotism and policy – helped to shape the mind of the younger Richard Hakluyt. The ruling passion of his adult life was to explain how, with the blessings of God, the English had discovered the globe, searching (as Hakluyt said himself in 1589) 'the most opposite corners and quarters of the world'.[24] For him it all went back to that schoolboy day in his cousin's chambers.

Hakluyt's talent was to turn what were often simply the fits and starts of exploration into a grand providential narrative. The reality, not surprisingly, was more complicated than this, beaten into shape by false starts and hopes, fantasies and illusions. Few understood this reality as personally and painfully as a merchant cosmographer Richard Hakluyt himself knew and admired. He was a man whose fortunes in the end were broken by commercial speculation and voyaging, and by the unforgiving power of the queen's court and the city of London. His name was Michael Lok and, like so many others before him, he wanted to find Cathay.

CHAPTER THIRTEEN

The Unknown Limits

Nothing better illustrates both the strengths and the limitations of mercantile London than the Frobisher adventure of the later 1570s. The city's strengths were formidable: great resources of money, mercantile energy, political will, ingenuity and bravery. Its limitations were all of those things left unchecked: greed, over-confidence, politicking and ignorance. Martin Frobisher's venture was an extraordinary one: three voyages in three years out into the wild seas of the Canadian Arctic, at first in search of a north-west passage through to Cathay, but then devoted to what, with a huge fanfare, was believed to be the greatest discovery of the age – the supposedly vast reserves of gold in the islands of the Labrador Sea.

It was the superlative mercantile failure of a generation: gold fever, a fantastic speculation in which thousands of pounds were invested by London's merchants as well as by some of the most powerful families in the kingdom. Today it would register as a major corporate scandal, shaking the political class and the financial world. In Elizabethan London it was merely a hard lesson learned, and one best quickly forgotten. Frobisher later sailed into other waters; his investors looked to other ventures. The character who suffered most for it was Michael Lok, Frobisher's strategist and money-raiser. In Lok's career it is hard to miss elements of classical tragedy: vaunting ambition brought crashing down by human flaws and the intervention of fortune – we might think of Holbein's *Triumph of Riches* and the hovering presence of the goddess Nemesis.

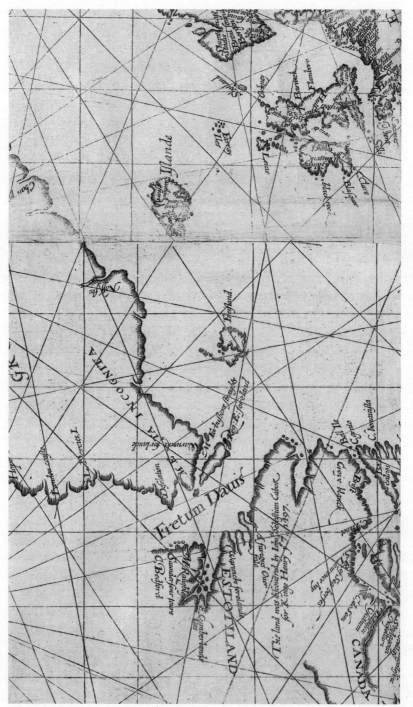

The north-western seas explored by Martin Frobisher, 1576–8.

Michael Lok's failure was emphasized by the height from which he eventually fell. He was a son of one of the most successful families of the city establishment, the great-grandson of John Lok, a fifteenth-century sheriff. Michael's father William was a mercer with a house and office on Cheapside at the sign of the padlock – a pun on the family name that doubtless worked as a kind of trademark, resonant of security and solidity. William Lok was well connected at the court of Henry VIII, able to negotiate for himself the exclusive licence to import silks and jewels for court revels. He was (like any sensible leading merchant with an eye on the bigger picture) a correspondent of Thomas Cromwell. He was also a man who was demonstrably loyal: in Dunkirk in 1533 Lok tore down from public display a copy of the papal bull excommunicating King Henry for his marriage to Anne Boleyn. As wealthy as they were politically astute, in middle Tudor London, families like the Loks and the Greshams were cut from identical cloth – and a very fine and textured cloth it was too.

Michael was a son of William Lok's second marriage, born in about 1532. His father gave him a thorough apprenticeship in the business of being a London mercer. It was not to be for Michael Lok, as it had been for young Thomas Gresham, a taste of university life in Cambridge followed by carefully structured years in Antwerp – son as courtier-merchant protégé. After Michael's education in grammar up to the age of thirteen, William Lok sent him to Flanders and France in order to 'learn those languages and to know the world'. After that, probably suited to this type of life by temperament, he threw himself at mercantile Europe, in fifteen years 'passing through almost all the countries of Christianity, namely out of England into Scotland, Ireland, Flanders, Germany, France, Spain, Italy and Greece, both by land and by sea'. His last command was a ship sailing the Levant seas of the eastern Mediterranean.[1] It was the kind of life – busy, adventurous and full of danger – that Anthony Jenkinson, only three years older than Lok, knew so well.

Lok was a thinker as much as he was a mercantile adventurer. He pushed himself to learn languages and to discover foreign lands. His ambition (so he explained in middle age) was to extend England's trade to its furthest limits.[2] He became a scholar of cosmography and navigation, and built up for himself what would have been one of the largest libraries in and around London, full of books in Spanish, French, Italian, Latin, Greek and even Arabic.[3] The parallels with John Dee and the two Richard Hakluyts are insistent; Lok was very much of their world.

So here was a London merchant a little out of the ordinary, though he probably seemed conventional enough. He was admitted to the freedom of the Mercers' Company in 1562, continuing the family tradition and affiliation. By the 1570s he had a lucrative office as London agent of the Muscovy Company, with a stipend and benefits (rent-free housing, for example) valued at some £400 a year. For this huge executive salary, his job between 1571 and 1576 was to supervise all the company's cargoes coming in and out of London.[4]

If Martin Frobisher had all of Michael Lok's taste for adventure (and perhaps more besides), he possessed at best a fraction of Lok's intellect. The two men were much the same age. Frobisher, just three or four years younger than Lok, was born near Wakefield in the West Riding of Yorkshire, but he went to London, aged fourteen, to live with his maternal grandfather, Sir John Yorke, at Walbrook near the Thames. Yorke was a city grandee of immaculate pedigree: a sheriff of London in Edward VI's reign (William Lok had been sheriff the previous year), a merchant taylor and a prominent financier. Yorke was busy, important and rich. One of the founding charter merchants of the Muscovy Company, a few years earlier, in 1552 and 1553, he had helped to fund trading voyages out to the Barbary coast and Guinea. It was on these that the teenaged Martin Frobisher sailed. Early on Frobisher found his métier, discovering a talent for life at sea that led to privateering and then to piracy, for which he was imprisoned in London in 1569. He was able a year later to negotiate his freedom, thanks to the intervention of powerful men at Elizabeth's court. One of Martin Frobisher's other talents was always to thrive and prosper against the odds.

What was Frobisher's secret? It is hard to know. He was fearless, impetuous, violent and volatile (indeed, at times frankly unstable), with a yearning after glory and recognition, and only the tiniest reserve of respect for merchants. His education had been atrocious. But this was the man who in 1574 went to the Muscovy Company with that familiar proposal: like Anthony Jenkinson and Sir Humphrey Gilbert before him, Frobisher wanted to find the empire of Cathay.

Frobisher's pitch to the company was as blunt as the man himself. He confronted the grandees of the Muscovy Company head-on. He knew that any northern voyage to find Cathay was reserved to the company by its charter. He knew, too, that in twenty years no such voyage to furthest Asia had been successful, though the company had begun to map the northern coasts of Russia east of the White Sea, and an early voyage, led by the intrepid Stephen Borough, had sailed in 1556 as far as Nova Zembla (Novaya Zemlya).[5] Frobisher would go west, to find what he and his backers believed would be a straightforward north-western passage to Cathay.

London's Russia merchants paid Frobisher the courtesy of hearing his case in person; one of the officials in the room was Michael Lok. But, not surprisingly, the company refused. A decade earlier that would have been the end of the matter – Gilbert and Jenkinson had got nowhere. But with powerful support, Frobisher kept on pushing, with the result that the company was told by the queen's government either to send out its own expedition to find Cathay or to allow Frobisher a licence to make the attempt himself. The Muscovy Company agreed to that licence in February 1575. Really it had little choice: at Muscovy House there was now nothing less than a sizeable corporate earthquake, for its monopoly on the exploration and exploitation of the northern seas and continents, two decades old, was at last broken.[6]

But the challenge in early 1575 was really Martin Frobisher's. To have a licence to find Cathay was one thing, to put together an actual expedition able to get to Asia was something else entirely. Someone had to knock the project into shape – to raise money, to find ships and crews, and to put in place all the training that was necessary for such an ambitious voyage. That someone was Michael Lok, who must have detected in Frobisher's pitch at least the germ of a viable expedition. Lok later wrote about his own role, admittedly with some self-puffing. He explained how he had taken Frobisher under his wing:

> finding him sufficient and ready to execute the attempt of so great matters, I joined with him, and to my power advanced him to the world with credit, and above my own power for my part furnished him with

things necessary for his first voyage lately made to the northwestward for the discovery of Cathay and other new countries, to the intent the whole world might be opened unto England which hitherto hath been hidden from it by the slothfulness of some, and policy of other.[7]

Here was a project for the clever and restless Michael Lok to get his teeth into. He rallied his contacts in London's mercantile world, characters like Thomas Randolph (a former ambassador to Russia who had loathed his time in Moscow), Anthony Jenkinson and even Sir Thomas Gresham. Lok worked hard to get the support of the city establishment.[8] The task he set for himself was formidable: as well as putting ships to sea, it was to turn an unpredictable gentleman-pirate into the plausible discoverer of the empire of the Great Khan.

There was no quick or easy success. At first, in 1575, Lok and Frobisher failed to raise money for the venture. But in 1576 that began to change, and Lok at last found investors willing to put their money into the expedition, 'divers persons of honour and worship', men and women of noble and knightly rank as well as city merchants.[9] This in itself was a major step forward, for one of the many challenges to overcome was Frobisher's unsavoury reputation and doubts as to his abilities as the captain general of such a voyage.[10] Interest in the venture began gradually to build. In early 1576 the poet George Gascoigne wrote a preface to Sir Humphrey Gilbert's until then private paper on his own proposal for a Cathay voyage ten years earlier. Entertaining himself one day in Gilbert's library in Limehouse, a few miles out of London, Gascoigne came across Sir Humphrey's old Cathay manuscript. Knowing, as he put it, that 'Master Frobisher (a kinsman of mine) did pretend to travail in the same discovery', Gascoigne asked for Gilbert's permission to read it.[11] Sir Humphrey allowed him to do more than that, and with Gascoigne's introduction it was printed in London in April 1576. John Dee noticed the pamphlet: 'a little English book,' Dee called it, 'containing some very probable reasons, tending to the persuasion of the same course and voyage'.[12] The possibilities were at last beginning to click.

Supporting what Dee called the 'probable reasons' for the likely success of the voyage was a map of the northwest passage shown in

Gilbert's short book. It has the distinction of being the earliest map of the globe printed in England. It was in fact a greatly simplified copy of the world map Abraham Ortelius had produced in Antwerp in 1564. The beauty of Gilbert's map – the secret of its psychological power – lay precisely in that simplicity, for it showed a clear route to Asia north-west from England, at about the latitude of 60 degrees north, through a long strait between Greenland and America, and on to Japan, the Spice (Molucca) Islands and Cathay.[13] No recent power had sailed the passage, though Gilbert (thanks to the elder Richard Hakluyt of the Middle Temple) had evidence of its navigability from Roman and medieval sources – the old cosmographical authorities still had their uses, at least when it suited the moment.[14]

Michael Lok threw himself at the project. They had two ships only, the *Michael*, which was specially refitted for the voyage, and the *Gabriel*, newly built by the royal master shipwrights Matthew Baker and John Ady. These vessels were impossibly small: *Michael* was a bark of between 20 and 25 tons; *Gabriel* a little larger at 30 tons, towing a 7-ton pinnace. What defies modern understanding is that these tiny wooden sailing ships were expected to sail through Arctic waters all the way to the other side of the world.

The two ships would carry men, food, weapons, trade samples of cloth, books and instruments. The instruments were of the kind that John Dee, Richard Chancellor and Anthony Jenkinson would have known so well: a terrestrial globe, armillary spheres, a universal dial and astronomical rings, an astrolabe, eighteen hour glasses and twenty compasses of various kinds, some of them bought from William Borough of the Muscovy Company, others made by Humphrey Cole, a talented London goldsmith who fashioned in his workshop devices as beautifully ornate as they were necessary for the survival of the ships and their crews.

The books Lok gathered together to take with them are an indication of the ambitions of the expedition, as well as of the obvious limitations of the Elizabethan understanding of the world. The pilots and other senior men of the venture, including Frobisher himself, were given crash courses in navigation, cosmography and geography in books that over the years any Londoner could have bought from the shops in Paul's Churchyard: Robert Recorde's treatise on the sphere,

Castle of Knowledge (1556), William Cunningham's *Cosmographical Glass* (1559), Thomas Hacket's translation of André Thevet on America (*The new found worlde*, 1568), and even (though it seems extraordinary) the medieval *Travels* of Sir John Mandeville, picked up for a shilling, and complete with late fifteenth-century woodcuts of strange beasts. The only specialized texts were originals of Thevet in French (*Cosmographie universelle* and *Les Singularitez de la France antarctique*) and the Spanish *Regimiento de navegación* by Pedro de Medina, but these must have been of pretty limited use: Frobisher, for one, could barely read English.[15]

Lok and others worked with Frobisher and his masters on their skills in cartography and navigation using the great maps of Mercator and Ortelius, and providing blank sea charts to be filled in on the voyage. William Borough, an experienced pilot and cartographer who had worked in Russia, northern Lapland and the Baltic, drew a sea card on vellum for the northern portion of the British Isles, the west coast of Norway and various parts of the Arctic coasts. His brother, Stephen, was also recruited to give advice.

At Lok's house in London in late May, the experts met the ships' officers who would go into those northern seas in *Gabriel* and *Michael*. John Dee was one of those experts, volunteering to help in any way that he could. Lok (so he wrote later) explained to Dee the purpose of the expedition as he saw it: the opening up of trade to the countries of what Lok called East India by way of a north-west passage, evidence of which Lok set before Dee in the form of books, charts, instruments and his own notes. Dee, according to Lok at least, was impressed, and shared his own researches. Dee himself wrote a few months later of Lok as 'a virtuous gentleman and merchant, with zealous intent, for the advancement of God his glory, and the great commodity, and honour of this kingdom', who had 'procured unto him, worshipful, yea and honourable aid also: to set forth ships, for a northwest discovery'.[16]

By the summer of 1576 everything was ready. There was, naturally, a substantial outlay of money, for the ships, their rigging, weapons and ammunition, navigational instruments, food and drink, the crews' wages and cloths to trade.[17] Lok appeared to be meticulous in keeping the accounts. So confident was he that he put over £700 of his own money into a voyage that, on 6 June 1576, set off to find Asia.

That first voyage was not the great breakthrough to Cathay that Lok and Frobisher had expected it would be. It turned out to be a four-month reconnaissance of Arctic waters and islands, during which the crews of *Michael* and *Gabriel* encountered great icebergs and Inuit in kayaks. It was the first encounter with unknown places and strange peoples: tentative, noteworthy, but hardly the beginning of a mercantile revolution for London, queen and kingdom. And yet within a few days of the arrival home of *Gabriel* in London, there quickly came into view a new possibility – not of Cathay, but the discovery of gold.

It began with a rock the size of a small loaf of bread. The sailors had brought back from their adventure all kinds of souvenirs. When they had gone ashore, some had collected flowers, others grass. On Little Hall Island in the Labrador Sea, Master Robert Garrard had picked up 'a piece of a black stone, much like to a sea coal in colour which by the weight seemed to be some kind of metal or mineral'. At first Frobisher had thought nothing of it, but he and Garrard kept the stone 'in respect of the place from whence it came'.[18] Back in London, it was on board *Gabriel* that Frobisher gave the stone to Michael Lok. The day was Saturday, 13 October 1576.

It changed everything. What Frobisher had found, or so it seemed, were islands full of precious metals, confirmed as such from the single sample by a Venetian goldsmith living in London who tested the stone and found it to contain a grain of gold. Now Lok and Frobisher worked furiously to rally interest and support, and Lok secured a licence to transport the ore to England.[19] He became a frequent visitor to the queen's secretary, Sir Francis Walsingham, who was a very long way from being entirely convinced by Frobisher's ore; but nevertheless Elizabeth's Privy Council threw its weight behind a second voyage, even going so far as to order grain from Essex to London to make biscuit 'necessary for the furniture of certain barks of Martin Frobisher and others now intending a voyage to the seas'.[20]

In the spring of 1577 Frobisher and Lok were busy in London planning the next phase of the expedition. Lok drew up a constitution for what he called the 'company of Cathay', modelled on the charter of the Muscovy Company. This was plausible enough to take a few minutes of Lord Burghley's precious time, but really the company was a corporate illusion; it never existed in any practical sense.[21] The search for Cathay was slowly becoming a secondary consideration, though notionally Frobisher's ambition was still to discover Asia. At about the time Lok was drawing up his company's charter, Richard Willes, editing one of Richard Eden's translations, put into print his view that Master Frobisher's forthcoming 'prosperous voyage, and happy return' would once and for all decide the old debates about the northwest sea route to Cathay.[22] A writer in Frobisher's circle, George Best, was much nearer the mark: 'the hope of more of the same gold ore to be found, kindled a greater opinion in the hearts of many, to advance the voyage again'.[23]

On the decidedly wobbly foundation of the company of Cathay, Michael Lok built up a formidable group of investors: nine of Elizabeth's privy councillors, a good number of the English nobility and court gentry, city grandees such as Sir Thomas Gresham, veteran merchants and travellers like Anthony Jenkinson – and indeed the queen herself, usually parsimonious to a fault, to the tune of £1,000.[24] On the instructions of the Privy Council, every element of the voyage – navigation, shipping and budgeting – was closely inspected by experienced men, of whom Lok and Jenkinson were two.[25] Once again, corporate and mercantile London fitted hand in glove with the political establishment in Westminster: neither could afford for Frobisher to fail.

The Royal Exchange and Paul's Churchyard were buzzing with news and gossip. Scribblers were busy, as printers dashed off to the Stationers' Company to register poems and ballads like 'Farewell to Master Frobisher and the other gentlemen adventurers who labour to discover the right way to Cathay'.[26] (Thomas Hacket would certainly have done a better job with the title.) Hopes for the voyage were huge. It was the beginning of the celebrity of the redoubtable Martin Frobisher.

And the second voyage was indeed suitably heroic, with great storms and battles with 'fierce and bold people'. Frobisher himself went ashore and returned to his ship 'with good news of great riches' he had discovered in the bowels of the barren mountains of Baffin Island.[27] The expedition even returned months later to England with Inuit captives: a man and a young woman with her baby. This became global news. Frobisher's capture of these people of the Arctic – 'those that killeth the seals' – was known in Moscow, from a Russian source, over a year later.[28]

Frobisher was interested above all in the ore that was ready to be mined. About 200 tons of it was loaded onto the ships. Frobisher's belief (and surely Lok's too) was that this precious cargo would pay for both the first and second voyages as well as offering 'sufficient interest' to the expedition's investors. One of the members of the crew wrote, with the kind of prescience he himself was unlikely to have recognized at the time: 'The stones of this supposed continent with America be altogether sparkled, and glister in the sun like gold: so likewise doth sand in the bright water; yet they verify the old proverb: All is not gold that glistereth.'[29]

Frobisher was back in England in September and embraced at Elizabeth's court, where the news was that he had returned with ore to the value of anything between £80,000 and £100,000. Rewards and a knighthood seemed certain.[30] He had pushed through into 'Meta Incognita'. And in those 'unknown limits' was fantastic wealth waiting to be gathered in. At an audience with the queen herself, Frobisher spoke of the riches he had brought home 'and so great promises of the infinite treasure of this new land, whereof he would possess her majesty surmounting the treasure of the Indies of the king of Spain, whereby he would make her majesty the richest prince in all Europe'.[31]

Frobisher's three Inuit captives added to his celebrity. They were gaped at by the people of Bristol and painted in watercolour by the artist John White. All died within weeks of arriving in England, the man of injuries sustained during his capture, the young woman probably of measles. A wet nurse was provided for her baby boy, and they were taken up to London and lodged at the Three Swans Inn. The baby died in late November 1577 and was buried in the churchyard of St Olave, Hart Street, in the shadow of Muscovy House.[32]

In London a few months later, one printer obtained a licence for 'A description of the portraiture and shape of those strange kind of people which the worthy Master Martin Frobisher brought into England'.[33] To Elizabethans, they were at best specimens and curiosities.

Of greatest importance was the ore 'from the parts of Cathay discovered by Martin Frobisher', which, on the special orders of the queen's Privy Council, was brought to London in conditions of high security.[34] In and around the city it was smelted in purpose-built furnaces, and Michael Lok recruited for that task specialist German miners, of whom the most senior was the Saxon metallurgist Jonas Schutz, with the help also of the goldsmith Humphrey Cole.[35]

By now the stakes were very high indeed. A great deal rested on the success of extracting precious metals from the ore: money for the two voyages, the hope of funding a third, handsome returns for the investors, and of course riches, honours and plaudits for Frobisher. By February 1578, with little sign of much progress, Frobisher's fragile patience was frayed, so much so that he marched to Lok's house 'in great rage' and dragged Lok and others over to Schutz's workshop on Tower Hill. There they found Schutz stripped almost naked because of the heat and choking on the poisonous fumes. Frobisher, by Lok's account, 'reviled him with villainous speech for that he had not finished his work and drew his dagger on him and threatened him with oaths, that he would strike it in him' if he failed to complete the job quickly. Frobisher was desperate for everything to be settled in preparation for a third voyage.[36]

Three weeks later, in a happier encounter, Frobisher and Lok met the commissioners of the venture at Muscovy House to receive the final judgement on the ore. It was held to be valuable.[37] This test was key; the numbers were everything. The ore had produced grains of silver that suggested a ton of it would make £23 and 15 shillings. Taking into account the costs of transporting the ore back to England, for every £8 spent on the venture, each investor would receive £5 more. So the effort was worth it. The commissioners made their report to the queen's Privy Council, and the council approved the third voyage whose purpose was to exploit 'the great riches of the mines of gold found in the new countries'.[38]

A couple of years later, Michael Lok wrote of how Frobisher had carried himself before that third voyage:

> And now Captain Frobisher having the thing that he so much hunted for, grew into such a monstrous mind, that the whole kingdom could not contain it, but as already by discovery of a new world, he was become another Columbus, so also now by conquest of a new world he would become another Cortes.[39]

These were the sentiments of a man then broken by hubris and stung by failure. The reality, as both Michael Lok and Martin Frobisher would soon discover, was that the riches of Baffin Island fell a very long way short of those of Spanish Mexico.

CHAPTER FOURTEEN
Master Lok's Disgrace

In the spring of 1578 the confidence of Frobisher's investors was at its peak. Michael Lok's accounts read like a Who's Who of the political and mercantile elite: privy councillors, earls, countesses, barons, knights, esquires, a royal customs officer, London mercers, skinners and haberdashers. Queen Elizabeth committed a further £1,350 of her own fortune, and Sir Francis Walsingham, her secretary, was the most ambitious investor of the council. One of the great men of mercantile London, Sir Lionel Duckett, was a venturer. Of even greater standing than Duckett was Sir Thomas Gresham, who invested as much in the voyage as Walsingham. Other smaller investors were experienced hands in trade and exploration like Anthony Jenkinson and John Dee. Michael Lok continued to pour into the venture huge sums of his own money. Indeed, the whole of Lok's extended family bought into the enterprise.[1]

More now than simply a voyage to the other side of the world, this third expedition was really planned as a mining operation for which a colony would have to be established. Three ships – *Judith*, *Gabriel* and *Michael* – carried with them food, drink, weapons, ammunition and tools, and, for worship and edification, bibles, books of common prayer and twenty-four catechisms.[2] The whole business was taken very seriously indeed, and Lord Burghley himself amended early instructions for the voyage. The objective was clear: 800 tons of precious ore would be brought into the River Thames and unloaded near London.[3]

Frobisher's celebrity was thus secure. He was a hero, lauded by the poet Abraham Fleming as a new Ulysses 'in skill and martial might', a voyager 'through brackish seas' who had returned home with riches: 'The golden fleece (like Jason) hath he got.'⁴ Complementing this overblown verse was Frobisher's portrait, painted by Cornelis Ketel a little over a year earlier. In golden doublet and hose, Frobisher stands ready for action with a pistol in hand and his rapier in its scabbard, strident and aggressive, though just a little distracted, perhaps with his eyes on the islands of the north. Ketel set up the picture to suggest activity and purpose: a bosun's whistle marks Frobisher's command at sea, a globe on the table behind his right arm makes the viewer mindful of the greater ambition. Here was a man of steady purpose – and most certainly not a man to be crossed without consequences.⁵

For some months the venture appeared to be going smoothly. After some hair-raising moments of danger at sea, Frobisher was back in England in September 1578. He went first to see Elizabeth at Richmond Palace, and then travelled to London. Frobisher's reputation shone in glory. His admirer and publicist Thomas Churchyard rushed to his printer in London and added a few lines of verse to a book already in press:

> O Frobisher, thy bruit [reputation] and name
> shall be enrolled in books,
> That whosoever after comes,
> and on thy labour looks
> Shall muse and marvel at thine acts,
> and greatness of thy mind.⁶

It was Michael Lok who saw to the practicalities of smelting and refining the ore, lodging at the Bull inn in Dartford in Kent. Meanwhile four Saxon metallurgists worked nearby under the supervision of Jonas Schutz and Humphrey Cole.⁷

But progress was slow – so slow, in fact, that by November Lok's ingeniously built house of cards began to look precarious. No success in the smelting at Dartford meant that the main investors withheld the money they had promised. Without the money, Lok could not pay the sailors' wages. Petitioned daily by the mariners, Lok returned to London. Then he went to Elizabeth's court to persuade the 'venturers' to pay their money. Only two would do so, one of whom (improbably, given her iron grip on money) was the queen herself. By this time Frobisher himself was, according to Lok, 'utterly destitute of money', and on the third Thursday in November he came to London and practically stormed Lok's house 'in great rage and fury', making serious allegations of corruption and false accounting, calling Lok 'a bankrupt knave', and swearing by God's blood to pull him out of his house by the ears. It was in fact a mild enough threat by Frobisher's standards, but Lok thought his sometime partner and protégé either drunk or mad. Lok later wrote: 'And so Captain Frobisher departed, and proclaimed all these slanders against him [that is, Lok], in the [royal] court, and in the Royal Exchange, and everywhere in London and other places where he came.'[8]

For Lok, the rumour and innuendo was worse than any physical assault. There began a slow breaking down of his reputation in London and at court. Within two days the queen's Privy Council knew that something was awry. At first they gave Lok the benefit of the doubt. Knowing the mariners and miners of the Frobisher voyages were complaining that Lok had not paid them, their lordships, though sure of his 'honest dealing . . . in that behalf', merely wanted to know the facts of what lay behind the complainants' 'clamorous disposition'.[9] In what was surely the most discomfiting interview of his life, Lok appeared before the council to explain how he had handled the investors' money, facing at the council table a number of those very investors. Whatever he said, it was not enough. The council was unconvinced that Lok's sums added up, and auditors were called in to check his accounts.[10]

Lok later described the depression and acrimony in the workshops in Dartford in the months that followed, too neatly distancing himself from any responsibility for the mess by casting Frobisher as a kind of pantomime villain, playing, as Lok put it, 'his part of general misrule', continually pressing Jonas Schutz for a piece of refined gold that he could present to the queen as a new year's gift, desperate for his knighthood. It was a sorry picture of ambition thwarted. No part of the operation was left unexamined by the auditors appointed by the council, and they were beginning, with 'much enquiry', to wonder why Schutz and his team were failing to produce precious metals.[11]

Perhaps more alchemy than metallurgy, buoyed up by inflated hopes and pushed and pulled by Frobisher's ego and Lok's misplaced optimism, the few grains of silver that Schutz had found in spring 1578 could not be turned into the huge quantities imagined by the adventurers. But the fact was that by now there were tons of worthless ore sitting in the workshops at Dartford. Investors had put tens of thousands of pounds into the venture, though what brought about its final collapse was the refusal of those investors (for very good reasons) to give up their latest commitment of money. There was something heroically hopeless in Lok's efforts to persist for another couple of years in trying to make everything work, while his humiliation was deepened further by tangled accounts, audits, reports, petitions and explanations, allegations and counter-allegations, slanders and efforts (always unsuccessful) at saving face. A number of reputations – Michael Lok's above all others – were ruined. Lok himself wrote: 'Great storms were raised in the court and in the city, both against Master Lok and against Jonas and the workmen.'[12] There was no mention here of Martin Frobisher, the consummate survivor of storms both at sea and at court.

It all looks like a crazy speculation: a gold fever that addled the brains of courtiers and London merchants who should have known better. Their speculations were built, in turn, on the navigational fantasy of being able to sail easily and quickly to Cathay. But this was the reality of discovery. Travel was, in a familiar Elizabethan pun, travail: it was difficult, even deadly, in its seriousness. Frobisher and his men sailed tiny ships through ice and fog using navigational techniques that were at best experimental, and at worst deeply flawed. Easy as it is to smile at the notion of Frobisher being likened to Ulysses, those voyages were by any standards heroic. And the expeditions did bring back to England the features of a new world. What they produced by way of literary output, in books and pamphlets printed and read in London, was remarkable, counterbalancing – for us, though not at the time for Michael Lok – the losses of a spectacular misadventure.

And so, buried in the failure – though at first this was not at all obvious – was an achievement that could stand on its own feet: like those encounters with faraway places that a young Richard Hakluyt would have discovered in the bookshops of Paul's Churchyard, there was in accounts of the Frobisher voyages a meeting of city, exploration, trade and literature. Elizabethan Londoners were able to continue to make sense of remote parts of the world. They were developing a feeling of purpose: part trade, part exploration for its own sake, part civilizing mission. Young gentlemen continued to volunteer for projects like Frobisher's or Sir Humphrey Gilbert's, in the hope of colonizing new lands.

The poet Thomas Churchyard celebrated this impulse in 1578, the year Gilbert obtained a new patent, a licence from the queen, for 'planting' America with a colony of settlers. Searching for inspiration, Churchyard sends his servant off into London to find news. The boy went, naturally, to where people talked in the city about the latest happenings:

> My lackey had not walked in Paul's
> not twenty paces then,
> But heard that sundry friends
> of mine, had taken leave
> At court, and were all shipped away.[13]

The draw of adventure was a powerful one for gentlemen who wanted to make their mark on the world. And the same thought had occurred to the London bookseller Thomas Hacket a decade earlier: true men left behind everything dear to them in order to seek out new lands. In two lines Churchyard expressed beautifully and tellingly a mixed bag of motives for exploration:

> For country's wealth, for private gain,
> or glory seek we all.[14]

Was this trade? Certainly it was for London's merchants who invested in new ventures and companies in Russia and Persia, the far eastern Mediterranean, Africa and later America and the East Indies. Was it the seeking out of knowledge? That was also what it represented for the younger Richard Hakluyt, driven by a sense of mission to discover the whole sphere of God's creation. Was it to bring true Christianity to infidels? Churchyard most certainly embraced that motive: 'the purpose of manifesting God's mighty word and majesty among those that feed like monsters (and rather live like dogs than men)'.[15]

Two books about the Frobisher voyages stand out. One, by Thomas Ellis, 'sailor, and one of the company', was printed in the workshop of Thomas Dawson at the Three Cranes in the Vintry – the Thames wharf where for decades wine from France was brought ashore into London. The second pamphlet was by George Best, the son of the Muscovy Company's first Russian translator Robert, and by 1578 a protégé of the influential Elizabethan courtier Sir Christopher Hatton.

Ellis's account of Frobisher's last voyage out to Meta Incognita was introduced by the kind of verse that spoke powerfully to literary London, full of exaggeration and conceit, and heavily encrusted with allusions to classical mythology: Frobisher was 'A martial knight, adventurous, / whose valour great was such' – Hercules, Perseus, Jason and Ulysses all rolled into one angry Elizabethan.[16] But the book itself was in fact a narrative as spare and jagged as Ellis's own line drawings of 'great and monstrous' pieces of ice they had found floating in the Arctic seas. Ellis articulates a self-conscious and doubtless deliberate stoicism in the face of danger and travail: 'narrow straights, perilous ice, and swift tides, our time of abode there in snow, and storms, and our departure from thence . . . with dangerous blustering winds and tempests . . . was . . . uncomfortable'.[17]

George Best's book about the Frobisher voyages was a manual of exploration and discovery. Best wanted his readers to find out how to discover new countries, to provision a voyage, to deal with strange peoples 'be they never so barbarous, cruel and fierce', and to navigate frozen seas and mountains of ice. New discovery was perilous for all kinds of reasons – from thieves and robbers, wild beasts, unsavoury meats, storms, mountains and darkness – but most of all (with here a nod to his father's work for the Muscovy Company) because of 'the ignorance of the language, the want of interpreters'. Trade was only on the edges of Best's mind. What came first for him was the thrill of knowledge uncovered:

How pleasant and profitable it is, to attempt new discoveries, either for the sundry sights and shapes of strange beasts and fishes, the wonderful works of nature, the different manners and fashions of diverse nations, the sundry sorts of government, the sight of strange trees, fruit, fowls, and beasts, the infinite treasure of pearl, gold and silver, the news of new found lands, the sundry positions of the sphere, and many others.[18]

Incidental to George Best was what he called, three times in his book, 'the supposed continent of America'. He, like everyone else, embraced Frobisher's ambition to get to Asia. A crude but highly effective wood-cut map in his book showed Arctic islands stamped all over with the names and ambitions of the voyages: Queen Elizabeth's Foreland, Hatton's Headland, Cape Walsingham, Lok's Land, Countess of Sussex's Mine, Cape Best (of course), Mount Oxford, and even, to the south of the island Frobisher had named West England, Charing Cross.[19]

We might imagine that the Frobisher debacle shook some sense into mercantile London and the keen investors of Elizabeth I's court, that they would concentrate instead on returning to the old trade with Europe, which was still necessary in spite of war and rebellion in France and the Low Countries and England's deteriorating rela-tions with the kingdom and empire of Spain. Sensible and pragmatic Elizabethans would surely turn away from fantasist obsessions with faraway places that were impossible to get to. But the impulse to set out on improbable sea journeys became difficult to resist, all the more so with the return home in 1580 of Sir Francis Drake from his spectacular circumnavigation of the globe. Drake's was an example of a certain kind of financial investment made by Elizabeth and her courtiers – privateering – that actually succeeded.

So much of all this moved in fits and starts: some successes, many failures; opportunities and possibilities embraced, others ignored. It was a great jumble of motives and factors. Certainly there was no long-term plan in Elizabeth's reign for seaborne dominion or empire, no easy nineteenth-century narrative of England's world dominance. But there was in Elizabethan London a spark of an ambition to do something – or at least a kind of vocabulary and set of assumptions more or less common to theorists and writers who thought about why it was important to sail off to far parts of the world and what they should do when they got there. What those things were Elizabethan writers articulated in words that would later cause robustly self-confident Victorians to prick up their ears. In 1578 George Best asked Sir Christopher Hatton 'to behold the great industry of our present age, and the invincible minds of our English nation, who have never left any worthy thing unattempted, nor any part almost of the whole world unsearched'.[20] Best really had his eye (like most others writing his kind of book) on Spain and Portugal: if those two global powers could dominate the south-eastern and south-western parts of the world, then it was up to England to discover and hold the north-east and north-west.

Only John Dee called it an empire, but few could hope to keep up with the complicated manoeuvrings of Dee's mind in the later 1570s, years when he went to and from Elizabeth's court carrying great piles of papers of abstruse scholarship and scrolls of evidence, all to prove the queen's dominion over the northern seas and oceans. Dee was interested in Elizabeth's claim to the north, fixing on the possibilities for trade and colonization, a 'British Empire', 'the incomparable island of the whole world'.[21] For Dee's contemporaries, the ambition was as extravagant as his prose. And it was not a simple model of empire, but one with all kinds of permutations and subtleties that reflected the intricate mechanisms of Dee's brain.

And so, while John Dee saw in his mind's eye a great territory in northern oceans discovered and then colonized by England – calling that territory a British empire – pedestrian thinkers tended to run along more well-worn tracks of ambition. The Frobisher voyages did not squash the hope of Cathay. In fact the failure of Frobisher and Lok – or perhaps, more to the point, their brief sniff at success – may even have been the reason the Muscovy Company at long last, in 1580, put its corporate muscle behind another expedition to reach the court of the Great Khan. It went through all the familiar phases: the help of experts (this time Dee and the elder Richard Hakluyt of the Middle Temple), the endorsement of authorities (Gerard Mercator wrote that 'The voyage to Cathay by the East, is doubtless very easy and short'), the gathering of resources, and the unforgiving reality of sailing into impenetrable north-eastern waters.[22] A single entry in the voyage's navigational log is especially revealing: 'This day all the afternoon we sailed under a great land of ice, we sailed between the land and ice, being not able to cross it.'[23] That entry was made in the harsh waters of the Kara Sea in late July; sailing along the top of Russia was now shown to be as futile as it was terrifying.

But, like the Frobisher voyages, there is still so much we can learn even from the failure of this last Cathay expedition. That Elizabethans persisted in the fantasy of sailing easily to Asia is, on its own terms, telling. Experts like Mercator and Dee were persuasive. The maps Dee made for Sir Humphrey Gilbert's voyages in the late 1570s were as beautiful as they were deceptive. In a briefing document for officers of the Muscovy Company's Cathay voyage, Dee set out in words of authoritative certainty the route to the capital city of the Great Khan, Cambalu, and suggested that maps and charts printed in Cathay and China would allow the expedition then to sail on to Japan.[24]

In this way, Cathay had for Elizabethans a physical presence. It existed; it was a reality. It was, of course, waiting for the blessing of English trade, as it had been for decades. What the merchants and experts at Muscovy House expected to find and to do in Cathay tells us all kinds of things about their own world. It is a truism that the way we prepare for and record our encounters with others says as much about ourselves as it does about the people we meet, and probably the effect is only deepened when we have at best an impression of who those others are and what they are like – a model fashioned by our own imaginations, assumptions and prejudices.

The briefing paper for the north-eastern voyage was prepared for the company by the elder Richard Hakluyt. In it we find an expedition on its best behaviour, ready to show a famously splendid and accomplished people the civilities of England. On board the company's ships lying at anchor in the harbour of Cambalu, the English officers would dine the great and the good of those fabulous cities of Cathay; the ships would be perfumed, the guests sprinkled with 'good sweet waters'. Here the English and the Cathaians would meet in peace, their friendship marked by the giving of gifts. Books showing the herbs, plants, trees, fish, birds and animals of Europe would 'much delight' the Great Khan, his nobility and merchants. But all the gifts and the charm was to one purpose: to convince the rulers of Cathay of the benefits of English trade.[25]

This was a mercantile voyage of the old-fashioned sort. The ships would go out to Asia stocked with the kinds of commodities that arrived every day into the port of London: kerseys, frieze cloth, felts, taffeta, sailors' caps, quilted caps of Levant taffeta, globes, shoes, purses, pewter, English and Venetian glass, looking glasses, spectacles, hour glasses, combs, linen, handkerchiefs, knives, buttons, needles, English coins, locks, keys and bolts. The elder Hakluyt saw the benefits of trade extending even beyond 'the gain of the merchant'. It would offer employment and a way out of poverty for those currently supported in London's charitable hospitals – of 'more worth to our people', he wrote, than Bridewell and the Savoy. A healthy market for sailors' caps, Hakluyt reflected, 'would turn to an infinite commodity of the common poor people by knitting'.[26] He – and others – saw in trade and colonization an answer to pressing questions of poverty and crime.

Hakluyt emphasized that the expedition should advertise the kingdom and the great city from whence it had sailed. 'Take with you the map of England set out in fair colours,' he wrote, 'one of the biggest sort I mean.' They should also take a large map of London 'to make show of your city', with the Thames 'drawn full of ships of all sorts, to make the more show of your great trade and traffic in trade of merchandize'.[27]

After 1580, two proposed destinations, more concrete than Cathay – America and then the East Indies – came to preoccupy mercantile London. America had for a long time been at the edges of the Tudor understanding of the world. But something had shifted by the early 1580s, thanks in good part to Sir Humphrey Gilbert's success in securing his royal patent in 1578 to plant a colony in the territory somewhere between what is now southern New England and the Strait of Belle Isle.[28] John Dee helped with the project, and drew in 1582 a polar map that gave geographical shape to his notion of a great northern empire of English colonization and trade. The Gilbert patent helped also to rehabilitate Michael Lok, who had been struggling with debt and periods of imprisonment after the ignominious failure of his Cathay company. Lok produced in 1582 a map of Meta Incognita and America that served as a kind of real estate brochure for prospective investors interested in putting their money into this new colonial project.[29] In the few years after the Frobisher debacle Lok, like many others in London and at the queen's court, became a convinced Atlanticist. After some dark days for Lok, he could at least enjoy the praise of the younger Richard Hakluyt:

> The map is Master Michael Lok's, a man, for his knowledge in divers languages and especially in cosmography, able to do his country good, and worthy in my judgement, for the manifold good parts in him, of good reputation and better fortune.[30]

America now became the latest challenge and new opportunity. The soldier and adventurer Christopher Carleill was a committed Atlanticist. Himself the son of a founding charter member of the Muscovy Company (and stepson of Sir Francis Walsingham), in 1583 he urged London's Russia merchants to redirect their efforts to America. Where ten ships sailed annually between England and Russia, he wrote, within decades twenty would go out to America twice a year.[31] Michael Lok, writing in the early 1580s a long apologia for his part in the Frobisher voyages, neatly reinvented the purpose of that expedition. The 'natural riches and infinite treasure and the great traffic of rich merchandize' to be found in Cathay, China and India were well known from 'every book of history or cosmography of those parts of the world, which are to be had in every printer's shop'. Waiting to be discovered, however, was America, as full of people and 'such commodities and merchandize' as the territories of Russia and beyond: it offered raw materials, potential for colonization, and the hope of future transatlantic trade.[32]

It also preoccupied the younger Richard Hakluyt, who in 1584 wrote for his patrons at court a highly speculative paper on the benefits of 'planting' America with English colonies. Hakluyt, by now in his early thirties, was well connected both in London and court, supported at Oxford by the skinners' and clothworkers' companies of London (one of his great supporters in the clothworkers became later a prominent founding merchant of the East India Company) and close to the influential Sir Francis Walsingham.[33] Hakluyt's first book, *Divers voyages touching the discoverie of America* (1582), became a source book on the new continent.

Hakluyt's agenda was an overtly colonizing one. This was not surprising given developments over the last thirty years: the desire for new markets and trade, the experimentation with new structures of royally chartered corporate organizations like the Muscovy Company, increasing expertise in England on techniques of navigation, the notion of Christian civilizing missions, and the prospectuses for 'proprietorial colonies' under the Crown, with patents like Gilbert's for America.[34] Now, for the courtier Walter Ralegh, Hakluyt wrote about the possibilities of colonial ventures. He saw all kinds of interlocking benefits for a kingdom like England, being squeezed hard by the power of King Philip II's Spain, and set out a strategic case for the push on America. He saw the likelihood of being able to clip Spain's wings, especially in the Caribbean. He perceived a way for English merchants to escape the stranglehold of Spanish power, and to engineer a fantastic boost for the kingdom's trade. Like his cousin of the Middle Temple, he saw the social benefits of employment for the poor, making commodities to trade. He imagined rising customs revenues for the queen's government, the development of her navy, and the precedence of Elizabeth's title to foreign dominions over that of King Philip. But he called too for quick action in planting America before other powers began to settle their own colonies. His first reason for this 'western planting' across the Atlantic was what he called 'the enlargement of the gospel' – the spreading of Protestant Christianity to far parts of the world.[35]

And so the scene was set, the foundations laid down. Colonial ventures could appeal to any English merchant throughout the kingdom. This was a national project: for a long time, experts like Hakluyt had been thinking and writing for the good of the whole kingdom. But London, in its concentration of families, capital and experience, was ideally placed to enter brave new worlds of discovery and trade. It was in the city, and for these reasons, that two of the greatest Elizabethan colonizing and trading ventures, the Virginia Company and the East India Company, came into existence.

CHAPTER FIFTEEN

Shylock's Victory

The sad boast of Michael Lok in the years following the Frobisher debacle was that he had seen the inside of every gaol in London. Burdened by debt for the rest of his life, he never recovered his position. The Cathay voyages had broken a man who, in his own way, was as visionary as Richard Hakluyt or John Dee. The problem was his venality, for which Nemesis had her revenge, with a further instalment to follow in the twentieth century. For the esoteric conspiracy theorists who believe that Shakespeare's plays were written by John de Vere, 17th Earl of Oxford (even by the often unimpressive standards of the Elizabethan nobility one of most appallingly arrogant, conceited and superficial men of the time), Lok was the model for Shylock in Oxford's *The Merchant of Venice*. That he had conned the earl out of £1,000 was indeed one of the many bitterly contested allegations made by Frobisher. Resurrected from his tomb to face this further stain upon his reputation, poor Michael Lok must have shuddered at the humiliation.

Both Lok and Shakespeare's Shylock lead us by different paths to the same point and place. Elizabethans worried about money: about how it was made and how it corrupted good Christians. But attitudes towards money were changing in the sixteenth century. The old fixed position on usury was under attack: language was evolving to reflect the loosening of some old moral restraints. Elizabethans may still have said that love of riches put a soul in peril, but did they really mean it?

Though these new and more lenient attitudes surprised Elizabethans, they should not surprise us. As the limits of their experience were expanded through travel and exploration, Elizabethans were obliged to confront alien peoples and places. At home Londoners were able to read new books on subjects that would have been unthinkable at the end of the fifteenth century: the arresting translations by Thomas Hacket of Jean Ribault's and André Thevet's accounts of America were a very long way from Mandeville's fabulous monsters. Yet the effort to fit everything they were discovering into the rigid structures of old assumptions was immense. Their world was all the time being reshaped in wonderful and unexpected ways, and only slowly and falteringly did Elizabethans come to terms with the consequences of the changes that they themselves were helping to engineer.

Mercantile ventures entrenched a new vocabulary of money: of capital, stocks, shares, dividends, interest – all words we take for granted now, but whose unfamiliarity was felt by anxious Elizabethans. Of course the opportunities were fantastic; but still money was a problem. Great riches had long troubled the values of Christian Europe, or at least afflicted the consciences of theologians and preachers. Money could be a corrupter of souls and an instrument of power over others, something shown so powerfully by Hans Holbein the Younger in his allegory of *The Triumph of Riches*. Money could subvert morality, even turn the world upside down. In 'yellow, glittering, precious gold' there was, as Shakespeare saw, the power to make 'black white, foul fair, / Wrong right, base noble, old young, coward valiant' (*Timon of Athens*, IV. iii. 26–30).[1]

Slowly something changed. By increments attitudes shifted. Shylock had his victory – but not without a fight.

* * *

As we saw in earlier chapters, emperors, kings and princes across Europe had long relied on wealthy merchants for credit. This had been the reality for centuries, where bankers (at first Italians and then Germans like the Fugger and Welser) kept up the pretensions of monarchs by loaning them huge sums of money at interest. When it came to matters of state, however, questions of usury were conveniently put to one side.

On the face of it, the high finances of princes were governed only by principles of pragmatism and necessity. Going crown in hand to one of Europe's great banking houses was a marriage of convenience voluntarily entered into; but, like a real marriage in the sixteenth century, all the power rested with one partner only. For monarchs, the short-term sigh of relief at the prospect of money in the royal exchequer was always followed by the long-term regret of years of painful repayment – or worse still, loan default. The Tudor Crown was indebted to foreign bankers for three decades. Even monitored and massaged by Sir Thomas Gresham, the interest alone was eye-watering: it was, as one of Elizabeth I's councillors once told the House of Commons, an 'eating corrosive' and 'a most pestilent cancer that is able to devour even the states of princes'.[2]

The royal agents in Antwerp managed the day-to-day realities of royal debt. As Stephen Vaughan wrote from Antwerp in 1546, 'The Fugger is never from me, the house of Bonvisi . . . pulleth me by the sleeve.'[3] Gresham or Vaughan or their factors could not really afford to ponder the theology or canon law on usury. Their job was to negotiate favourable terms for loans, and it could be thankless work. Vaughan, for example, experienced the indignity of making late payments to Henry VIII's creditors, as well as having the bankers' factors rifling through chests of money in order to determine which coins they would and would not accept.[4] Gresham's official accounts tell their own story – setting out the loans taken up, brokers' fees to be charged and the interest to be paid. His letters to Sir William Cecil prickle with the anxieties of high finance in Antwerp. Sometimes the bankers were nervous, spooked by business bankruptcies or the churning fear of loan defaults by great sovereign debtors like the king of Spain. Gresham described 'great bank routs', and the miseries of Elizabeth's own wobbling creditors, keen to get rid of the queen's bonds.[5] And all this was before the Dutch Revolt and the Spanish assault on Antwerp, which further shook what until then had been the greatest financial centre in Europe.

Thomas Gresham was superbly accomplished at advertising his mastery of the Antwerp exchange. But even his hope was to wean the English Crown off foreign loans and to look for credit instead at home. If the queen used her own merchants to raise money, Gresham maintained, she would show to the whole of Europe what 'a prince of power' she was.[6] Gresham had long prided himself on his skill at influencing and manipulating the Antwerp exchange in Elizabeth's favour. Now he believed that she – and he – should use her 'money merchants' both tactically and strategically 'for the service of the prince'.[7]

English merchants came later to banking than their continental counterparts. One clever London mercantile analyst of the early seventeenth century, Gerard de Malynes, looked back to the reign of Henry VII (1485–1509) and found that 'in his time the bankers had their beginning, who did invent the merchandizing exchange, making of money a merchandize'.[8] Malynes meant by this the lending out of money to make more money.

In the 1560s Gresham was able to raise loans from merchants in London, who lent money – naturally at interest – in order to make payments to the queen's creditors in Antwerp and Augsburg. These 'money merchants' were the city's super-rich: serving and former lord mayors, aldermen, governors and masters of the livery companies, leaders and financiers of new endeavours like the Muscovy Company. Here were merchants at once rooted in the old mercantile world of Europe and investors in the new corporate ventures. And they were as hard-nosed as a Fugger: Gresham set out the terms of their loans in exactly the form he used in Antwerp – with the sum taken up, the broker's fee charged for negotiating the loan, and the sum eventually payable in interest.[9]

Gresham knew that he was working at the far boundaries of the law. The queen's merchant creditors had to be given special protection from prosecution under a statute of King Edward VI that prohibited outright the charging of interest.[10] Gresham was, however, a pragmatic man who believed that there needed to be, in the words of his own factor Richard Clough, 'some reasonable interest between man and man'.[11] To Cecil, Gresham emphasized that he needed to be able more easily to accomplish 'her highness's enterprises' – in other words, he needed the right tools for the job he had been given. Cecil, however, was of the old school, believing, like most people, in the need for vigilant protection at law against usury.[12]

Usury was not for Elizabethans a pretty word or notion. It was also a complicated one. Though lending out one's money for one's own financial return was very difficult not to class as usury, it was still a tricky thing to define precisely – in part because so many inventive minds and ingenious practitioners had spent centuries trying to get round it, finding loopholes in the law. The nearest we have to a dictionary definition of usury as Elizabethans understood it is by Dr Thomas Wilson, writing in 1572, a year after the law in England was relaxed to allow for an increase of interest up to 10 per cent: 'usury is committed only where lending and borrowing is, and that when any overplus or excess is taken over and above the principal that was lent, for the very respect only of lending, and in consideration of forbearing money for time'.[13] The 'principal' was the capital sum lent and the 'overplus or excess' the interest charged for the loan of it. But was all interest usury, as Wilson seemed to be suggesting, or was it really just excessive interest? Did it extend to more than money? Wrestled with for centuries, questions like these (and many more too) occupied anxious Elizabethans.

And so Sir Thomas Gresham's pragmatism bumped up against one of the great taboos for the Church and Christendom. Money was as necessary as it was problematic. And it was problematic because how it was made was under the scrutiny of God, from which there was no escape.

The Merchant of Venice (1596/97) illustrates beautifully Elizabethans' ambivalence over usury, interest and money. The brilliance of Shylock is that he is an outsider, embittered and isolated – a rich Jew, that stock figure of fear and hatred in sixteenth-century Europe, who despises Christian society and its codes and values. In the characters of Shylock and the merchant Antonio, Shakespeare gives us two extreme positions on money. Where one is monstrously grasping, the other is admirably generous but hopelessly naive.

Antonio and Shylock operate their two businesses on entirely opposing principles. Shylock grumbles that Antonio's Christian scruples are bad for the city's moneylenders:

> ... in low simplicity
> He lends out money gratis, and brings down
> The rate of usance here with us in Venice. (I. iii. 43–5)

By 'usance' Shylock means the period of the loan that determined the amount of interest to be paid on it. Easy to miss – but in fact the most significant thing to notice – is how being a merchant is very different from being a moneylender. Antonio is an old-fashioned merchant adventurer: he trades in commodities and puts ships out to sea. He is an amateur lender of money (and for good and just reasons), where Shylock is the professional moneylender, grasping and unscrupulous. There is a world of difference between the methods employed by the two men. Shylock simply uses his money to make even more of it. Trade plays no part in his business, and he is contemptuous of it. Where the moneylender is in this sense passive, the merchant is active. Antonio takes risks, whereas in merely lending money Shylock risks nothing. What Shylock calls his own 'well-won thrift' (I. iii. 50–51), Antonio calls 'interest'. It was a word and a concept that would have been as offensive and oppressive as usury to many in Shakespeare's audience.

For Southwark's playgoers in the 1590s, Antonio's practice of lending money for free would have seemed long out of date. Shylock's business model was well established not only in London but throughout Europe. There was little difference in technique between a Shylock and a Fugger (though the Fugger, as tough as they were, stopped short of cutting chunks of flesh out of their debtors).[14]

'Interest' was a significant word for the Elizabethans, who worried about the degrading of honest language. Some felt that sharp financial practices were being blunted by weasel words, and that clever obfuscations were disguising old sins. There is nothing, after all, like a euphemism to distract one's attention from what is really being said or going on. One writer, in 1594, believed that gentlemen and merchants were using 'fine terms' to cover up their usury: 'they will not say, let their money to *usury*, but to *interest*; or put it to *usance*, or *they take consideration, rent or an honourable reward*'.[15] Usury, said another, was being covered up by a 'goodly cloak to cover the shame thereof': 'I mean the name of interest, or profit of money.'[16] The idea that the purpose of money was simply to facilitate trade and commerce went all the way back to Aristotle. But what if trade played no part in making fortunes? What was frightening was the idea that money could simply regenerate itself, 'multiplied by drawing of continual profit upon the use of the principal stock from month or month, or year to year, by the loan of money till it be repaid'. For the moralists, this was usury under the newly invented name of interest.[17]

It is here that we can begin to see how Elizabethans made moral sense of the fortunes built up by merchants and traders. *The Merchant of Venice* helps once again. Antonio's fortune means something: his merchant adventuring was red-blooded, vital, alive. Trade was hard-won and tangible. Textiles and spices, furs and oil, ships and caravans, encounters with foreign merchants and princes, risk with legitimate reward, or loss and misfortune according to the will of providence: goods and wares, and the wealth that came from them, spoke to mercantile prosperity and the common good. There was all the difference, in the Elizabethan mind, between sitting on ever-growing piles of money (like Shylock or any other usurer) and the hard slog of Anthony Jenkinson fighting his way to the silk road with the Muscovy Company's fardels of London cloth.

London's preachers saw before them a city infected by the love of money. Usury, they believed, was a special pestilence, a plague of vice and sin that threatened destruction. At Paul's Cross, during the plague time of 1577, one preacher opened his sermon with stark words:

> Woe to that abominable, filthy and cruel city, she heard not the voice, she received not correction, she trusted not in the Lord, she drew not near unto her God, her rulers within are as roaring lions, her judges are as wolves in the evenings.[18]

The devil stalked the streets of London in search of worldly men to get into his clutches. One morality play has Satan celebrating the 'worldly man' who is able to avoid being entrapped by usury law. Satan continues with a warning:

> All you worldly men, that in your riches do trust,
> Be merry and jocund, build palaces and make lusty cheer:
> Put your money to usury, let it not lie and rust,
> Occupy yourselves in my laws while ye be here.[19]

London's usury sermons are common enough to be called a genre, and the most compelling of them was preached by the minister of the city parish of St Peter's Cornhill, Richard Porder, from Paul's Cross in 1570. The striking thing about the sermon (or at least the book of it, which ran to nearly 40,000 words) is that Porder gave Londoners something more than the usual preacher's fare of biblical text, godly exhortation and doom. Porder was a young graduate with a sharp eye and a clear brain, and he looked closely at how merchants did business with one another, discerning their sleights of hand, and watching Christian morality give way under the weight of gold.

Porder was not at all sure that it was possible to be both a good Christian and a clever merchant who did deals in the marketplace or bourse. Too many merchants, he believed, convinced themselves that what made them their money was the lucky uncertainty of markets and exchanges. What Porder saw, by contrast, was 'the malice of men, who spying their neighbours' need do make gain thereof to themselves'.[20] For Porder, the 'market' was something tangible and physical, that space and place where merchants and others went to buy and sell, regulated by rules for good behaviour – quite literally 'The laws of the market'.[21] But for him, it was also a place where people made moral choices about how they treated others, for which they had to take personal responsibility.[22] Elizabethan dramatists took the same kind of view – a rare alignment of the values of playwright and preacher.

Richard Porder was swingeing in his condemnation of what he saw round about him in the city, recognizing the pernicious work of run-of-the-mill usurers who (in one of Porder's illustrations) might on a loan of forty shillings take in interest five shillings a week.[23] Elizabethan moralists like George Whetstone believed that this kind of small-scale loan-sharking was endemic in London. He explained with great passion how young and naive gentlemen were drawn into the clutches of 'brokers', bankrupt citizens or other indebted gentlemen who got their victim 'to credit' with their own creditors and then took a share of the spoils.[24] 'Broker' used in a different sense meant pimp: one kind of broker procured money for his clients, the other sex.

Most striking in Porder's sermon is that he engaged in a full frontal assault on the way merchants used the foreign exchange. Criminal loan-sharking was one thing: anyone could condemn a grasping moneylender. But to treat the use by merchants of bills of exchange as illustrations of usury was something else entirely.

The bill of exchange was the bread and butter of the trading merchant, for decades making possible English trade with the Low Countries. It was the instrument of Antonio, not Shylock – the means by which hard-working merchants earned their living by buying and selling commodities at the Antwerp and other fairs. Without the bill, Thomas Wyndout, Richard and Thomas Gresham, Gregory and John Isham and thousands of other reputable merchants could never have conducted the kind of trade that they did.

But Porder offered a different perspective. He used the example of a bill drawn up in London between two merchants. One was the 'deliverer', the other the 'taker'. The taker 'took up' from the deliverer a sum of money in pounds sterling. The bill was the taker's promise to pay back that sum of money in Antwerp in the local currency, the Flemish groat, calculated according to the exchange rate between the two currencies. It looks like a simple enough transaction, described thus by an Elizabethan expert: 'money is delivered in one country plainly and simply . . . and bills delivered and received for the payment of the same in another country, according as money is current by merchants' valuation [i.e. the exchange rate] between those two countries'.[25]

Crucial to any bill of exchange was the date agreed by the two merchants for repayment. They used the word Shylock used: 'usance'. The taker might pay the amount to the deliverer's factor or representative in Antwerp after the standard period of a month ('at usance') or perhaps fifteen days ('half usance') or two months ('double usance').

Porder saw the bill of exchange for what it really was: a temporary loan of money from one merchant to another. And so it was: bills of exchange had allowed generations of merchants, in need of money but anticipating good sales, to go over to Antwerp to sell their cloth. Porder's objection was that, because of the nature of business on the bourse, and the way exchange rates worked, the sum the taker would almost always pay back in Antwerp was in fact more than he had borrowed in London. In the transaction Porder saw that the taker was in reality a debtor borrowing money from a creditor (the deliverer), paying an amount of money on top of the 'principal' for the privilege of taking out a fixed-term loan. He was certain that this was usury.[26]

He knew that the merchants would respond by citing risk. By long tradition, usury was committed only where the lender was guaranteed a profit without regard to the borrower's risk.[27] The risk, merchants might say, was the variability of the exchange rate. Instead

11. A detail from Anthony Jenkinson's groundbreaking map of nearest Asia, 1562. The pictures (which include an Elizabethan galleon sailing on the Caspian Sea) and cartouches give a narrative of his perilous return journey from Moscow to Bukhara.

13. A universal instrument made by the goldsmith and cartographer Humphrey Cole, 1582. Cole, a superlative craftsman, was closely involved with Martin Frobisher's three voyages of the late 1570s.

12. Cosmographer, editor and colonial theorist: the younger Richard Hakluyt commemorated in Victorian stained glass by C. E. Kempe.

14. Cornelis Kettel's 1577 portrait of a
robust Martin Frobisher, ready to conquer
the globe.

15. Shakespeare's 'yellow, glittering,
precious gold': an Elizabethan sovereign.

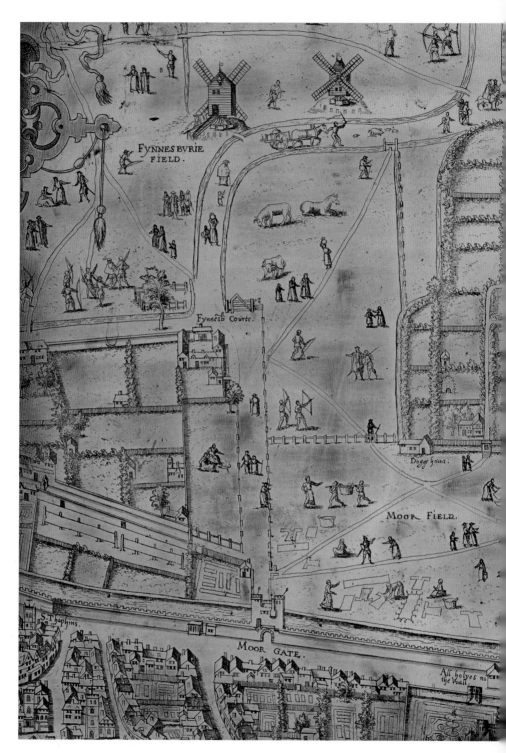

FYNNESBVRIE FIELD.

Fynnesb Courte.

Dogge hows.

MOOR FIELD.

S.T paphins.

MOOR GATE.

All holyes ni the Woll.

16. A reverse image of the printing plate used for the 'Copperplate Map' of London, showing the city suburbs outside Bishopsgate, including Bethlehem Hospital (Bedlam) and the insalubrious Moorfields.

SHOR

S. M. Spittel

THE SPITEL

Busshoppes gate Strete

Blak hows

Bedlame

Bedlame Gate

Giardin di Piero

S. Buttet

BVSSHOPPES GATE

17. The consummate corporate operator: Sir Thomas Smythe, Jacobean governor of the Muscovy, East India and Virginia companies.

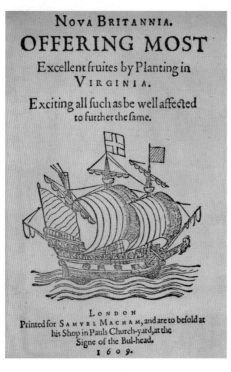

NOVA BRITANNIA.

OFFERING MOST

Excellent fruites by Planting in
VIRGINIA.

Exciting all such as be well affected
to further the same.

LONDON
Printed for SAMVEL MACHAM, and are to be sold at
his Shop in Pauls Church-yard, at the
Signe of the Bul-head.
1609.

18. Colonizing Virginia: trade leads to empire, with the hope of a New Britain planted by London's merchants and investors. Title-page of *Nova Britannia*, 1609.

19. The church of St Andrew Undershaft, the last resting place of the London antiquary John Stow, today in the shadow of 30 St Mary Axe.

20. Looking earnestly to heaven: effigy of Paul Bayning (d. 1616), a Levant and senior East India Company merchant and London alderman, who shares a tomb with his brother Peter (d. 1610) in the church of St Olave, Hart Street.

of a deliverer taking 'overplus' (yet another word for interest), the sum of money paid back by the taker might not be worth the sum borrowed.[28] Porder brushed aside the objection. He recognized what he called the 'hazard' of the market. But he knew – as the standard authorities on the workings of the exchange also knew – that it was so much more likely for a deliverer to take a profit than to make a loss.[29] Porder saw no difference between a 'plain usurer' (someone who simply lent out a sum of money at interest) and the 'exchange usurer'. In both cases, in his view, the expectation of profit easily outpaced the likelihood of loss.[30]

Though he was no financial analyst or exchange expert, Porder thought his way through and around a subject that continued, even after the later change in the law in 1571, to perplex and worry Elizabethans. He saw how the value of money might be said by merchants to vary with the exchange. He made his own estimate of risk in exchange transactions. He sensed the power relations between a deliverer (as creditor) and a taker (as debtor). He refused to accept as an excuse for exploitation the workings of a market or exchange. And he saw how, at huge moral and spiritual cost, money could be used simply to make more money by being moved 'to and fro upon the exchange', so making it 'a continual trade to gain by'.[31] Here was the danger of Antonio developing the instincts of Shylock: a merchant with enough capital to keep bills running between exchanges, in order – without doing much by way of trade – to make a profitable return.[32]

Like Richard Porder, what offended his exact contemporary Thomas Wilson (widely recognized as the most distinguished Elizabethan expert on usury) was that money was being traded like a commodity, 'making the loan of money a kind of merchandize'.[33] Wilson's great work, A Discourse upon Usury (1572), is a brilliant companion piece to Porder's sermon. Where Porder was a minister, Wilson was a lawyer, as well as a classical scholar and a government official. Porder's parish of St Peter's Cornhill was not so far away from Wilson's apartments in the hospital of St Katherine near the Tower of London. Both men saw usury and its toxic effects all around them. Both spoke in and to the city in stridently moral terms, trying to put money back under the control of God and law.

Wilson's *Discourse* is a long dialogue between a merchant, his kinsman apprentice, a preacher, a dilettante gentleman acquainted with the inns of court, and a 'civilian', an expert in the civil (or Roman) law. The cleverest and most astute speaker, not surprisingly, is the civilian: that, after all, was Wilson's specialism.

Wilson's setting for his dialogue is the merchant's townhouse on a hot London afternoon, following a morning sermon on usury. The merchant and his guests enjoy a good lunch, after which the apprentice lays out cushions in the beautiful garden. The merchant, welcoming and cheerful, is 'merry as a pie', and looks forward to their conversation, happily complacent in admitting the preacher's charge that he minds 'nothing so much as getting of money'.[34] They talk about merchants' bills and about uncertainty on the exchange. The merchant's guests (and Wilson himself) are as dismissive as Richard Porder is of the defence of risk: what the exchange really exposed was 'the greediness of man, and the covetous desire which he hath to enrich himself by hook or crook'.[35] Wilson's position is clear: the mechanisms of trade and finance could not be used to argue away an individual's moral responsibility to act according to divine and human laws.

Wilson enjoyed a savage joke at the city of London's expense, telling the story of a famous preacher who gave a sermon 'wholly against usury'. The preacher dined that same day with a rich and important merchant. After dinner the merchant thanked the preacher for his sermon, saying that 'he had done great good that day in speaking so much against usury'. One of the merchant's friends asked him why he had said such a thing, given that no one in London made more from usury than the merchant himself. 'Tush,' said the merchant to his friend, 'you are a fool. I do thank him, and thank him again, for wot you what? The fewer usurers that he can make, the more shall be my gain, for then men shall chiefly seek me out.' Did his friend really think that *he* would 'leave so sweet a trade for a few words of his [the preacher's] trolling tongue'?[36]

The merchant in the *Discourse* presents as his common-sense defence the way he actually treats money. What trade would there be if merchants were deprived of the hope of gain? 'What man is so mad to deliver his money out of his own possession for naught?' His kinsman apprentice goes a step further. What was the point of risking everything in the travail, toil and hazard of trade and merchandise? 'I am young,' he says, 'and gladly would I learn of mine elders to get goods with ease, and gain money with money, which I take to be a good gain.' This was a notion made all the more shocking by the young man's unembarrassed bluntness in saying it.[37]

If we take preachers and writers like Porder and Wilson at their word, cold money was triumphing over the warmth of Christian charity. City and society were tempting God's judgement. The preacher says in Wilson's *Discourse*: 'It is very certain, as I take it, the world is almost at an end.' His attitude is in sharp contrast to the merchant's cheerful complacency and full belly. But Wilson meant what he wrote; in dedicating the book to his noble patron, he wrote: 'I do verily believe, the end of this world is nigh at hand.'[38] Like so many of his contemporaries, Dr Wilson was reluctant to let go of some deep moral assumptions and associations.

It is striking how peculiar all this febrile moral commentary is when we set it alongside the trading ventures of Elizabeth's reign, the complexities of Crown finance, the workings of exchanges and the new chartered trading companies. But old habits and values were hard to cast off: a society soaked in Christian morality, viewing usury as sin, could not very easily attune itself to new economic thinking. Such an adjustment took time, and people had to be prepared to think in new ways – someone like the author of a policy paper of *c.* 1570 on the need for a stern look at the law, who cut through the fug of moral outrage to a reality that to him was clear as day. An absolute prohibition on usury encouraged merchants to conceal their profiteering in complicated exchange dealings: such 'Usury tendeth to the destruction of the commonwealth, but the borrowing of money or any other thing, yielding to the lender true and just interest, is one of the commodities which issued by the society of man.'[39] Contained in this sentence were deep traditions and new ways of thinking about economic realities – and a blurring of some old moral and theological certainties.

To add to the complexity, London's late Elizabethan merchants themselves defy simple categorizations. Porder called them plain usurers and exchange usurers, where Wilson produced two caricatures, one the full-bellied merchant, the other the morally bankrupt apprentice. Both the preacher and the lawyer must have known that they were using tabloid generalizations, and that in London in the 1570s and 1580s they were very much more likely to encounter earnest merchants all too conscious of the city's need for moral reformation. Many of London's late Elizabethan merchants were inclined to puritanism, and they spent as long in churches listening to impossibly long sermons as they did in their counting houses.

In fact there was a pronounced godly feel to the city's aldermanic elite, thinking on God and justifying to their consciences and to others the kinds of business dealings that scrupulous preachers worried about. London's godly merchants looked out to the world, hoping to export Christianity to godless savages. At the turn of the new century, London would help to take trade and the true faith out to the new world. They attended also to London itself: to their own parishes and the lives of fellow parishioners in a growing and changing city, policing lives and morals and offering charity.

CHAPTER SIXTEEN

St Bartholomew the Less

Imagine a city whose population is swollen by migrants from an English countryside ravaged by crop failure and starvation, crammed into squalid tenements in ever-growing suburbs. It is a city without any kind of social safety net beyond the resources of parishes and charitable hospitals, and where poverty, riot and the fear of crime so terrify the government that martial law is sometimes declared; where men are conscripted for foreign wars, and those lucky enough to make it home have, like so many others, to beg on the streets; where wages keep falling and prices rising, impoverishing many thousands; where everyone from the poorest to the richest – but especially the poorest – feels the sting of plague epidemics that claim so many families and stalk parish communities: imagine that city, locate it on the River Thames just over 400 years ago, and you have imagined London in the 1590s, in the punishing *fin de siècle* of the Tudor century. This, supposedly, was the Golden Age of Queen Elizabeth I.

No one living in London in the 1590s could for a moment have doubted that the city all around them was changing. The social fabric was under strain; by temperament and long practice conservative and reactionary in matters of governance, London's elite felt themselves to be at the dangerous edge of things. And rightly so: their city faced challenges that would test even a modern state with infinitely more resources. Between 1594 and 1597 there were four consecutive failed summer harvests; rising food prices, hunger and suspicions of grain-hoarding for profit were real and present. Before this, in the years 1592 and 1593, plague had killed thousands of Londoners – something like 14 per cent of the city's population – and it returned in 1601 and 1603 to kill in even greater numbers. During these times, when London was 'hot' with the plague, the city was in quarantine; those able to abandoned it for safety.[1] Thomas Dekker wrote in *The Wonderfull Yeare* (1603) that Death 'marched even through Cheapside, and the capital streets of Troynovant'.[2] For Elizabethans, those long Paul's Cross sermons on London's sin, and the judgement of God it invited, were not hollow rhetoric: the city, many felt, was being scourged by providence.

And yet, for all this London's population continued to grow unchecked: on balance it was better to take one's chances in the city than to starve in the countryside. Between the haves and have-nots there were, needless to say, massive inequities. The have-nots were entering the city in great numbers, settling especially in the parishes outside the old walls; they were the outsiders, the strangers, the foreigners and the migrants, clinging on by their fingertips to some kind of existence. Even the securely established of London, the privileged citizenry of tradesmen, retailers and merchants with money and a voice in the affairs of the city, were feeling the sharp pinch of the times. In 1596 the city government wrote to the queen's Privy Council:

> The great dearth of victual which hath been continued now these three years, besides three years' plague before, which hath so impoverished the general estate of this whole city, that many persons, before known to be of good wealth, are greatly decayed and utterly disabled for all public service, being hardly able by their uttermost endeavours to maintain the charges of their private families in very mean sort: divers of them being enforced to relinquish their trades, and to dissolve their households, which public calamity is greatly increased by the decay of traffic in foreign countries.[3]

Dearth, plague, impoverishment, fragile European trade: merchants were suffering. This cry of anguish was a response to a request by the royal government for money. In other decades it might be read as exaggerated special pleading by a comfortable elite. But the 1590s was a decade unlike any other, and the pain, though shared out unequally across London society as a whole, was felt by every Londoner.

It seems remarkable that out of these conditions there came the kind of creativity that seems a world away from the grimness of late Elizabethan London. The plague years of the 1590s were a kind of enforced leave of absence for William Shakespeare. The theatres of Southwark were closed in 1593 a week after performances of Thomas Kyd's *The Spanish Tragedy* and Christopher Marlowe's *The Massacre at Paris*. When a few months later they reopened, Shakespeare returned to London to give his audiences *Love's Labour's Lost*, *A Midsummer Night's Dream* and *Romeo and Juliet* over the years that followed.[4]

Poverty was one of the greatest tests for London. The levels of impoverishment and deprivation in the city were profound, particularly in the large and overcrowded parishes outside the wall. Elizabethans inherited and deployed notions of the 'impotent' and idle poor that, mediated through the century of Charles Dickens, are still very much with us today. Some, poor through no fault of their own, deserved help and support, where others – those who chose to be idle – deserved only to be beaten into obedience and work. Elizabethans worried endlessly about 'masterless' men lurking outside the patriarchal hierarchy of family or trade, subverting the social order and cocking a snook at rank and degree. Henry Arthington, in his *Provision for the Poore* (1597), set out the criteria for deserving poverty in such a way as to suggest a checklist precision in being able to identify those who might be offered help. He held up the London stranger churches as examples for others to follow: 'for they are so careful to keep their country people, both from idleness, and begging, that such as can work, neither want work, nor yet wages, and so soon as any fall in decay, their state is imparted unto their company'.[5]

Using criteria like Arthington's, London's 'impotent poor' were helped by parishes and hospitals. More problematic for the city and its leaders were marauding bands of criminal vagabonds and apprentices who gathered in and around London. This at least was how they were characterized by the city elite and the queen's government: 'multitudes of a popular sort of base [low] condition, whereof some are prentices and servants to artificers [craftsmen] . . . and some others wandering idle persons of condition of rogues and vagabonds, and some colouring [disguising] their wandering by the name of soldiers returned from the wars'.[6] Orders were given in 1595 and again in 1598 that such men, who evaded ordinary justice, should be summarily executed upon the gallows. Demobilized soldiers from the wars in the Low Countries and in France, especially those who feigned injury in order to beg, were a familiar sight in and around London.[7] The plan concocted by the character of Brainworm in Ben Jonson's *Every Man In His Humour* (1616) would have struck a chord with the playhouse audiences. Disguised as a soldier, Brainworm goes off to the insalubrious Moorfields, just outside the city wall, to lie 'in *ambuscado*' for his master and beg for charity. He plays his part well: 'I am a poor gentleman,' he says, 'a soldier, one that (in the better state of my fortunes) scorned so mean a refuge, but now it is the humour of necessity, to have it so' (II. iv. 44–7).

Polite society feared those outside its boundaries as subversive of hierarchy and order. In 1598, Parliament's Vagabonds Act gave local officials the powers to apprehend all kinds of wandering minstrels, actors, jugglers, tinkers, pedlars, chapmen, 'Egyptians' (Romany gypsies), 'rogues, vagabonds, and sturdy beggars'. The emphasis was on punishment in houses of correction or even banishment. But for most vagabonds, all the law prescribed was a sound whipping. The test of innocence was a willingness to work, the guilty 'being persons able in body, using loitering, and refusing to work for such reasonable wages'. In dealing with such vagabonds and idlers, the parish had an important part to play, administering the whipping, completing the formal paperwork that followed it, and then sending the offender on to his or her home parish.[8]

Youthful disorder also stalked the streets of London. Every so often disaffected apprentices or apprentice drop-outs congregated to cause trouble. There were frequent rumblings of threat and intimidation; riots took the form of organized gatherings advertised in advance. The victims of this kind of hostility were those on the outer edges of the city and its society, particularly the strangers; here was the still familiar pattern of the impoverished resenting the dispossessed. Anonymous libels threatening violence were taken so seriously that in 1593 the queen's Privy Council authorized the use of torture in discovering their authors.[9] In the play of *Sir Thomas More* (1600), Shakespeare and other dramatists were not afraid to challenge Londoners 'in the ruff' of this kind of anti-immigrant prejudice (II. iii. 85).·

The big issues and the statistics suggest a city on the edge of collapse, near social breakdown. At times the whole hierarchy was felt by the city elite to be in danger, with the instruments of law and order likely to be overwhelmed. The stability of London's society seemed so often to hang precariously. But that collapse never came.

The secret of London's robustness lay in part in the life of its parishes, that close patchwork of urban villages which made up the city. They, too, felt the weight of the times, raising money to pay for troops on service in France, the Low Countries and Ireland, and carrying the expense of looking after maimed soldiers as well as their own poor. The calls for money were especially insistent and regular: purses, as well as some old social bonds, were under strain. It was lucky that the prosperous and well-to-do kept up the long-established practices of charity.

Yet for all of the stresses and strains, parish communities were tenacious. Elizabethan parishioners kept their city going, feeling their way through a decade of crisis, surviving against the odds, as people so often do. We know about these Londoners mostly from written accounts, but sometimes (if we are very lucky) also from pictures – revealing men and women, masters, mistresses and servants, the well-to-do and those in straitened circumstances, the young and the old, strangers and natives.

The church of St Bartholomew the Less, or St Bartholomew near the Exchange as it came to be known, was a street away from Sir Thomas Gresham's grand bourse. It was a parish packed full of all kinds of people, where in the early 1580s tax officials recorded a fair mix of prosperous Londoners (a city alderman, a number of well-to-do merchants, a wealthy widow), a rump of comfortably off tradesmen, and a handful of settled and busy strangers. Left off the record, however, were the parish poor.[10]

The church itself was an early medieval foundation rebuilt in the fifteenth century, with a chapel added at the beginning of the reign of Henry VIII by a lord mayor, Sir Giles Capel, to house his tomb. St Bartholomew's was a typical city church – neat and well cared for, and packed with brasses and memorials that spoke to that familiar sense of long continuity over centuries, the rich and successful of London's citizenry marking out their plots for eternity.

Some families had been in the parish for a very long time. James Wilford, sheriff in 1499, gave money in his will for a sermon to be preached on Good Friday for ever, and so every year the parishioners gathered between six and nine o'clock in the morning to hear the preacher talk about Christ's passion, with the reward (other, of course, than spiritual nourishment) of a grand parish lunch. The church was full of Wilford family graves, and as late as 1598 the original Wilford bequest was still providing money to feed and clothe the worthy poor of the parish, thanks to the efficiency of the Merchant Taylors' Company. Stripped of any flavour of Catholic idolatry (as Elizabethans would have called it), Wilford charity had been pared down to essentials to suit the new scrubbed and scoured post-Reformation world of bare walls, simple communion tables and plain glass.

A parish like St Bartholomew's gave its parishioners a degree of security in unsettling and uncertain times; it was a community and a neighbourhood with a broadly settled hierarchy. Its people and families were well known and acknowledged. They belonged: the church and parish fixed them. St Bartholomew's jostled for its own identity in a great city, preserving its own space, something reaffirmed each year when the children of the parish were walked around its boundaries. This, once again, was an excuse for a good meal: after the parish circuit the parishioners went off together for breakfast, choosing in 1600 the Ship tavern as their venue.

Each year, too, the wardens and other officials of the church took an inventory of its possessions, a necessary stocktaking of communion cups and a communion cloth, a cushion of green velvet and two surplices for the parson, a parish Bible, two Books of Common Prayer, the register of births, marriages and deaths, the account and vestry minute books, a book of homilies and the big volumes of Erasmus of Rotterdam's *Paraphrases* on the New Testament (which, given that the last edition was printed in 1549, were probably looking rather worn by the 1590s), as well as a cupboard full of buckets, ladders, hooks and baskets. This was part of the orderly conduct of the parish and there was some sense of common ownership here: the church as a place of community, busy attending to its parishioners in life and death, the steady rhythm of christenings, marriages, burials and bells – bells for funerals, bells for the queen's birthday every 7 September, her accession to the throne on 17 November and the anniversary of her coronation each 15 January. The noise of the bells ringing out from the square tower of St Bartholomew the Less competed for attention with hundreds just like them across London.

Every day there were jobs to keep the parish officers busy. There was always maintenance to be done: mending the pews, fixing locks, repairing the bells, cleaning windows, restocking candles and attending to the church's hourglass. Holly and ivy were brought into the church each year for Christmas. For some of the jobs the churchwardens employed local plasterers, painters, joiners and smiths, but much of the day-to-day work was done by the humblest of the parish's officers, the scavenger and the raker, whose tasks included cleaning the church, digging graves and carrying dead dogs and cats and rubbish out of the churchyard.

Read John Stow's description of St Bartholomew's and its parish in the later 1590s and one might imagine that everyone and everything gleamed with the lustre of urban prosperity. Bartholomew Lane, at the south-east corner of which stood the church, was described as having 'divers fair-built houses on both sides'; here we might think that some of the glamour of the Royal Exchange and Austin Friars had long rubbed off on the parish.[11] Stow was silent, however, on the parish's network of small lanes, like Legg Alley, Potts Alley and Copthall Alley, and these were where the poorer parishioners lived, away from the grand thoroughfares. It was in these corners of the parish that plague, when it came, was felt the hardest. And the plague most certainly was felt on the streets and in the houses of St Bartholomew the Less: in 1603 it took away ninety-one parishioners.[12]

Wander along the streets bounded by Throgmorton Street and Broad Street in the middle 1590s and we find at work the busy parishioners of St Bartholomew's. Some were humble but keen to do their bit, like the three women who cared for an illegitimate baby girl whose welfare was parish business – Goodwife Williamson, Goodwife Bramley and Goodwife Preston. For punishment, the little girl's mother, Katheryne Wrench, was put in the parish stocks and sent to Bridewell

Hospital for correction at parish expense: she, for one, felt the shame of breaking all the moral norms.[13] There was little leeway in London society to reject the social conventions of the day: men and women – perhaps especially women – had to take the consequences of their actions. There is little doubt that the matrons of St Bartholomew's would have spent much of their time gossiping about local goings on and remonstrating with wayward neighbours. Few private affairs were left unexamined by the parish 'goodwives' of high morality. In the vestry records, there was no more neighbourly appreciation of the local standing of poorer parishioners than the prefixes 'Goodwife' (or 'Goody') and 'Goodman' – forms of polite and respectful address used for otherwise modest and very ordinary Londoners.

The parish tried to support its own. Out of the parish chest, kept topped up by regular assessed contributions from the wealthiest parishioners (as well as their gifts and posthumous bequests), came support for the deserving elderly. The poor received food, clothes and, in the especially harsh winters at the turn of the seventeenth century, an allowance of coal to heat their rooms. Parishioners were also keen to help one of their young men at Cambridge University. He was John Preston, the son of Goodwife Preston, and after studying at St Paul's School, he went off to Peterhouse at Easter 1594 as a sizar, the poorest class of scholar. The parson of St Bartholomew's, Dr Dix, had taken John under his wing, recommending to the vestry meeting that a sum of money would help him to take his bachelor's degree. A couple of years later, still in Cambridge and studying for his MA, John was given a further grant, recorded by the vestry as a gift from all the parishioners. This clever son of the parish, the boy of a highly respectable mother who looked after foundling children, went on to a Cambridge fellowship and a career as a minister, thanks in part to the generosity of people he had grown up with.[14] Likewise, young Thomas Becke, Goody Becke's son, was fortunate enough to be given sufficient money out of parish funds to pay for a new suit of clothes in order to set him up in service.[15]

And so the parish moved steadily through that punishing last Elizabethan decade, diligently recording the decisions made by the local worthies who held the keys to the parish chest. They looked after lost children and sick beggars found in the precincts of the Royal

Exchange. They dealt, too, with the wandering idle of the city streets just as the law prescribed. In May 1598, when a meeting of the parish vestry agreed unanimously to pave the street around the church, they also consented to 'a new post to be set up for the punishing of rogues at the church wall', a response to Parliament's Vagabonds Act. Whoever did the whipping was to receive a fee of sixpence; flogging was, after all, hard work.[16] Thanks to the book of Parliament's most recent statutes bought by the parish for two shillings and sixpence, no one would have missed the precise wording of the law: the offender was to be 'stripped naked from the middle upwards, and shall be openly whipped until his or her body be bloody'.[17] One example is that of Elizabeth Justice, who was punished outside the church in 1600 before being moved off to the parish of her birth.[18] Though showing Christian charity to those unfortunates who could not help themselves, the goodmen and goodwives and worshipful of St Bartholomew's are unlikely to have had very much sympathy for Elizabeth: in a city marauded by vagrants, they would have said, the idle got what they deserved.

Thomas Dauncer was an assiduous attender of parish vestry meetings. He was a substantial man, a citizen and a liveryman, a proud freeman of the Girdlers' Company. He was also a God-fearing man, 'a sinful wretch and a mortal creature of the creation of Almighty God, my saviour and redeemer', as he put it in his last will and testament. He died, probably of plague, in the winter of 1592, and was put into his grave in St Bartholomew the Less five days before Christmas. If his testament was followed to the letter – and there is little doubt that his wife Anne did everything that he expected of her – then his corpse was attended to its grave by sixty poor men dressed in specially made gowns of 'comely cloth' priced at five shillings and sixpence a yard. Even faced with eternity, Dauncer maintained his eye for detail to the end.[19]

We can only guess who else was standing at Thomas's graveside on that cold Wednesday: Anne, their sons Peter, John and Thomas, their daughter Elizabeth. Thanks to Dauncer's brothers and sisters and their wives and husbands, he had a whole squadron of nephews and nieces, as well as Anne Dauncer's side of her family: in neat and tidy St Bartholomew's there might have been a great gathering of Dauncers, Gostmans, Bradleys, Garnons and Malleryes, along with all the worthies of the Girdlers' Company and Thomas's friends and neighbours. But the plague had been devastating, with the rising number of deaths over the course of the year leading to a grim administrative process of recording mortality – matrons of the parish inspected the corpses of the dead and reports were then being sent on to the city government. The attendance at Thomas's funeral was probably very much thinner than it would have been at other times and in other circumstances.

To the officials in the Guildhall, Dauncer was a statistic, one of thousands of Londoners killed by the epidemic. To his family and former servants, he was the man who remembered, among others, his uncle John Bradley, then in Holland, and Robert Wattune, his gardener, as well as leaving money for London's poor and imprisoned.

And so near Christmas 1592, a few days before the theatres of Southwark reopened with a performance of Thomas Kyd's *The Spanish Tragedy* (the play was always popular with London's theatre-goers), Anne Dauncer began her life as a widow. Death was nothing new to her; she and Thomas had lost children in infancy and they were buried near to her husband in the chancel of the church. As a widow, she now had an identity of her own, making contributions of money to the vestry, and even in 1595 buying property – a house on Broad Street, near Austin Friars, with some land that once upon a time, probably before Anne was born, had belonged to the monastery of Our Lady of Grace near the Tower of London.

But Anne Dauncer knew that she was merely the custodian of her husband's fortune. Her responsibility was to look to the next generation, and she spoke in the last year of her life of her 'natural cares' for her children, her good friends and her kindred. John, their eldest son, would of course inherit the family's principal home in the parish, which was next door to the church; certainly he was living there by 1602. For Thomas, one of John's younger brothers, their mother provided the handsome sum of £300 to buy 'some annuity or pension'. Anne's daughter Elizabeth received money from the will, but also inherited what was perhaps her mother's most precious possession: a gold ring set with a white sapphire which had been bequeathed to her by one Mistress Greene (a relative or a friend?) precisely on the condition that it would one day pass to Elizabeth. Anne's was a house full (as so many mercantile houses were) of basins, ewers and standing cups and stocks of pillows, beds, bolsters and blankets; she was comfortable in her widowhood. The best of these things she would use to mark especially close relationships, like the gilt silver pot engraved 'T A and D' (for Thomas and Anne Dauncer) she gave to her sister, and a gold ring for her brother, as well as charitable obligations to the parish poor. The respectable matrons of St Bartholomew's were not forgotten: Goodwife Peter and Goodwife Isaacke received in Anne's will ten shillings apiece – a fortnight's wages for a carpenter and thus a small fortune in hard times.[20]

As much a part of parish life as the Dauncers was the family and household of Jacques Wittewronghele. They were different, of course: the Wittewrongheles were strangers and aliens. Jacques had been a successful notary in Ghent before bringing his Protestant family to the safety of London in about 1564. His was not the kind of émigré family that struggled on the margins of the city, out in Bishopsgate near the asylum of St Bethlehem's Hospital, where many poorer stranger families congregated. The Wittewrongheles were living in the parish of St Bartholomew the Less by the early 1580s. It was a good place in which to settle: Jacques had only a short walk to Austin Friars (he was a member of the Dutch congregation), and he was even closer to the Royal Exchange, always a magnet for notaries and their clients.

Jacques Wittewronghele did very well for himself in a new life in a foreign city. Ten years after leaving Ghent he was prosperous and comfortable: a man in his early forties, heavily built, with cropped auburn hair, a neatly trimmed beard and moustache and a keen eye, serious and purposeful.[21] The family acclimatized themselves to London. Jacques's eldest son Jacob was a little boy when they left Ghent, later going off to study in Oxford and then returning to London to run a successful brewing business; able neatly to bridge two identities, Jacob became a citizen of London as well as an elder at Austin Friars. And he made his mark on the parish, thanks to his naturalization as a subject of Queen Elizabeth I, doing his bit in 1591 and 1592 in the humble but necessary office of parish constable.[22] It was a small mark of belonging, fixing Jacob to the identifiable cluster of streets in the great tangle of the city, a place with a name whose boundary was walked each year by its parishioners.

We know what Jacob Wittewronghele looked like in these years of the 1590s. He was slimmer than his father had been at much the same age, his hair was darker and greyer, though he wore the same style of beard and moustache and his eyes possessed the same steady quality as Jacques's. Jacob's portrait is as individual as it is commonplace: the standard suit of expensive black, the left hand holding beautiful gloves, his right resting on a skull, the clock on the wall ticking away time. The portrait of Jacob's father twenty or more years earlier had conveyed the same message: 'By the hour, thus life flees', as Jacques's clock had been inscribed.[23]

Death in the 1590s was never far away. In a city always growing, plague could take friends and neighbours by the score. Life was uncertain; God's judgement was present, and order and hierarchy seemed at times too fragile. A successful man like Jacob Wittewronghele would have known all this. Like so many citizens, he understood that riches were weighed in the balance. He was not insulated from the great shifts and challenges of his time – all about him the city was changing.

CHAPTER SEVENTEEN
Change and Nostalgia

About ten minutes' walk from St Bartholomew the Less was Bishopsgate and the long road out to the village of Shoreditch and the countryside north of London. Just outside the city gate was the Dolphin Inn, popular with travellers, across the street from which was St Botolph's church and next to that the complex of the Bethlehem Hospital. Close by the city ditch was Petty France, where many of London's poor Dutch and French strangers settled themselves, and the point of reference when in 1603 Thomas Dekker wrote of 'a Dutchman . . . who (though he dwelt in Bedlam) was not mad'.[1] Near to the hospital lay the Moorfields.

Moorfields did not enjoy a happy reputation. It was fen, a wet and marshy expanse of 'waste and unprofitable ground' that over the centuries had been drained with modest success.[2] Various projects in the fifteenth century helped to turn the fields into a just about serviceable space for Londoners to walk and work; a fine copperplate engraving of Moorfields from about the time of the Muscovy Company's founding in 1555 shows citizens promenading along its pathways, men practising archery and women pegging out great cloths and clothes on tenterhooks.[3] But just as likely to be found in the fields were furtive criminals and spies, relishing so isolated a spot, and rogues and vagrant soldiers. It could be a dangerous and threatening place: one has the impression at times of Moorfields as the setting for the great storm in *King Lear*, with Poor Tom borrowed from Bedlam. And perhaps there was a kind of doom in the fen damp.

Falstaff, in *1 Henry IV* (1598), speaks of 'the melancholy of Moor-ditch', the muddy sewer that drained the fields (I. ii. 77–8), and John Taylor wrote twenty years later of his mind 'attired in moody, muddy, Moorditch melancholy'.[4]

Moorfields was a meeting place between wealthy and comfort-able citizens and the city's prolific underclass. In 1616 Robert Anton imagined the poor haunting the footpaths through the fields: 'walk Moorfields, / The shades of malcontents; whose causes [i.e. cause-ways] yields / Whole shoals of travellers'. Here, Anton continued, the poor might dream about the rich:

> Cast here and there with envious characters,
> On limping soldiers, and wild travellers,
> That sit a-sunning under some green tree,
> Wondering what riches are, or rich men be.[5]

This was the outer limit of London psychologically as well as geo-graphically; it was the place on the edge, the disconcerting shadow over the wall.

Ten years before Anton's verse, the city fathers had decided to do something about Moorfields. The trees under which Anton's maimed soldiers and masterless men dreamed of different lives were planted by citizens and gentlemen like John Sanderson, for most of his life a merchant out in the Levant, who put his own tree into the ground on Monday, 20 October 1606; close by, forming a triangle, were the trees of Sir Leonard Halliday and his son. Sanderson made a small sketch which shows a neat formal garden of walks, rails, trees and grass plots just outside out Bethlehem gate. 'Be this', he wrote, 'for remembrance thereof.' Halliday was lord mayor, and Sanderson, not surprisingly, wanted to mark the honour.[6]

So here was a wild and troubling place now subdued and reclaimed: ten acres measured out, made level by a plough and enclosed with gardens.[7] For a city so used to the sting of plague epidemics in the dec-ade between 1593 and 1603, the new Moorfields project, to cleanse the noxious fen, was a prophylactic against infection. But it presented, too, an opportunity for London's rich to enjoy themselves in a modest parcel of *faux* countryside, where they built, as one observer wrote rather sniffily, 'many fair summer houses, and as in other places of the suburbs, some of them like midsummer pageants, with towers, turrets and chimney tops, not so much for use or profit, as for show and pleasure'.[8] Just like the Royal Exchange, the new Moorfields was an opportunity for conspicuous display and (as for Ben Jonson's Mistress Littlewit in *Bartholomew Fair*) fashionable promenading on fine summer evenings (I. ii. 5–6).

At first this looks like privatization by the rich of the newly bucolic Moorfields, upon which London's worthies stamped their own identities, marking it forever: the trees, for example, bore the names of those who had planted them.[9] But the city fathers wanted to emphasize that Moorfields had been reclaimed for every decent Londoner. In 1607 Richard Johnson published *The Pleasant Walkes of Moore-fields*, dedicating his work to the right worshipful the knights and aldermen of London: 'Those sweet and delightful walks of Moorfields . . . as it seems a garden to this city, and a pleasurable place of sweet airs for citizens to walk in, now made most beautiful by your good worships.'[10] Johnson's earnest dialogue between a country gentleman and a citizen of London explains how it all came about:

> GENTLEMAN: . . . of all pleasures that contents me, these sweet walks of Moorfields are the chiefest, and the causes thereof deserve much commendations.
> CITIZEN: Those be the worthy aldermen and common council of London, who seeing the disorder used in these fields, have bestowed this cost, and as occasion requires intends further to beautify the same.
> GENTLEMAN: In so doing, they purchase fame after death, and much pleasure to posterity. But to what use are these fields reserved?
> CITIZEN: Only for citizens to walk in to take the air, and for merchants' maids to dry clothes in, which want necessary gardens at their dwellings.[11]

If there is pride here, there is also still a whiff of the Moorfields' old reputation. Welcome were the citizens and merchants' servants going about their proper business; unwelcome were those who disturbed the recreation of respectable people. Why, Johnson's country gentleman asks, are there stocks chained with iron to the wall? 'Only as punishment for those that lay any filthy thing within these fields,' the citizen replies, 'or make water in the same to the annoyance of those that walk therein, which evil savours in times past have much corrupted man's senses and are supposed to be a great nourishing of diseases.'[12]

On the face of it, this new London was merely the old London, improved and beautified, whose ancient foundation made sense of contemporary grandeur. 'Many things might be spoken of this famous city,' wrote the cartographer John Norden in 1593: 'It is most sweetly situate upon the Thames, served with all kind of necessaries most commodiously. The air healthful, it is populous, rich and beautiful; be it also faithful, loving and thankful.'[13] But who really, in 1593, would have believed that? With the strains of poverty and war, vagrancy and riot, fears of grain-hoarding, famine and plague, Norden's brief sketch of the city for that and the following years was simply a fantasy.

All this happy complacency speaks in fact of a disquiet and anxiety lurking just beneath the surface commentary. London was growing. Suburbs menaced the city: the very word, used commonly in a neutral way to describe the topography of other cities, was for London laden with negative meanings. Suburbs meant vice and disease. Poets and playwrights knew this. In *Catiline His Conspiracy* (1611), Ben Jonson wrote of the 'suburb-brothels' of ancient Rome, a reference full of meaning for Elizabethan Londoners (II. i. 275). The same is true of Shakespeare's *Measure for Measure* (1604), where there is a proclamation by the authorities of Vienna for the suburbs to be 'pluck'd down'. About to be put out of business, Mistress Overdone is horrified:

MISTRESS OVERDONE: But shall all our houses of resort in the suburbs be pull'd down?
POMPEY: To the ground, mistress.
MISTRESS OVERDONE: Why, here's a change indeed in the common-wealth! What shall become of me?
POMPEY: Come; fear you not; good counsellors lack no clients. Though you change your place, you need not change your trade . . .
(I. ii. 95–108)

Shakespeare's fictional Vienna was really the city he and everyone knew: 'houses of resort' were the kinds of brothels familiar throughout London, by reputation to be found especially in its outer reaches.

What troubled the rulers of Elizabethan London, apart from the sin, was the sense of their city spreading almost beyond control. John Stow, whose great *Survey of London* was first printed in 1598, wrote nostalgically of the earliest medieval city suburb of houses, gardens and trees, pastures, meadows and water mills – a graceful blending of town into country. How different that was to the suburbs 400 years later, when

> the beauty of this city on that part [outside Aldgate, near the Tower of London], is so encroached upon, by building of filthy cottages, that . . . in some places it scarce remaineth a sufficient highway for the meeting of carriages and droves of cattle, much less is there any fair, pleasant, or whole way for people to walk on foot.[14]

By the end of the sixteenth century, every possible space in and around the city was being used. Near the Tower, the city ditch, once so deep that some unwary riders and their horses had drowned in it, was filled in and let out, Stow observed, 'for garden plots, carpenters' yards, bowling alleys and divers houses'. Of the once wide ditch there was practically nothing left but a small channel 'and that very shallow'.[15]

The first instinct of both city and royal government was to prohibit any new building in London, threatening to fine or even imprison builders and workmen. But new building was only part of the problem. Existing buildings were being divided up and let out for rent. The very poor, living in tiny chambers, were 'heaped up together, and in a sort smothered with many families of children and servants in one house or small tenement'.[16] Always packed with people, especially during the law terms, London was at the best of times exposed to plague and sickness. At the same time it was – and for centuries had been – a city of temporary lodgings, especially for country gentlemen.[17] Poverty only heightened the danger. For decades those in authority wrestled with what they knew would be the consequences of growing numbers of people crammed into every square inch of London. Disease, poverty and crime stalked the elite. In 1596 the queen's Privy Council called the attention of local magistrates to the 'great number of dissolute, loose and insolent people harboured in such and the like noisome and disorderly houses, as namely poor cottages and habitations of beggars and people without trade, stables, inns, alehouses, taverns, . . . dicing houses, bowling alleys and brothel houses'.[18]

The reality for many thousands of Londoners was a tenement life of overcrowded squalor in a city where all available buildings – former monasteries, churches, grand townhouses – were subdivided up into tiny apartments and chambers over and over again. The story of one former religious house, the priory of the nuns of Holywell, not so far from Bishopsgate, was true of so many others like it across the city. Founded by a medieval bishop, rebuilt in the fifteenth century by one of Henry VII's chief advisers, it was surrendered to Henry VIII in 1539. By 1598 it had been gutted and put to new use in a city under strain: 'The church thereof being pulled down, many houses have been builded for the lodgings of noblemen, of strangers born, and other.'[19]

For the poor, exploitation by landlords, violence, theft and prostitution flourished. Privacy, too, was a rare thing in circumstances where servants lived with families, chambers and beds were shared, and moral lapses were the business of parishes and church courts. Local resentments prickled with anger. In Katherine Wheel Alley on Thames Street, close to the river, nine tenements once occupied by 'honest citizens' were converted after 1584 into forty-three tenements. Locals complained about overcrowding and the dangers of infection: 'The poor tenements . . . receive many inmates and other base and poor people of bad conditions to the great trouble and annoyance of the honest neighbours.' Reputable parishioners wanted 'the reformation of the said alley by plucking down such unnecessary buildings' – doubtless a phrase spoken and heard over and over again by 'honest' Londoners when they moaned about the nuisance of squalid tenements.[20] Citizens worried about disease, disorder and the amount of parish charity that was being consumed by the begging poor. The wealth of decent citizens, after all, would stretch only so far.

Making sense of all this change at the very end of the sixteenth century was John Stow, citizen and antiquary, whose *Survey* covered every nook and cranny of London, celebrating the city's antiquity, prosperity and beauty. Like all antiquaries he was an instinctive recorder and classifier, and he wanted the London of his book, all its wards and parishes, to be packaged up neatly and tidily. But the rapidity of change in the city had given places once so familiar to Stow new 'mongrel natures which frustrated a [i.e. his] categorical mind', in one historian's memorable phrase.[21] For Stow, the ordered past was in very great danger of being broken apart by an unpredictable and disconcerting present.

John Stow was a son of the city, born in 1524 or 1525 in the parish of St Michael Cornhill to a citizen father, Thomas, a tallow-chandler. The Royal Exchange was on John Stow's doorstep: he saw it begun and completed with his own eyes. He was a boy when Thomas Cromwell lived close by (Cromwell in fact took without asking or recompense some of Thomas Stow's garden to build himself a new grand house), and in his twenties and thirties John witnessed the reformation of London's churches, regretting the forcible cleansing by zealous Protestant iconoclasts of tombs and memorials that bore witness to the deep continuities of the past. His was not an outstanding career: he kept a low profile, quietly beavering away at books and manuscripts, reading and writing. The son of a decent and respectable family, though not quite a gentleman, he was unable to boast of a school or a university or his freedom of a livery company – something of an irony, perhaps, for one whose cause was to set down forever the achievements of mercantile London. But he was tireless in grasping every last detail of his subject, a mastery he attained by walking and observing. *A Survey of London* was the distillation of the hundreds of perambulations Stow made of his city over decades.

We might be tempted today to read Stow's *Survey* as a sort of hybrid of Baedeker's guides and Pevsner's architectural handbooks, with the volumes of the Royal Commission on Historical Monuments thrown in for good measure, and missing only the photographs. We could also add to these venerable institutions Alfred Wainwright's twentieth-century guides to the English Lake District, because like them the *Survey* seems to look to every contour and detail, missing nothing. Both Stow's and Wainwright's projects were long labours of love, even of obsession. Wainwright and Stow shared a devotion to landscape – the formet for fells and mountains, the latter for a city (though Stow, too, loved the countryside), as well as a deep and unapologetic conservatism. In Stow it was the conservatism of age as much as of temperament. In 1598, when his great book was first printed, John Stow was in his middle seventies; it was a remarkable run of years given that most Londoners were lucky to reach forty, and in a society that set great store by ancient memory it made him a formidable authority.

It is easy to read Stow's *Survey* as a comprehensive inventory of what was there in his city, a kind of antiquary's catalogue. That is how it looks from the Contents page, moving from London's origins and history to its sources of water, its ditch and walls, bridges, gates and so on, before embarking on a study of the city wards (really the main body of the *Survey*) and the names of the lord mayors, aldermen and sheriffs. The book considers, too, old games and pastimes, evoking a comfortable sense of a lost merry England; Stow was nothing if not nostalgic for that which had once been.[22] It is so obviously the work of an antiquary: a book written by someone who knows his history and is reluctant to leave out any fact, as well as a man who has used up a huge amount of shoe leather in walking the streets, noting and recording houses and halls, crosses and conduits, and inspecting every crevice of London's churches in search of monuments and inscriptions. Stow's *Survey* is a masterpiece of first-hand observation, fact and detail.

But actually Stow's *Survey* is more than this. It is an effort to mark change and to record loss. The place we know as Stow's London was located somewhere in a past of his own making, and it was being eroded away before his eyes. And it was not just the built city that was changing. Londoners of Stow's present were not quite up to the mark of their predecessors. For Stow, old social bonds of charity and generosity were loosening. Behind Stow's celebration of 'Troynovant' ('New Troy'), with its fair merchants' houses, fine churches and great livery company halls, was the sense of new and disconcerting forces at work. The most corrosive of these was private profit.

Stow wanted to record in 1598 the London he had known as a boy and a younger man, the city fast disappearing. He read in the memorial inscriptions of London's churches old traditions of city piety. Now the city was choked with people, Stow clung to the security of the old benefactors who had built London and made it great.[23] He saw what he wanted to see, and he was frank in ignoring what did not interest him. 'In Addle Street or Lane [close to Silver Street, where Shakespeare lodged] I find no monuments' – and that was that.[24]

Stow knew where the new Londoners were living. He had seen in the course of his life open spaces covered over with houses and tenements, and suburban filth and congestion ruin a city once all the more magnificent because of its surrounding countryside. He was disturbed by the enclosing of common land 'all which ought to lie open and free for all men'.[25] Nowhere, he felt, was immune from change. The country farm, near the Tower of London, from which as a boy he had collected fresh warm milk, was a memory. It was a vision almost of the Golden Country, an idealized lost world of imagination, to which Stow was able to add memories of old families and characters he had known.[26]

Yet this was more than simply a private nostalgia. At stake, indeed, was the very identity of the city. This Stow understood in his own peculiar way, both compressing and telescoping centuries of the city's history. In many ways Stow was more at home with his records of twelfth-century London (especially the work of the chronicler William Fitzstephen) than he was in the city of the late sixteenth. London's distant and recent pasts seemed to coexist for Stow; it was the present and the future that disturbed the fragile equilibrium of history, place and people. This was what he wanted to record in his *Survey*. Completing it was to Stow as necessary a task as it must have been for him a dislocating one. His book was in some ways a eulogy for a better London – and better Londoners – dead and gone.

And yet even this new London stood out impressively. No other English town or city came close to it, and by the end of the sixteenth century it ranked in European terms. Stow concluded his *Survey* with an 'Apology' – a defence – of London against the charge that it was too big and powerful for England's well-being. Stow being Stow, he offered to his readers a long and elaborate essay on the origins of towns and cities and their benefits to humanity as instruments of civilization, commerce and charity. True, some complained that London possessed too much money and power; true also that other English towns, especially the trading ports, complained that London had ruined their livelihoods – and Stow admitted that probably they were right. But it was no wonder, in Stow's view, that so many retailers and tradesmen left their home towns for London. The queen's court, so often positioned near to the city, was greater than ever. The Thames and its ships helped to make London 'the nurse' of the navy. The southern counties of England flourished because of the city. It was a reserve of money and taxation for the royal government, as well as an engine of charity for the poor and support for the universities. 'It only is stored with rich merchants,' Stow wrote, 'which sort only is tolerable: for beggarly merchants do bite too near, and will do more harm than good to the realm.'[27] London's self-evident success was in the end an easy justification for the disproportionality of its size and power.

For a Londoner who felt all the discomforts of a changing city, it was a bravura defence by Stow of London's uniqueness: all the regrets and the nostalgia were for the moment forgotten.

To compare John Stow and Richard Hakluyt in 1598 is to put side by side two Londoners of different generations with strikingly similar talents, but very different obsessions. One was an old man for whom London meant everything. The other, thirty years younger, was a church minister whose vocation was to serve God by chronicling English navigations across the globe. Both Stow and Hakluyt were the sons of London citizens, but where Stow was a self-taught antiquary who moved in fairly humble circles, Hakluyt was a university-trained scholar who had the knack of securing high patronage. He was able to impress the great men and women of Elizabeth I's court, dedicating the first edition of his masterly *Principal navigations* (1589) to Sir Francis Walsingham and its hugely expanded successor (1598–1600) to Lord Howard of Effingham, Lord High Admiral of England, and Sir Robert Cecil, Elizabeth's influential secretary and the son and protégé of Lord Burghley.

The three volumes of *Principal navigations* Hakluyt produced between 1598 and 1600 exceeded in ambition even Stow's *Survey*. The work was colossal: 1.76 million words, ranking in scale with the English Bible and John Foxe's *Acts and monuments*, the famous 'Book of Martyrs'. It is perhaps the largest repository we have of Elizabethan prose. Each of the volumes took a portion of the globe: the first, the north and north-east, the second, the south and south-east, the third America. Hakluyt had spent years gathering together the sources from navigators, mariners, merchants and diplomats. His skill was to let their voices be heard, carefully cueing them in for the reader, but then stepping unobtrusively into the background. He was not shy about the hard work he had undertaken, or about what he had achieved. He saw it as a task of national importance, preserving 'certain memorable exploits of late years by our English nation achieved, from the greedy and devouring jaws of oblivion'.[28]

Hakluyt knew that he had to dig deeply into the past to look at very old sources, sources which helped to explain the present. Like Stow, Hakluyt was able to compress the centuries into a single reflex, moving with surprising speed from a voyage back in the mists of ancient British history to an expedition of one of the great Elizabethan navigators – Drake, say, or Frobisher. His book is a celebration of achievement, something plain enough from the title page: *The principal navigations, voiages, traffiques and discoveries of the English Nation, made by Sea or over-land, to the remote and farthest distant quarters of the Earth, at any time within the compasse of these 1500. yeeres.* He had used the same title in 1589: a decade later nothing had changed, other than that Hakluyt had gathered so much more evidence with which to prove his point.

Lurking over England's shoulder were Spain and Portugal, and Hakluyt knew what those sea powers had achieved. 'True it is, that our success hath not been correspondent unto theirs,' he admitted. But in fact England had had to work harder than its rivals, showing grit and determination in sailing tough northern seas. What he called the 'golden success' of Spain and Portugal – the colonies and the conquests – would come. English mastery of a 'convenient' sea route to Russia was comparable in his mind to Portugal's discovery of the East Indies.[29]

At the beginning of this great project, Hakluyt introduced a roll call of heroes like Richard Chancellor, Sir Hugh Willoughby and Anthony Jenkinson.[30] Of these, only Jenkinson was then alive, having retired to a country manor near Northampton after a busy second career as a royal diplomat. It was thanks to Jenkinson, Hakluyt wrote, that English merchants had pushed even beyond 'the farthest eastern and southeastern bounds of that huge empire' to the unknown and dangerous Caspian Sea.[31] In *Principal navigations* Hakluyt completed the script of a century, one that had been put together over decades by Hakluyt himself, as well as his cousin Richard of the Middle Temple, Richard Eden, John Dee, Anthony Jenkinson, Sir Humphrey Gilbert and Michael Lok. It was by now a familiar narrative: England, the plucky outsider, was quickly catching up with the once great powers. Global supremacy would come, the evidence was clear – it was only a matter of time.

For Hakluyt, it was all part of a greater endeavour blessed by God's providence, in which, as he had shown in his long and important 'Discourse on Western planting' (1584), the ambition was to plant colonies in America. Proceeding by fits and starts, thanks to men like Gilbert and Sir Walter Ralegh, at the turn of a new century this was at long last becoming realizable. A convinced Atlanticist from the beginning, Hakluyt's purpose in the third volume of the new *Principal navigations* was to understand all the efforts made so far in discovering America. He printed all the sources he could on what had been found so far on that continent: a fair portion of them had to do with Sebastian Cabot of the Muscovy Company and Martin Frobisher's heroic voyages in the Canadian Arctic, the various patents granted by Elizabeth I to explorers in their claims to the new continent, as well as to Ralegh's voyages to Virginia in the 1580s. Virginia, as we shall see, was of special interest to Hakluyt.

London had a central place in Hakluyt's big project. He believed that English global ambition had deep roots in history: 'But that no man should imagine that our foreign trades of merchandise have been comprised within some few years, or at least wise have not been of any long continuance.' For proof of this, he asked his readers to turn to a later page of the volume. There they read the Latin of the Roman historian Tacitus, and with it Hakluyt's English translation: ancient London, 'which though it were not honoured with the name and title of a Roman colony, yet was it most famous for multitude of merchants and concourse of people'.[32] John Stow used the same short passage in his *Survey* to make the identical point: London was historically unrivalled in England as a city of merchants.[33]

The great volumes of Stow's *Survey* and Hakluyt's *Principal navigations* were on sale in London at the beginning of a new century. Both were serious works, full of meaning. They articulated something stirring in the ancient city – and that was change, a force that by instinct Elizabethans found disturbing and uncomfortable, but one that they somehow managed to embrace. London was not quite what it had once been. But in the transformation there were fresh possibilities – the hopes of a future there to be discovered, new ventures, new commerce and new worlds.

CHAPTER EIGHTEEN

To the East Indies

When John Sanderson planted his tree in Moorfields in 1606, he was more or less retired from trade. He was a native Londoner; his father's house, where he had been born, was in the shadow of St Paul's Cathedral, and he had attended St Paul's School in the churchyard. His experience there was not a happy one: he wrote of his 'unaptness' for study and of beatings so severe that they left him scarred for life. Work out in the far eastern Mediterranean was a kind of freedom for Sanderson. It brought standing and responsibility. On his first posting to Constantinople in 1584, when he was twenty-four, the queen's ambassador there had made him steward of his household. Over the following decades Sanderson went on to explore the East, learning languages, travelling to Egypt (where he saw the Sphinx) and touring the villages and towns of the Holy Land. In his time there, he journeyed overland through Asia Minor to Antioch and Aleppo, and visited Tripoli and Damascus.

Sanderson never married. Once as a young man there had been a servant girl, but any hope of marrying her had been squashed by her mistress. In 1606 that must have seemed a lifetime away: by then he was in his middle forties and settling down as well as a restless temperament would allow him. He was never an easy man to rub along with – his temper could be ferocious and he had a long memory for old scores and grievances. By middle age he knew that marriage was not for him. He remarked in a letter of 1608 that the rich widows of London were being quickly snapped up by new husbands: 'I look not after any,' he wrote, 'better liking a free single life than with more wealth to be subjected to a woman's humours.'[1] That independence he celebrated with the occasional visit to the theatre. Often he played his lute, which was something of a passion. And he never quite let go of the mercantile life: in London, where he lodged with his brother, he went to the Royal Exchange to hear the latest news and kept in touch by letter with old contacts in Constantinople.

No great sense of vocation had originally taken the young John Sanderson out to the Mediterranean. Bound as an apprentice in his late teens, he had been turned over by his master to a syndicate of London merchants trading with the Ottoman Empire without his knowledge or consent. Before the first journey out to Constantinople, he and the gentlemen passengers got 'merry drunk' in the cellars of the governor of the Isle of Wight, Sir George Carew.[2] On the voyage they came close to disaster when the ship ran aground; the master's mate had fallen asleep at his post. It was not the only shipwreck Sanderson experienced. Another was near Rosetta on the voyage between Alexandria and Cairo. For all the danger, he took pretty well to his new life; he was a robust traveller, even if his short temper tested the patience of his seniors. Sanderson was a man who could not leave an argument alone.

Once upon a time Venetian ships had sailed up the Thames carrying the spices and silks of the East. In the sixteenth century, London's merchants went instead to buy them in Antwerp. Some Tudor merchants went further, trading and sailing in the East, two of whom were Anthony Jenkinson and Michael Lok. In Aleppo, Jenkinson had seen Suleiman the Magnificent the best part of a decade before John Sanderson was born. But for English merchants, Mediterranean trade was a tentative business and highly risky. Pirates operating from the coast of North Africa captured ships and enslaved their crews. And negotiating with the great Islamic power of the East, the Ottoman Empire, was fraught with hostility. For Elizabethans, Turkish power was both fascinating and repellent. As one writer put it, 'Many men do wonder at the great power and puissance of the Turks', a people 'most rude and barbarous'.[3] The poet Thomas Nashe called the Ottoman Empire 'the adamantinest tyranny of mankind'.[4] Any merchants who wanted to open up direct trade with Turkey had somehow to persuade the Ottoman sultans that Anglo-Turkish trade was a worthwhile enterprise to be protected and nourished. It was not an easy pitch to make.

John Sanderson was sent out to Constantinople by tenacious and hard-working merchants who recognized that in order to succeed with the Ottomans they would have to work with them. The chartered company model was well established by the 1580s: as London's Muscovy Company had shown, pooling resources and expertise was vital to the success of long-distance trade, where huge amounts of capital were necessary to rig out ships, establish local bases and pay staff. There were disasters, endemic problems of corruption (the Muscovy Company in the 1570s and 1580s was plagued by its agents and factors in Russia running their own private businesses), and foreign competition. In the eastern Mediterranean, French and especially Venetian merchants ran long-established and formidably efficient trading operations. They were naturally hostile towards a new syndicate of English merchants trying to muscle in on the eastern spice business.

The visionaries of this new Levant trade were two London merchants called Edward Osborne and Richard Staper. They were rich and successful, each with a large portfolio of commercial interests: Osborne in Spain and Portugal; Staper in Spain also, as well as North Africa and Brazil, where, in the 1580s, he, other Londoners and aggressive privateers were trying to break into the trade of the once-powerful Portuguese empire. Osborne and Staper had their eyes on Constantinople, and sent one of their factors, William Harborne, there in the late 1570s.

Harborne was an inspired choice: fearless, robust, flamboyant, his self-confidence formidable. He was a merchant-diplomat, the queen's man whose job it was to look to English commercial interests. On the model of the ambassadors sent out to Moscow, he took his instructions from the government, but his salary from the merchants. It worked: in 1580 Sultan Murād III agreed to a licence for English merchants to trade in his empire. Harborne, like everyone else, knew that this kind of commercial breakthrough had to be recognized by gifts for the sultan and his officials, and the new syndicate of Levant merchants paid thousands of pounds for silver tableware, fine cloths of blue, scarlet, violet, green and black, greyhounds, spaniels, mastiffs and bloodhounds; obviously Murād was fond of dogs.⁵ News of the sumptuousness of these gifts spread throughout London, with Ben Jonson giving one of the characters in *Every Man In His Humour* (1616) the line: 'I have such a present for thee (our Turkey Company never sent the like to the Grand Signior!)' (I. ii. 69–70)

Harborne's style and flamboyance made him something of an Elizabethan celebrity. In 1599 Thomas Nashe wrote that, thanks to Harborne, 'not an infant of the curtailed skinclipping [i.e. circumcised] pagans but talk of London as frequently as of their Prophet's tomb at Mecca'. 'So from the prepotent [pre-eminently powerful] goddess of the earth, Eliza,' Nashe continued, 'was he sent to set free the English captives and open unto us the passage into the Red Sea and Euphrates.'⁶ In Constantinople, William Harborne was young John Sanderson's boss.

In 1581 the goddess Eliza as plain Queen Elizabeth I gave to a small group of London merchants a commercial monopoly on the Levant trade for a period of seven years.⁷ Hopes were high, and in 1582 Elizabeth lent to Osborne and three other merchants a little over £42,000 worth of fine silver bullion, to be paid back over five years.⁸ Success came quickly. In its first half-decade, the new company's business thrived. It boasted of employing nineteen ships and 782 mariners in making twenty-seven voyages, paying £11,359 in customs to the royal exchequer. The cargo of one of its ships in 1588 was valued at over £70,000.⁹ Either those figures were inflated or trade tailed off a little. Still, the Levant operation was a sizeable one. In the middle 1590s, 900 tons of English shipping and 216 mariners sailed between England and Alexandria, and a further 1,130 tons and 264 sailors navigated the ports and islands of the Aegean Sea. The *Jewel*, *Centurion*, *Royal Exchange*, *Great Susan* and *Margaret and Elizabeth* brought home from Syria commodities like raw silk, indigo (in high demand by London's dyers), medicines, mohair, cotton wool and yarn, spices and currants. Cloth and tin were exported out of England, and the company's ships moved between Constantinople, the island of Chios, Syria and Egypt. For all its successes, the company was always keen to remind its friends in Elizabeth's government of the enormous costs of the Mediterranean trade. In the 1590s cost of the hire of all the ships and their crews came to the huge sum of £16,910.¹⁰

Thanks to its commercial clout and the success of the embassy in Constantinople, this first Turkey Company (as it was commonly known) was recognized in a new charter of 1592. This opened up the monopoly to a few more London merchants and set a further limit of time before its renewal – the company could not afford to sit on its hands as the Muscovy Company had done in its ventures and navigations.[11]

One of the fifty-three members of this newly reshaped Levant Company was Ralph Fitch. Of all of them, as grand as they were (the company boasted a number of London aldermen), Fitch was the most extraordinary. In 1583 he and three others had set out to travel east, reaching as far as Fatehpur Sikri, the city of the Mughal emperor Akbar. They had travelled out from London to Aleppo, and then on to Basra and Hormuz. Taken prisoner by the Portuguese authorities in Hormuz, the party was sent to Goa, from where they escaped to Bijapur, going northwards to Agra. After that they divided. John Newberry, co-leader of the expedition, took the overland route back to Aleppo, while Fitch travelled down the Jamuna and Ganges rivers to Bengal, Burma and Malacca. Fitch and Newberry agreed to meet, two years hence, in the city of Pegu in Burma. Newberry, however, disappeared, and so Fitch made his own journey back to London. He arrived, in April 1591, eight years after leaving.[12]

Fitch's account of his fantastic journey was printed by Richard Hakluyt in 1599. Fitch made it sound as routine and unremarkable as taking a boat across to Antwerp:

> In the year of our Lord 1583, I Ralph Fitch of London, merchant, being desirous to see the countries of the East India, in the company of Master John Newberry merchant (which had been at Hormuz once before) . . . being chiefly set forth by the right worshipful Sir Edward Osborne knight, and Master Richard Staper, citizens and merchants of London, did ship myself in a ship of London called the *Tiger*, wherein we went for Tripoli in Syria . . .[13]

The familiar names of Osborne and Staper are important here: two of the masterminds behind the Turkey Company of 1581, both were naturally members of the newly chartered Levant Company. Indeed, they were largely responsible for the Levant commerce in the first place.[14] Fitch's travels opened up possibilities of which Osborne and Staper must have dreamed for a decade. The Levant charter of 1592 allowed the company to operate on land and at sea in the eastern Mediterranean 'and also by land through the countries of the said Grand Signior [the sultan] into and from the East India, lately discovered by John Newberry [and] Ralph Fitch'.[15] Here was the prospect of overland trade from the eastern Mediterranean all the way to India. There had been nothing like it before.

But there was another obvious route out to the east. For decades, the English cosmographers and navigators of the northern voyages to Cathay had mocked the arduous efforts of the Portuguese in sailing all the way around the southern tip of Africa to get to their territories in the East Indies. By the 1590s, however, such a journey around the Cape of Good Hope to the Indies looked like an opportunity waiting to be seized by English navigators; Drake, after all, had managed to sail all the way around the world, and privateering expeditions out to the Caribbean and the coasts of South America were common.

It was nevertheless a heavy slog. An early effort, in which John Sanderson himself invested, failed in 1590. A more successful attempt, at least in reaching the Indies, was that of James Lancaster four years later. Lancaster sailed to the island of Penang, off the west coast of the Malay Peninsula, circling back to England via the Caribbean. The keynotes of his expedition were scurvy, disease, desertion and capture: a miserable and punishing failure, it was emphatically not an heroic breakthrough to Asia. But Lancaster's efforts at least suggested that it might be viable for London merchantmen to sail all the way to the East Indies. By a coincidence – or was it for Elizabethans a sign of providence? – Lancaster's vessel was the *Edward Bonaventure*, sharing the very name of the ship that Richard Chancellor had taken to Russia forty years earlier.[16]

Yet by now old habits were hard to break, especially in a time of Anglo-Spanish war. Organized privateering was a long-standing instrument of aggression against Spain. It offered a great opportunity for making huge amounts of money (for captains, merchants, the queen and her courtiers alike) by smashing up Portuguese ports and plundering Spanish ships for gold and silver (Philip II had absorbed

Portugal into his empire in 1580). Certainly it was much less demanding of money and infrastructure than the building up of long-term
trade with the East Indies.[17] In the middle 1590s the kind of East
Indies syndicate that made such a success of the Levant business did
not exist in London or anywhere else in England – at least not yet.
But circumstances would soon prod London's merchants to get themselves organized very quickly indeed.

In trade in the sixteenth century there were always competitors.
French and Italian merchants were busy in the Mediterranean, and
for a decade at least Richard Hakluyt had worried about France's
colonial ambitions. Printing in 1599 a letter sent by Ralph Fitch from
Goa in 1583, Hakluyt allowed himself a marginal comment: 'The
Italians our great enemies for the trade in the East.'[18] But at the end
of the sixteenth century, Hakluyt and everyone in London knew that
in the Indies competition came from one nation only: the Dutch of the
United Provinces, England's ally in the war against Spain.

The Dutch were themselves reacting to difficult circumstances.
Spanish military action around the Scheldt river in 1585 meant the
end of the Antwerp spice market, encouraging Dutch merchants to
find a new way to trade – this time directly – with Asia. This meant
challenging Portuguese dominance of the Cape sea route to the East
Indies. A 'Company of Far Lands' based in Amsterdam sent four ships
out to the east in 1595; three returned in 1597 with a cargo of pepper, nutmeg and mace. Other merchants organized themselves for
the Asian trade, a second in Amsterdam and others in Zeeland and
Rotterdam. The Amsterdam companies merged to form an organization known as the 'Old Company'. Its expedition of 1598–9 was a
huge success: profit on investment in the voyage was estimated at
about 400 per cent.[19]

And so Dutch merchants began to embed themselves in East Indies
trade. By the late 1590s they had built for themselves a base in the
city of Bantam in western Java, a map view of which was printed
in Amsterdam in 1598. It was a modest enough beginning. They
shared a western suburb of the city with the Chinese, protecting their
interests with a stockade. But what the Amsterdam merchants had
done – and what London's merchants soon desperately wanted to

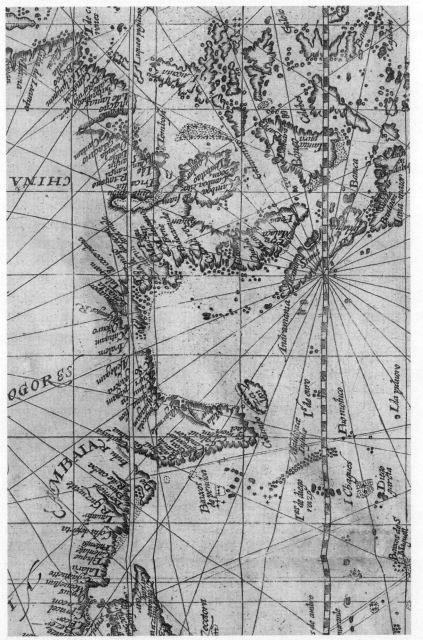

The East Indies, 1599.

do – was to position themselves in a nexus of Asian trading routes that extended out to China and Japan. East Asia was waiting to be opened up to north-western Europe, with pepper from the Malabar coast of India, Sumatra and Java, and cloves, nutmeg and mace from the Molucca Islands.[20]

It was Dutch success in the East Indies that shocked London's merchants into action. In 1599 a pamphlet was on sale in Paul's Churchyard, a translation of the latest Dutch voyage called *A true report of the gainefull, prosperous and speedy voiage to Java in the East Indies, performed by a fleete of eight ships of Amsterdam*. The final paragraph of the expedition's journal made clear the scale of what was involved, as well as the fantastic potential of trade. The ships had arrived home, 'having performed in the short space of one year, two months and nineteen days, almost as long a voyage as if we should have compassed the globe of the earth, and bringing home with us our full freight of rich and gainful merchandize'.[21] One of John Sanderson's contacts in London wrote to him from Constantinople: 'The Flemings have found traffic in the East Indies and have come home very rich . . . and [are] going again in good readiness.' He was pessimistic: 'It will be a hurt to your company.'[22]

The Dutch seemed to be everywhere. The Levant merchants had felt them nipping at their heels for some time. The Levant Company complained in 1595 that their Dutch competitors wanted for free what it had cost the company tens of thousands of pounds to build up from scratch: a hugely expensive and complex trade involving a Mediterranean fleet, teams of consuls and agents throughout the Ottoman Empire, and an embassy in Constantinople. And the Dutch were even seeking English government protection for their ships voyaging between Amsterdam and Turkey. If such a thing were allowed to happen, the company complained, the national interest and Elizabeth's treasury were bound to suffer.[23]

Now, in 1599, the situation looked worse. The London Levant trade relied on long and expensive caravans to carry its spices overland from the Euphrates and the Persian Gulf to the Mediterranean coast. A more straightforward (if still long and perilous) journey by sea from the East Indies to Holland threatened to cut off at the knees England's Mediterranean trade. This was what worried the Levant

Company's agent in Aleppo in November 1599: 'I assure you our Aleppo trade is such as is not worth the venture, except it amend this year, whereof there is no great likelihood.'[24] He was convinced that the city's spice trade would collapse. And he was not alone in this belief. Another of his and John Sanderson's colleagues gave a sombre analysis a month later:

> The Flemings are returned richly laden from the East Indies, and six great ships were to depart out of London for those places in September last. This trading to the Indies have clean overthrown our dealings to Aleppo, as by experience ere long we shall see; and by means thereof our company shall not be able to undergo the charges they are at.

If spices found their way into England by any route other than Aleppo, he continued, the company would not be able to cover half of the heavy charges it incurred in the Mediterranean.[25] This was global trade in the raw: the commercial breakthrough by the Dutch in the East Indies was a direct threat to what had been a valuable English trade in the Mediterranean.

Sanderson was not himself one of the doom-mongers, treating as a bad joke the report that the Dutch had returned from the Indies with a cargo of indigo merely as ballast for their ships.[26] The senior merchants of the Levant Company agreed. They wrote in March 1600 that Dutch success was not inevitable:

> We see not any reason why that [the Dutch voyages to the East Indies] should be any just discouragement . . . there are many impediments that may hinder their voyages of so long courses and great adventures, and may move the Dutch merchants rather to frequent a known and peaceable trade in Turkey than hazard the danger of seas and enemies of so long a circuit and infestious climates.[27]

That, at any rate, was the official line. But we might compare those sober words to Hendrik Cornelisz Vroom's scene of the homecoming of the Dutch expedition in 1599. Doubtless stylized, but nevertheless brimming with pride and self-confidence, the picture shows a festival of boats around the four great galleons returned to Europe from the East Indies. There were no such celebrations on the River Thames.

* * *

The official position of the Levant Company gave away not a hint of how many of London's Levant merchants were beginning to organize themselves into action. In the autumn of 1599 the city's mercantile elite was being recruited for a new venture into the East Indies. In September a full list was produced of all those merchants who were committed to the enterprise. For the record, each man wrote out his name in his own handwriting, adding the amount of money he would lay out 'to venture in the pretended [i.e. intended] voyage to the East Indias'. The first name in the register was that of the lord mayor, Sir Stephen Soame. One of the biggest investors was Leonard Halliday, who seven years later would plant a tree close to John Sanderson's in the new Moorfields. Halliday put £1,000 into the voyage. Most others invested between £100 and £500, and five men sums between £800 and £3,000. The total amount raised was £30,133.

Many of the investors met together two days later on Monday, 24 September. They set out what they wanted to do. For the honour of their native country and for the advancement of English trade, they proposed to make that year a voyage 'to the East Indies and other the islands and countries thereabouts'. A board of fifteen directors was elected, along with a treasurer to handle the sums invested.[28]

The following day they agreed a plan to petition the queen's council for support. Their reason for action, they said, was the successful Dutch voyage out to the Indies. They understood that a second Dutch expedition was being planned; in fact, several ships for that new voyage had been bought in England. 'Stirred up with no less affection to advance the trade of their native country than the Dutch merchants were to benefit their commonwealth', they proposed to make their own voyage out to the East Indies. What they wanted most was recognition as a single and united company, 'for that the trade of the Indias being so far remote from hence cannot be traded but in a joint and united stock'.[29] The venture was to be right from the beginning a robust pooling of resources and resolve.

There is a sense from the minutes of their meeting of an iron resolution to get on with the job. They found ships and crews and petitioned the Privy Council. They made progress. But because Elizabeth's government was negotiating a peace treaty with Spain, there was a temporary stall. Too politically and diplomatically sensitive to support for the moment, the East India project was put to one side for the time being. The merchants looked instead to a voyage the following year.[30]

Driving the ambitious new company were some of the most experienced merchants of the Mediterranean trade. Five of the fifteen directors had been Levant Company men for the best part of a decade. One was Richard Staper, who had spent twenty years petitioning queen and Privy Council to support the Turkey merchants; it was no surprise that Staper was one of the team of new East India directors whose job it was to lobby Elizabeth's advisers. Two other East India directors would join a newly chartered Levant Company in 1605 and 1610, showing that the weave of overlapping commercial interests in London was as dense as ever.[31] The Levant merchants drove the East India project, which needed their experience and above all their capital.

On Wednesday, 31 December 1600, a new international trading company was born and another was given a fresh charter: the Governor and Company of Merchants of London trading into the East Indies, and the Governor and Company of Merchants of Levant.[32] For the East India Company, preparations for a voyage to Asia began in earnest: with nearly £70,000 by now raised in capital, every detail was looked to in fitting out the ships and recruiting their crews. Those preparations drew on London's already extensive international connections: the cordage for rigging ships bound for the East Indies was supplied out of Russia by the Muscovy Company.[33]

Between 1601 and 1613 twelve voyages went out to the Indies: five ships in that first year, four out to Bantam in 1604, three to Bantam and the Red Sea in 1607. The company's chief interest was to bring home 'pepper, spices, gold and other merchandizes which are like to yield the most profitable return for the adventurers'.[34] But what developed was something more complex: a 'triangular trade' the three points of which were the Indies, England and mainland Europe. The company traded within the East Indies, brought goods home to London, and re-exported them to Europe. It recorded the export into Germany, the Netherlands, Spain, Italy and Turkey of nearly £220,000 worth of pepper, cloves, nutmeg and mace. That was in a fifteen-month period between 1613 and 1614.[35] This European business in spices, calico and indigo was the architecture for a sophisticated system of trade centred on London, where those commodities were exchanged for bullion and other export goods, further helping the company to invest in its port-to-port trade in the East Indies.³⁶ The company's charter permitted it for the first voyage to take out of the kingdom £30,000 of 'foreign coin of silver, either Spanish or other foreign silver' (in other words the spoils of English privateers), and quickly the company's export to Asia of coin and bullion became a prominent feature of its trade, as silver commanded a high price in Asia.³⁷ Between 1601 and 1624 the East India Company took out to the East bullion worth an astonishing £753,336.³⁸

All of this was a very long way from the days when London had been a satellite of Antwerp. The city was now standing on its own two feet. Of course there were new rivals, of which Amsterdam, soon to be a superpower in global finance and trade, was pre-eminent, and the Dutch founded their own truly formidable trading corporation, the United East India Company (Vereenigde Oost-Indische Compagnie, or VOC), in 1602. But London had at last plugged itself directly into a sophisticated system of global commerce; its merchants were dealing first-hand with producers and traders on the other side of the world. One estimate of the strength of the East India Company's fleet in 1615 put it at twenty-one ships with a combined tonnage of 10,516 tons; ten of those ships were new, two were being built.³⁹ Company trading stations were set up from the Red Sea to Japan: 'factories' in Bantam and in five cities in Moghul India, including Surat.⁴⁰ By 1621 Bantam was the head factory for the Molucca Islands, China, Japan, Borneo, Java and Sumatra, extending out to company trading posts in the Gulf of Bengal, Malabar and Goa. The Sumatra base supervised India, the Red Sea and factories in Persia and the Persian Gulf.⁴¹

Nevertheless it was a bumpy ride for the East India Company. The ups and downs of global trade over the decades meant that there were both good and testing times for the company. There was armed conflict between the company and the VOC in 1618, settled by an agreement that very obviously favoured the Dutch.⁴² Yet the scale of the East India's Company's achievement was immense. Even by the measure of Russia and the Muscovy Company's trade out of Persia, the company's operation represented an achievement of organization and communication never before encountered by London's merchants. Its administrative machine was impressive. Its printed

Lawes or Standing Orders set out in 1621 every aspect of the East India Company's corporate life, from its committees, courts, officers and accounts to its stores, shipwrights, joiners, wages, porters and clerks – the business of a global corporation in 335 rules and regulations.

In 1500 merchants from London had gone to the marts of Antwerp to sell their cloth and buy their luxury goods. Theirs was a prosperous but modest city on the edges of the great commercial powers. A century later, the mercantile elite of a growing, complex and at times febrile city looked for their riches to the furthest corners of the known world.

On Thursday, 29 January 1601, the East India directors gathered for one of their routine meetings. Joining them were the two most senior sea captains of the approaching voyage, James Lancaster and John Middleton. Present, too, was the old Levant hand Richard Staper.

It was in many ways an unremarkable meeting in which they discussed paying a bill for twenty-two shirts of chain mail and the price of timber. But that was not all, for they were joined by a special guest lecturer:

> Master Hakluyt, the historiographer of the voyages of the East Indies, being here before the committees [directors] and having read unto them out of his notes and books . . . was required to set down in writing a note of the principal places in the East Indies where trade is to be had.[43]

Hakluyt, not surprisingly, was involved at an early stage of the East India project; in the spring of 1600 he had written a paper on Spanish forts in the Indies. Now at their meeting Hakluyt gave the directors a synthesis of everything he knew about the East. He came before them with a huge pile of books and papers. One was Jan Huygen van Linschoten's *Discours of voyages into the East and West Indies* (1598), a hefty volume translated from Dutch at Hakluyt's request. It was full of close descriptions of places, peoples and customs. With maps of Madagascar, Sumatra and Java, and all sorts of engravings showing – amongst other things – elephants and the forests and fields of India, Chinese merchant ships and natives of Goa, van Linschoten's *Discours* was essential reading for the East India voyage: it gave an idea of who and what would be encountered. Another book was the best available history of China. And there was of course Hakluyt's own great work, *Principal navigations*, the third and final volume of which had been printed only a few months earlier. Of the papers, the most important were maps and documents that had come into his possession after being taken from a Portuguese East India vessel captured in 1592. Here privateering had its uses. For Hakluyt, and certainly for the East India Company of London, there was vital intelligence to be processed and understood.[44]

Within a fortnight of his meeting with the East India directors, Hakluyt drew up a full account of all the spices of the Indies and where they could be found; just as usefully, he helped to lobby the queen's Privy Council. He received for his work the handsome fee of £10, as well as thirty shillings for the delivery to the company of three maps. But Hakluyt was interested in so much more than the money. Always possessed of that drive to discover, he saw at once the new opportunities for trade in conditions unknown for two generations: the likelihood of peace with Spain, Europe's superpower, after half a century of hostility.[45]

How far they had come from Wynkyn de Worde's *Travels* of Sir John Mandeville, with its strange wondrous beasts, and from the early fantasy of Cathay. Here at last was the real East: in the place of the court of the Great Khan were factories in Java and India, and instead of cosmographical speculations on northern sea routes, a corporation was trading right across the globe. How altered the world looked from London in a century of fresh opportunities – and how different mercantile London looked too.

CHAPTER NINETEEN

Virginia Richly Valued

Standing on the city quays in the first years of a new century, a Londoner might have seen the *Dragon*, *Hector* or *Susan* being made ready for the long voyage around the Cape of Good Hope into the Indian Ocean, or the *Brave*, *Roebuck*, *Speedwell*, *Triumph* and *Cherubim* of the Muscovy Company's fleet coming up the Thames home from Archangel.[1] On the river wharves, cranes loaded and unloaded a fantastic range of goods and commodities. Sailors, workmen, merchants' apprentices, company factors and agents and customs officers moved between ships and warehouses, as passengers ferried by rowing boats and wherries climbed up quayside steps. The port was so busy that in the years of war with Spain Sir Robert Cecil had kept a watcher there to look for enemy spies and conspirators entering the city. So much was familiar: Southwark lay across the river, joined to London by the great carbuncle of its bridge that put Billingsgate in shadow. Yet the city was more crowded than ever; there must have been a great din of people, animals and bells.

Elizabethan London became Jacobean London. In 1603 Elizabeth I died, to be succeeded by King James VI of Scotland, the son of Mary Queen of Scots, now king of Great Britain. His accession was marked across London by churches like St Bartholomew near the Exchange, which spent six shillings and eight pence on ringing its bells 'the day the king was proclaimed'.[2] There was barely a slip in the rhythm of daily life. At St Bartholomew's there were still locks to be mended, pews to be repaired, the parish pump to see to, dead cats and dogs and other rubbish to be carried out of the churchyard. And in the first months of the new reign Londoners were stung by an especially sharp outbreak of plague. The poet and playwright Thomas Dekker called 1603 'The wonderful year' – a year full of change, of wonders and horrors.

London had for centuries reached out to the ports of France and the Netherlands, with whom it shared long histories. But now there were new horizons: Russia, Persia, north Africa, Brazil, the far eastern Mediterranean, India, China and Japan. With these new horizons came new challenges.

At Muscovy House on Seething Lane near the Tower of London the senior men of England's Russia trade met in May 1604 to untangle a tricky problem. Their chief agent in Moscow had warned them that the company's trading charter was about to be either cancelled or suspended until an ambassador was sent to renegotiate and confirm their privileges. They wrote urgently to Robert Cecil at court.[3]

For half a century the Muscovy Company had fought to maintain its exclusive commercial charter. It was always a hard fight. Agents and factors had filled their own pockets at the company's expense, just as merchants from other European countries had pressed ceaselessly to open up trade with Russia. Tsars and officials changed; some were friendly, others hostile. Elizabethans found Russian politics to be as brutal as it was mysterious. One former ambassador, Giles Fletcher, published in London in 1591 a scathing analysis of Russia and its rulers and people. So explosive was Fletcher's exposé of the tsar and his court that the Muscovy Company had gone to Lord Burghley to have the book suppressed. They were successful.[4] To upset the most powerful men in Moscow was to threaten the very existence of Anglo-Russian commerce; it was better to keep silent on the gothic violence and tyranny of the Kremlin than to lose valuable trade.

In 1604 King James's government acted with speed. At Greenwich Palace on 10 June (a month and a day after the Muscovy merchants' letter) the chosen ambassador, Sir Thomas Smythe, was presented by Robert Cecil himself to the king. James wanted to know all about Russia. When Smythe told him that he would be away for 'full fifteen months, by reason of the winter's cruelty', the king was surprised. 'It seems then that Sir Thomas goes from the sun,' he said; to which the Earl of Northampton quipped, with a courtier's talent for sycophancy, 'He must needs go from the sun, departing from his resplendent majesty.' At this James smiled and gave Smythe his hand to kiss.[5]

Sir Thomas Smythe was a merchant experienced in the Russian trade. This was his most important qualification for the embassy. His brief was to negotiate for the Muscovy Company 'all conditions of safety and profit' that he could, as well as to handle the tricky subject of Anglo-Turkish relations and the standing of the English embassy in Constantinople.[6] In Moscow he was suavely effective, suffering none of the anxieties over ambassadorial status that so often tormented thin-skinned courtiers or scholars. Given the labyrinthine politics of the Kremlin in 1604 and 1605, Sir Thomas had to have his wits about him. When he got there, he was, like Richard Chancellor and Anthony Jenkinson decades before him, feted and feasted. There were three qualifications for any effective English ambassador in Moscow. The first was a practical political intelligence, the second a vast reserve of patience in the face of diplomatic procrastination and maddening protocol. The third was the kind of stomach and head that could cope with great feasts and heavy drinking.

Half a lifetime before his Russian embassy, Thomas Smythe had had his portrait painted. He was then a young man of twenty or twenty-one. The artist was Cornelis Ketel, a Dutch émigré. Thomas's picture was one of a set of individual family portraits commissioned by his father, an elder Thomas who was the chief customs officer of the port of London. If Ketel got the senior 'Customer' Smythe right, he was the very model of the Elizabethan city man, all bulk, red beard and high colour, wearing the traditional uniform of a black merchant's cap and a heavily furred gown; he might have been John Isham's brother. In her portrait, Alice Smythe, young Thomas's mother, looks every inch the severe Tudor matron, with a gaze that could freeze the Thames. Where Thomas's sisters are miniatures of their mother, he and his brothers look very different from their father. Wearing a silver-grey slashed doublet and with short dark auburn hair, a pale complexion and reddened lips, Thomas Smythe seems more a poet than a merchant in the making.[7]

He became, however, every inch the man of business. Two decades later his name counted for everything – he was all substance and weight. No one in London was more able to exercise such huge influence with his grace and style. A feel and sense for the city, like money and connections, ran very easily in some families; it was a rule to which poor Michael Lok was the spectacular exception. The elder Thomas Smythe was an important man who knew London's trading world inside out, but even he was in the shadow of his father-in-law, the younger Thomas's maternal grandfather, Sir Andrew Judde. Judde had been lord mayor, a great power in the Skinners' Company and, like other fur traders, a founder member of the Muscovy Company. He was a man of great dignity – and very probably his daughter Alice's no-nonsense severity was a long-perfected family trait.

Judde's grandson might have followed in his mayoral footsteps had it not been for Robert Devereux, Earl of Essex, once the queen's favourite courtier. Disgraced and desperate, in 1601 Essex armed his followers and took to the streets of London in a farcical effort to force an audience with Elizabeth. Smythe was by then an alderman, one of the two sheriffs of London for that year and governor of the newly established East India Company. In search of support in the city, Essex and his men went to Smythe's house. When the coup collapsed, Sir Thomas did his best to disentangle himself from any association with the earl, strongly denying any contact beforehand, and telling his brother John that the only letter he had received from Essex was a recent one 'touching some matter of the East Indian company'.[8] But the damage was done. Sir Thomas Smythe was tainted by Essex's treason. Interrogated by the Privy Council, hours later he was dismissed as an alderman. He stood down from his other responsibilities as well, discreetly withdrawing from directors' meetings of the East India Company; his deputy took the chair, and a new governor was elected.[9]

For about two years he was out in the cold, but eventually the thaw came. One of Sir Thomas's formal duties as the king's ambassador to the tsar in 1604 was to maintain the royal dignity, and rarely were disgraced men allowed the honour of doing that. Half a decade later, Sir Thomas Smythe was seen to be a merchant grandee of extraordinary range. With a bulging portfolio of offices and responsibilities, he was the consummate mercantile bureaucrat. He was at least twice (before and after Essex) governor of the Muscovy Company. From the beginning one of the moving spirits of the East India venture, he was the company's governor for seventeen years. He was also governor of two later ventures, one to Bermuda, the other a further expedition in search of the Northwest Passage. He was a director of the Spanish Company and a charter member of the Levant Company of 1605. Few men were busier in the corporate power structures of early Jacobean London.

And then there was the New World. For eleven years Sir Thomas Smythe was the most senior official in a venture to colonize an as yet unexplored continent. This was the Virginia Company of London, whose corporate ambition was to settle America for God and English trade.

In the second and definitive edition of *The principal navigations* (1598–1600), Richard Hakluyt left the 'fourth part of the globe' to the final volume. This was America, the continent that had teased and tested cosmographers and navigators for a century following its discovery by Christopher Columbus.

Richard Hakluyt hated imprecision, and he tolerated the word America as at best convenient shorthand. In one moment of rhetorical excitement, he called the continent 'my Western Atlantis'. On balance, however, he preferred the functional 'New World'. Simply, America was new because Columbus had discovered it as recently as 1492, and 'world' reflected its size. The continent was huge and mysterious: 'to this day', Hakluyt wrote, it was 'not thoroughly discovered, neither within the inland nor on the coast'.[10]

Hakluyt knew that even he, with all his material, could not do justice to America. He recognized that the picture of it he presented in *Principal navigations* was a monotone lacking 'more lively and exquisite colours'.[11] The spectacular fold-out map that some purchasers of Hakluyt chose to buy separately and had stitched into the third volume – a map four times the size of the book itself – showed the land masses of Europe, South America, Africa and even South Asia in convincing detail. Yet so much of North America, on the map as well as in the text, was unknown, a blank waiting to be filled in. It was surely far from a coincidence that on the map the royal arms of

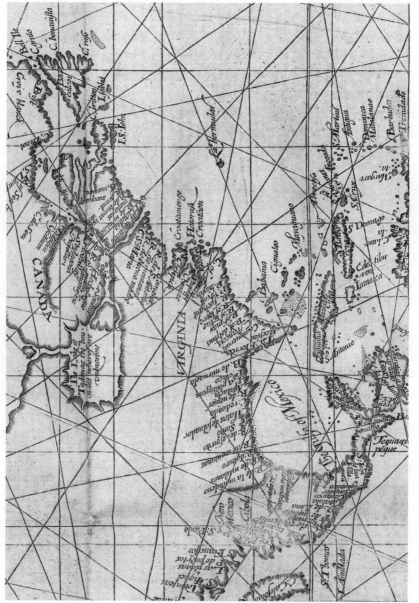

North America, Richard Hakluyt's 'fourth part of the globe'.

Queen Elizabeth hover over this terra incognita: surely soon enough America would be explored, mapped, colonized, farmed and mined, and the men, women and children who already lived there would have the honour of being civilized by the new settlers.

Hakluyt signed the letter of dedication to the third volume from London on Monday, 1 September 1600. His dedicatee, Sir Robert Cecil, was the latest of a number of powerful men that Hakluyt had courted since the 1580s. Pushing and pressing a colonizing agenda for twenty years, Hakluyt had dedicated his first book on America, *Divers voyages* (1582), to Philip Sidney and the single volume of *Principal navigations* (1589) to Sir Francis Walsingham. He and Michael Lok had helped Sir Humphrey Gilbert to put together his prospectus for settling the North American continent, and Hakluyt had done the same a few years later for Sir Walter Ralegh. His influential 'Discourse on Western planting' (1584), a briefing paper for Ralegh and his supporters, was completed during the course of the first successful English voyage out to the coast of present-day North Carolina. The two leaders of that expedition, Philip Amadas and Arthur Barlowe, had gone ashore in July 1584 'to take possession' of the American continent in the queen's name.[12] A month after their return home, Hakluyt presented Elizabeth herself with a special copy of his 'Discourse'.

There were all kinds of reasons to plant America with English settlers. One was missionary, converting 'infidels' to the true religion. Another was proprietary, adding to the size of the queen's dominions. Trade was also a powerful motive, as was the old idea (familiar in the books and papers about voyaging to no doubt chilly Cathay) of selling English woollen cloths in cold climates, where there was bound to be a healthy market. And there was the hope of further discovery and contact, trading beyond America with Japan and China. The elder Richard Hakluyt of the Middle Temple set out these interconnected objectives in 1585. Of course it was not going to be easy, and there would, he noted, be some difficult choices to make: 'To plant Christian religion without conquest, will be hard. Traffic easily followeth conquest: conquest is not easy. Traffic without conquest seemeth possible, and not uneasy.' Hamlet-like, he ended: 'What is to be done, is the question.'[13] There is no good reason to think that his younger cousin Richard thought any differently.

The first colonial efforts failed. High on rhetoric and ambition, Ralegh had secured in 1584 Queen Elizabeth's permission to settle a colony named in her honour, with the right to make a seal of his coat of arms with the legend (in Latin) of 'Walter Ralegh, Knight, Lord and Governor of Virginia'.[14] However, the realities of planting the new continent were stark. By 1587 there was a fledgling settlement of men, women and children on Roanoke Island. Two babies were born there; they were very probably the first European Americans. One was a girl, christened Virginia. But this tiny colony was lost: all of the settlers simply vanished, including little Virginia and her parents Ananias and Eleanor Dare. The English settlers of Roanoke were never seen again.[15]

And yet in spite of the horror of Roanoke and the failure of Ralegh's efforts, hope persisted: hope for a new continent rich in natural resources, hope for a flourishing Western trading satellite of England. There were fresh attempts after 1600 to explore and settle that portion of America which was so quickly fixed with the name Virginia. Ralegh's patent had expired in 1590, and so it was more than anything else a nod to Sir Walter's efforts that a voyage of 1602 sought his blessing. He gave it, writing of Virginia to Sir Robert Cecil like some colonial prophet: 'I shall yet live to see it an English nation'.[16]

Roanoke was not forgotten, for in 1602 the new explorers tried and failed to find the old colonists. But there was no room for sentiment or regret. Settling Virginia was too important an opportunity to let slip: a land of beauty and promise, it began to fire the Jacobean imagination much as Elizabethans had been possessed by the fantasy of the empire of Cathay. And, of course, Viriginia actually existed. Eating boiled fish and smoking strong tobacco with the local Virginians, the English explorers enjoyed an agreeable climate and saw all around them fantastic natural resources. They recognized very clearly what could be achieved with money, effort and God's will.

What strikes us today is the boldness of the pitch. The Elizabethan and Jacobean mind was brilliantly elastic. The writer and adventurer John Brereton, who published an influential prospectus on Virginia in late 1602, was undaunted by the huge challenges of distance and geography. Thinking a project achievable somehow made it so. There were no limits to ambition, which took on a reality all of its own.

And Brereton's ambition was considerable. By planting 'Christian people and religion' along the eastern American seaboard, he wanted to open up America to European trade. The North Atlantic would buzz with traffic. He saw in his mind's eye wines, fruits, spices, sugars, silks, gold and silver arriving in Virginia from Portugal and Spain, and English cloth and cattle crossing the ocean from the home country. Virginia would become America's entrepôt. Even more ambitiously, in the light of what even Elizabethans knew about the size of the continent, Brereton believed that Virginia would become a vital staging post for transcontinental trade between Europe, America and Asia. With that eternal hope of finding a navigable north-western sea route from America into the North Pacific and Indian oceans, Brereton predicted ships returning to England every four months, laden with 'the great riches of Cathay, China, and Japan, and the rest, which will be spices, drugs, musk, pearl, stones, gold, silver, silks, cloths of gold, and all manner of precious things'.[17]

Brereton's prospectus, in fact, was not far short of a plan for a system of English trade that circumnavigated the globe. It had all the optimism of the colonial patents of Gilbert and Ralegh and the charter of the East India Company, a year old when Brereton's pamphlet was put on sale in London by the leading printer of *Principal navigations*, George Bishop. Trade was the golden chain that tied kingdoms together in mutual friendship: the metaphor came from the pamphlet *Sir Thomas Smithes voiage and entertainment in Rushia* (1605).[18] Smythe and other East India Company grandees threw themselves at the Virginia project. East and West might be joined seamlessly together. That for London's merchants and investors was the hope of Virginia.

The Virginia Company of London came into existence on 10 April 1606 by virtue of King James's letters patent. It was a corporate hybrid, a kind of public–private partnership in which capital was raised by investment in a joint-stock enterprise (here it was very similar to the Muscovy or East India Companies), but where governance belonged to the king through a council responsible to him. The new company delicately balanced a number of interested parties. London grandees dominated, but merchants from Bristol and Plymouth wanted an equal say. To add to this complexity, the company and its royal council would supervise two separate plantations in Virginia. One part of the colony, to the north, was the West Country enterprise. The southern plantation was London's. Sir Thomas Smythe, Sir William Romney and John Eldred sat on the king's council. All three were East India Company men.

The poet Michael Drayton celebrated in 1606 the forthcoming enterprise. Having read accounts of Virginia in *Principal navigations* ('Industrious Hakluyt / Whose reading shall inflame / Men to seek fame'), he praised America as a place unique, a kind of Eden:

> And cheerefully at sea
> successe you still entise
> to get the pearle and gould,
> and ours to hould,
> *Virginia,*
> earths onely paradise.
>
> where nature hath in store
> fowle, venison and fishe,
> and the fruitfull'st soyle,
> without your toyle,
> three harvests more,
> all greater then your wish.[19]

Where poets made excellent propagandists, they could also be scathing satirists. Thanks to Hakluyt and probably John Brereton, Drayton's poetic imagination helped him to imagine Virginia's rich vines and tall cedars reaching up to kiss the sky. In their play *Eastward Hoe* (1605), George Chapman, Ben Jonson and John Marston instead poked fun mercilessly at the fantasy of Virginia. In the setting of the Blue Anchor near Billingsgate, Scapethrift asks the expert Captain Seagull all about America. 'But is there such treasure there, Captain, as I have heard?' 'I tell thee,' Seagull answers, taking his script straight from Sir Thomas More's *Utopia*, 'gold is more plentiful there than copper is with us.' Dripping pans, chamber-pots and prisoners' chains were all made of gold, while children collected rubies and diamonds from the seashore. The Virginian climate was excellent, and wild boar was as common as the tamest bacon in England, venison as plentiful as mutton.

But the humour also has to it a sharper edge. Captain Seagull makes an indirect but clear reference to Roanoke, even if he muddles his dates: 'A whole country of English is there, man, bred of those that were left there in '79.' And there is a swipe, too, at utopian dreams of the new freedoms of colonial society, with all the hopes of a life of rank and importance without the realities of low parish office and drudgery: 'And then you shall live freely there, without sergeants, or courtiers, or lawyers, or intelligencers [spies]. . . . You may be an alderman there, and never be scavenger; you may be a nobleman, and never be a slave.' Seagull hints at a community without law, order or moral self-restraint: 'Besides, there we shall have no more law than conscience, and not too much of either: serve God enough, eat and drink enough, and "enough is as good as a feast".'[20]

There is every reason to think that in 1605 Chapman, Jonson and Marston knew exactly what ordinary Londoners were saying about a new life in Virginia. Plenty of gentlemen sailed across the North Atlantic on the first voyage in 1606, but of the 295 settlers many were carpenters, blacksmiths, apothecaries, tailors, artisans, fishermen and labourers. These were the kinds of men who in the 1590s had had to work hard to scratch a living. Perhaps it was the desire for adventure that took them out to Virginia, or the hope of making their mark on a new continent. There is a high statistical probability that many had lost members of their close or extended family to plague in 1601 or 1603. And who, reading or hearing about pristine Virginia, would not have been glad to leave behind the filth, stink and disease of over-crowded London?

Of course it was less straightforward than that. The first Virginia colony was the furthest outpost of King James's new British kingdoms. To guard against Captain Seagull's vision of a society with no more law than conscience, it had the government of a president and council. Gentlemen and preachers were in authority.[21] The ministers with their bibles and prayer books gave the plantation a sense of godly mission. Almost certainly there were copies of Hakluyt's *Principal navigations* to edify and occupy the settlers.[22] Yet there were good reasons in 1606 and 1607 to imagine that Roanoke might happen all over again. The planters of 1606 relied for their survival on two supply voyages that arrived months apart in 1608. The quickest recorded sea journey from England to America was five weeks, the longest eighteen.[23] And the Virginian climate was far from easy and temperate. The winters of 1607 and 1608 were as brutal in America as they were in Europe. The Virginia adventurers in London shivered through cold so severe that it froze the Thames and turned the river into a playground, but also kept Londoners short of food, with depleted stores of fuel, and made it difficult for the city's trades and businesses to stay open. Thousands of miles away it was much worse: the company's planters had to cling on to survival.[24]

The Virginia Company of London pushed hard for money and support, and by the spring of 1609 it was orchestrating a major new effort to raise capital. This physical act of planting a continent was an 'adventure': here, once again, was the language of the Frobisher voyages and the joint-stock corporations. Certificates were printed, with blanks for names and for the amounts of money subscribed. These were processed by Sir Thomas Smythe himself as the company's treasurer. This subscription represented a permanent share in the colony that could be passed to heirs and successors. From 'time to time', so the certificate explained, there would be returns on Virginia's 'mines and minerals of gold, silver, and other metals or treasure, pearls, precious stones, or any kinds of wares or merchandizes, commodities or profits whatsoever'.[25] In London the whole venture looked promising; Sir Humphrey Weld, the lord mayor, was foursquare behind it. Thanks to Weld, at least five livery companies – including companies as distinguished and influential as the mercers, merchant taylors and clothworkers – took out institutional holdings in Virginia.[26]

In these early years of the colony, two motives for plantation jostled for pre-eminence and publicity. There was every belief that Virginia possessed wonderful raw materials that would in due course be brought home to England. Richard Hakluyt identified in particular mulberry trees, which could be used to feed silkworms, and sources for various dyes. The clue was in the title of his pamphlet of 1609, *Virginia richly valued*. Hakluyt found in the Virginia enterprise future commercial wealth – not a surprise for a man named in the company's 1606 charter and a Virginia shareholder.

But more than this, America was a virgin continent ripe for God's word. Richard Hakluyt had his adventurer's certificate in one hand

and the Bible in his other. Virginia, he suggested, was a test of Christian constancy and mission:

> . . . the painful [i.e. assiduous] preachers shall be reverenced and cherished, the valiant and forward soldier respected, the diligent rewarded, the coward emboldened, the weak and sick relieved, the mutinous suppressed, the reputations of the Christians among the savages preserved, our most holy faith exalted, all paganism and idolatry by little and little utterly extinguished.

Hakluyt had no great faith in the native Virginians; they were 'as unconstant as the weathercock, and most ready to take all occasions of advantages to do mischief'. Handling them gently was the best way forward. But if 'gentle polishing will not serve', then he thought it could be left to the trained English veterans of the Spanish wars 'to square and prepare them to our preachers' hands'.[27] God's work of converting the infidel was not for the faint of heart or purpose.

Everyone knew from John Stow and the other chroniclers of their ancient city that London itself had begun as a colony of busy merchants. Now, out of New Troy there grew a 'Nova Britannia', as the company called its American enterprise.[28] Future settlers of this New Britain were asked in 1609 to call on Sir Thomas Smythe at his London house on Philpot Lane. The invitation went out to potential planters across London, particularly men who could work with their hands. They were offered a portion of a single share of £12 and 10 shillings divided out between them. More compelling perhaps was the promise of a country life, with a house, garden and orchard and suits of clothes at the company's charge.[29] The company tried to recruit investors from across the whole of England. Towns and cities as well as individuals were given the pitch: 'it hath pleased God to encourage us to go on, in that great work and enterprise of planting colonies of our English nation'.[30] And this vast project all emanated from London: more precisely, from the mansion of a rich and influential merchant on the lane between the church of St Andrew Hubbard and Fenchurch Street, with future settlers and hopeful investors knocking on the gate and asking for Sir Thomas Smythe.

As well as unearthing the riches of a new continent, trading across the oceans and converting the infidel, the Virginia Company of

London really intended to plant a nation. In April 1609 many of the Virginia adventurers and future planters gathered in Whitechapel to hear a sermon by the preacher William Symonds. He took as his text three verses from the Book of Genesis (12:1–3):

> For the Lord had said unto Abraham, Get thee out of thy country, and from thy kindred, and from thy father's house, unto the land that I will show thee.
>
> And I will make of thee a great nation, and will bless thee, and make thy name great, and thou shalt be a blessing.
>
> I will bless them that bless thee, and curse them that curseth thee: and in thee shall all families of the earth be blessed.[31]

There was no more serious a project than this. Transcending trade and commerce, it was an exercise in global nation-building blessed by God, and a natural working out of a colonial project whose political, commercial, social and economic benefits had been sketched out by Richard Hakluyt in the 1580s. Only days after Symonds's sermon (and perhaps inspired by it), another Virginia propagandist explained how essential it was to

> seek after such adventures whereby the glory of God may be advanced, the territories of our kingdom enlarged, our people both preferred and employed abroad, our wants supplied at home, his majesty's customs wonderfully augmented, and the honour and renown of our nation spread and propagated to the ends of the world.[32]

William Symonds praised in his sermon the civilizing mission of the company's investors and settlers. He ended in rousing style: 'Be cheerful then, and the Lord of all glory, glorify his name by your happy spreading of the gospel, to your commendation, and his glory, that is Lord of all things, to whom be power and dominion. Hallelujah.'[33]

CHAPTER TWENTY

Time Past, Time Present

There is a wonderful panoramic view of London by Claes Visscher from 1616, the year of William Shakespeare's death. Engraved on copper and printed in Amsterdam, it looks as though someone has taken Anthonis van den Wyngaerde's view of London of seventy years earlier and given those impressionist strokes of the artist's pen greater depth, shadow and body. Visscher's city of the early seventeenth century was obviously still the one Wyngaerde had seen from his perch in Southwark, still the London of towers and spires, with the great bridge sitting across the River Thames as solidly as ever, and the quays and wharves of the port crowded with ships. Yet it is different too: much heavier and bulkier than the Tudor city, the adolescent city has filled out. But the change was more than a physical one. The worlds Londoners inhabited and imagined were simply far larger and more complex.

Panoramas like these tease us with the impression that they possess the accuracy of a photograph. This one does not: it was put together from old views of London and made by an artist who had probably never visited the city. Here, instead, was London as it was imagined to be, huge and impressive in all its mercantile glory, 'Celebrated throughout the world', to be viewed in ink on paper in that other remarkable commercial power of the seventeenth century, Amsterdam. London was a city of trade, activity and power; no longer was it merely a satellite, on the edges of Europe's – or the world's – mercantile life.[1]

By 1620 almost all of the Londoners we have met in this book, those born in the city as well as those adopted by it, were gone. Sir Richard Gresham had died in 1549, his son Sir Thomas in 1579, John Isham in 1596, John Stow in 1605, Anthony Jenkinson in 1610 or 1611, the younger Richard Hakluyt in 1616, and Michael Lok sometime between 1620 and 1622. Both Isham and Jenkinson had retired to country manor houses in Northamptonshire after distinguished careers. Stow died in the city he loved and celebrated and was buried in the church of St Andrew Undershaft. His monument survives, showing him writing in a book. The inscription reads (translated from Latin):

> John Stow, London citizen, piously awaits resurrection in Christ. Who having employed most careful diligence in bringing to light records of antiquity, deserved well of his own time and of posterity in writing with distinction the annals of England and the survey of the city of London.[2]

Like Stow, Richard Hakluyt achieved his life's ambition as the great expert on English navigations. He made his will in 1616, leaving his property and money to family, friends and charity. One of those friends was the younger Michael Lok, son of the unfortunate elder Michael, whose troubled career after the failure of the Cathay company led him to a disastrous posting as consul at Aleppo for the Turkey Company and ever-increasing debts. His life in a sense came full circle: he died on Cheapside at the sign of the lock.[3]

The richest of these men left memorials and tombs as earlier generations had done, and these served as summations and celebrations of their careers. But a very few have survived. Sir Thomas Gresham's beautiful tomb of alabaster and black marble in the church of St Helen, Bishopsgate, spoke to his contemporaries – and speaks to us today – of the riches and power of a merchant prince who had little need for ostentation or more words than were necessary: the mottled marble slab is simply carved with his name and the date of his burial.[4]

Any Londoner of 1620 with the inclinations of John Stow, wandering about the city, noticing and recording, could find dozens of tombs and memorials in every city church. To Jacobeans, many of them would have been relics of a bygone age, a time before the Reformation when Londoners still believed in purgatory and prayers for the dead – remote and perhaps discomfiting monuments to past errors and superstitions. In St Olave, Hart Street, for example, was the memorial brass to Sir Richard Haddon, showing Sir Richard and his two wives; Dame Katherine Haddon, once Katherine Wyndout, is on the left, kneeling in prayer with her children, Bartholomew and Joan, behind her. It would have seemed extraordinary to a Londoner of 1620 that a century earlier a priest had actually been employed in the church to say prayers for the Haddons' souls.[5]

Other memorials in St Olave, Hart Street, would have had more immediate significance for Jacobeans. One fine monument is striking even today, a double celebration of the lives of two merchant brothers, Andrew and Paul Bayning, who died in 1610 and 1616 respectively. The Baynings were Turkey and Levant Company merchants; and Paul, like Andrew a city alderman, was one of the first directors of the East India Company.[6] That Mediterranean and eastern trade would not have existed at all without the efforts of a merchant the Baynings knew well – Richard Staper, who died in 1608. A curious Jacobean would have found Staper celebrated in stone in the long disappeared church of St Martin Outwich: 'He was the greatest merchant in his time, the chiefest actor in discovery, of the trades of Turkey, and East India, a man humble in prosperity, painful and ever ready in the affairs public and discreetly.'[7] This would be an exaggeration for any merchant other than Staper, who had been tenacious and formidable over decades in pushing London's interests out to the East.

The legacies these grandees left were tangled up with the affairs of this world and the hopes of the next. Was it in the end vanity and self-aggrandizement, an effort to buy a kind of immortality? The glories of Sir Thomas Gresham's Exchange and the grand hopes of his endowed lectureships in the arts and sciences were all but scuppered by his widow Dame Anne, who, resenting the vast amounts of money her husband had thrown at them, dragged her feet as much as she possibly could and tried to undo the complicated provisions of her husband's will. A characteristic tussle occurred in 1581, when the queen's Privy Council was obliged, gently but firmly, to prod Lady Gresham into repairing crumbling portions of the Royal Exchange. The deal was simple, their lordships explained: her responsibility under her late husband's will was to maintain the Exchange, in return for which she received a portion of its annual revenue. At stake, for the comparatively tiny sum (for a Gresham) of about £20, were the honour of queen and kingdom:

> forasmuch as the charges and reparations of the said Exchange during her life are to be borne and supplied by her, and to that end a yearly revenue is accorded her out of that place: albeit they doubt not of her care to be had in the maintaining of that famous building in respect of the memory of her late husband . . . Yet for that it standeth with the honour of her majesty and the realm that so worthy a monument should not be suffered to fall into ruin and decay.[8]

It was not the last time that she had to be reminded of her duty.[9] But whatever grumblings and grievances she had, Anne Gresham was reconciled enough with Sir Thomas's memory to want to be buried with him in St Helen, Bishopsgate.

A merchant prince like Gresham wanted it all: wealth, legacy and heaven. But was it possible to have everything, and to reconcile the drive for profit with the expectation of eternal life? Those were the questions examined at Paul's Cross in August 1619 by Immanuel Bourne, in a sermon printed and sold a few months later at the shop of George Fairbeard at the north door of the Exchange. Bourne himself lived among the merchants as the minister of St Michael, Cornhill, next door to the Exchange. He knew that London was a city where merchants were driven to buy and sell for money. In that, of course, he saw sin and the temptation of covetousness. He likened gain – material riches – to the apple with which Eve had been tempted by Satan in the Garden of Eden. Prizing the pursuit of godliness above everything, Bourne was mystified by the kind of energy and effort that drove merchants to the far corners of the globe:

> if we look into these our times, what strange . . . enterprises are daily undertaken, both by sea and land, on horse and foot, as if they would tempt the God of heaven to see whether he will punish their desperate boldness or no? It is not foul nor fair, nor wet nor dry, not cold or heat, that can hinder men in their passage from one fair to another, from one city to another, from one kingdom to another, and all to get this much admired gain.[10]

Yet of course this was the secret to the success of a Bayning, a Gresham or a Staper, or any one of the merchants in this book: unflinching tenacity in the face of often apparently overwhelming odds. It was not generally the sort of energy deployed by the earnest godly preacher in his pursuit of heaven – though we should make an exception for the younger Richard Hakluyt, for whom discovery and mercantile endeavour represented God's will in action.

It would be easy at the end of this book simply to catalogue the dead: in the small churchyard of St Olave, Hart Street, the Inuit baby boy brought home by Martin Frobisher as a curiosity and buried without record, or the scores of parishioners killed by the terrible outbreak of plague in 1563, or even Thomas Hacket the stationer and translator, who in his lifetime had communicated to Londoners the promise of the new continent of America.[11]

But London was not in 1620 what Charles Dickens later called 'The city of the absent' – of deserted and spooky churchyards and quiet nocturnal wanderings.[12] The Jacobean city was very much of and for the living. In that year there were fifty-three baptisms at St Olave, Hart Street, and seventy-six at the Jesus Temple in Austin Friars. Multiply those numbers by over a hundred and take into account the thousands still arriving in London in search of work, and then mortality had its counterweight. Londoners continued to live, work and enjoy themselves. Parish life had its familiar structures and rhythms. At St Bartholomew the Less in 1620 the churchwardens dutifully recorded gifts and bequests from wealthy parishioners that were deployed for the benefit of the worthy poor. It was a busy time for the church, as a whole team of workmen spent three months repointing its steeple and replacing its windows.[13]

For those on the outside of city life things could be difficult. The government of King James saw in London's rich merchant strangers the opportunity to raise great sums of money. Between 1618 and 1620 a case rumbled through the court of Star Chamber in which it was alleged that strangers were sending bullion and coin abroad to the impoverishment of the kingdom: at one point the utterly fantastic sum of £7 million was mentioned. The king got money out of the strangers in two ways: first through loans, secondly by means of huge fines imposed on foreign merchants.[14]

As harsh as this was, perhaps in the end all was fair in trade and finance. Certainly London merchants in India and investors in Virginia had a far from straightforward time. To read the reports from 1620 of the East India Company's agents at their base in Surat is to encounter the growing pains of global corporate endeavour. They kept a close eye on Portuguese and Dutch competitors, fumed at negligent factors in Persia and complained about the 'inborn cunning' of the people of India and the corruption of their government. The commodities they were dealing with were far removed from the traditional English cloth trade, and included items such as glass beads, unicorn horn, ivory, polished coral, quicksilver (liquid mercury), animal hides all the way from Russia, cloth of gold, cochineal and sea-morse (walrus) teeth. They hinted at the need for an armed force to protect trade – a presage of the future.[15]

There were difficulties even greater, however, for the adventurers and planters of Virginia, for whom 1620 was a crunch year. In private session, the Virginia Company met in London to agree a plan for the better government of the plantation. They began with the need for unity by removing the company's 'late distractions' by 'partialities and factions' – corporate life was so easily disrupted by powerful characters and interest groups. In the case of the Virginia Company, the disagreements had been provoked by differences of opinion over how the colonies should be governed and the management of accounts.[16]

Like any struggling corporate endeavour, the Virginia Company published in the summer of 1620 a kind of investors' and planters' brochure that made Virginia sound irresistible. There had been 'many disasters', operations of divine providence in which the devil and his agents had tried to disrupt 'this noble action for the planting of Virginia with Christian religion and English people'.[17] But the Virginia narrative was as steady and as unwavering as it had been since the time of Hakluyt and the other early prophets of an English America:

> The rich furs, caviary, and cordage, which we draw from Russia with so great difficulty, are to be had in Virginia, and the parts adjoining, with ease and plenty. The masts, planks, and boards and pitch and tar, the pot-ashes and soap-ashes, the hemp and flax (being the materials of linen) which now we fetch from Norway, Denmark, Poland and Germany, are there to be had in abundance and great perfection. The iron, which hath so wasted our English woods, that itself in short time

must decay together with them, is to be had in Virginia . . . for all good
conditions answerable to the best in the world. The wines, fruit, and
salt of France and Spain; the silks of Persia and Italy, will be found also
in Virginia, and in no mind of worth inferior.[18]

The reality was more complex. America would be no easy substitute
for other continents, and England's trade with Europe was both fixed
and essential. But the spark of possibility is there in this luxurious
description: surely from the New World there was so much more to
be gathered in? The 1620 prospectus concluded with a long list of
noble, gentry and merchant investors. Who, this was meant to communicate, could resist such an opportunity?

One specific issue in 1620 especially exercised the Virginia
Company of London, and that was King James's well-known aver-
sion to tobacco: 'tending to a general and new corruption both of
men's bodies and manners', as the king put it in a proclamation of that
year. James's economic objection to tobacco was that it drained the
kingdom of bullion, as well as resulting in the trading of England's
staple commodities below their real value, thus enhancing the price
of tobacco, all to 'the great disturbance and decay of the trade of the
orderly and good merchant'.[19] The governing court of the Virginia
Company saw in the restrictions about to be placed on the unlimited
importation of tobacco, 'the utter overthrow and destruction' of its
plantations. It petitioned the king through the Earl of Southampton,
the company's treasurer (he had East India Company interests too,
and had been Shakespeare's literary patron); King James said that 'it
was never his meaning to grant anything that might be prejudicial
to any or both those plantations'.[20] Hard and coordinated lobbying
of the royal government was essential; it was clear in 1620 that the
lucrative tobacco leaf had friends in high places. And, with the nim-
bleness of powerful interests, the company prepared itself for new
markets: if it became impossible to import tobacco into England, then
they would shift their operations to Flushing and Middelburg in the
Low Countries. Where there was a problem, there might also be a
corporate opportunity.

After 1620, London continued to grow and fill out. Metropolitan
fashion took over. The 1630s saw the development of Covent Garden

near the Strand, outside the city boundary. London blurred into Westminster; its geographical weight was shifting. What we think of today as London was to Elizabethans a very long way from the old city, which, if we map it now, is bounded by a tiny handful of Tube stations. That change began in the seventeenth century. And so, where in a view of Westminster from the 1590s 'the Convent Garden' was shown as open space, by the time of Wenceslaus Hollar's captivating bird's-eye view of the new Covent Garden in about 1660, it was a tidy city planner's dream, with grand houses of three and four storeys, some with elegant arcades, built in an ordered way around gardens and a central piazza. There was, at long last, the sense of a city of order and design.[21]

Everything changed in September 1666 with a fire of barely comprehensible intensity. Though the suburbs beyond the Roman wall survived, the Great Fire reduced the old city to ashes. Almost all the buildings mentioned in this book, with the exception of those towards Bishopsgate and Aldgate and the Tower of London, were destroyed: the church of St Antholin and the hospital of St Thomas of Acon (where this book began), St Lawrence Jewry, Guildhall, the Royal Exchange and so much else.

The scholar and diarist John Evelyn watched the Great Fire from the safety of Bankside in Southwark. He tried to make sense of the scale of an event that struck him like a physical blow; the tautness of his prose only emphasizes the horror of what he and his family saw. 'We beheld that dismal spectacle, the whole city in dreadful flames near the waterside; all the houses from the Bridge, all Thames Street, and upward toward Cheapside down to the Three Cranes, were now consumed.' Nothing could stop the fire as it leapt 'after a prodigious manner' from house to house and street to street, burning 'the churches, public halls, Exchange, hospitals, monuments, ornaments'. 'The stones of Paul's,' he continued, 'flew like grenados, the melting lead running down the streets in a stream, and the very pavements glowing with fiery redness, so as no horse, nor man, was able to tread on them.' The destruction was so complete that John Evelyn felt he had witnessed in the Great Fire 'a resemblance of Sodom, or the last day'. But the other point of reference for Evelyn was the destruction of ancient Troy. Now New Troy, like the old, was gone: 'London was,' Evelyn wrote, 'but is no more.'[22]

And yet London survived. Just as the Romans had twice rebuilt Londinium after the rising of Boudicca and the first great fire, so, now, the city was carefully surveyed and the ancient streets and buildings meticulously recorded, along with the old ward boundaries. London grew up again around the streets and lanes walked by generations of Londoners. The Gothic leviathan of St Paul's Cathedral was replaced by Sir Christopher Wren's domed masterpiece. If Wren's proposed model for a new city had been used, London within the walls would have been tidied up into long boulevards and ordered piazzas, of which the focus would have been a new Exchange – from Newgate and Cheapside, Dowgate and the Customs House, London Bridge and Bishopsgate, all roads would have led to the merchants' bourse.

But it never happened; perhaps Londoners preferred the familiar tangle and jostle, a kind of deep ancestral imprint of disorder. Sir Joshua Reynolds later wrote of Wren's ideas that their 'effect might have been . . . rather unpleasing: the uniformity might have produced weariness, and a slight degree of disgust'.[23]

The story of London after the Great Fire belongs to other books. But one further event – this time in the twentieth century – should be mentioned. The Temple of Jesus at Austin Friars somehow survived the inferno of 1666, but in the early hours of the morning of 16 October 1940 it was hit by a landmine attached to a parachute. The last functioning part of London's medieval Augustinian friary – the simple church of rag-stone and chalk, with dressings of Reigate stone – was smashed by high explosive down to rubble.[24]

To try to navigate the modern city with Elizabethan maps and views is an utterly dislocating experience: even someone with decent skills in map-reading and a fair sense of direction will find himself or herself wandering backwards and forwards, frustrated and disoriented. We have to work hard to get our bearings. Old street names both direct and deceive.

It should be possible, more or less. Even given all the alterations, whether by fire, bombs, routine demolition and all the changes that are bound to happen over centuries, a portion of the old city's pattern and structure has survived, like the major bones of a skeleton upon and around which a new body has been built. When we do find small miracles of survival, like the city's few medieval churches, they seem tiny and shrunken standing next to enormous office blocks. They have been tenacious in holding back modernity from total victory – or at the very least showing that there was once something else here – another world, other lives. It is hard not to feel the vast historical distance between then and now, and with it a twinge of melancholy.

The incongruity is striking. The church of St Helen, Bishopsgate, lies in the shadow of 30 St Mary Axe, better known by its nickname of 'The Gherkin'. Very close by is the small church of St Andrew Undershaft. That, too, was a nickname, as John Stow explained: 'because that of old time, every year on May day in the morning . . . an high or long shaft, or maypole, was set up there in the midst of the street'. It was a practice abandoned after the anti-alien riot of 'Evil May Day' in 1517.[25] Stow's last resting place is today just across the road from the vast Leadenhall Building. As Stow wrote at the beginning of his *Survey*, 'What London hath been of ancient time men may here see, as what it is now every man doth behold.'[26]

It takes a very great effort now even to begin to imagine that such things might ever have happened in this place; what half a millennium ago was the tangle of townhouses, tenements, shops, halls and churches is now a topography of steel, concrete and glass – once a city on a human scale (though of course to its inhabitants fantastically huge) has become an impersonal megapolis. Now it has its own jostling life of bistros, restaurants, wine bars and preoccupied financiers, for whom money is in the abstract – on the screen and in the computer – and so often removed from the physical act of carrying commodities on ships across oceans and between continents. Just what would Elizabethan preachers, who found sin in something as innocuous as the merchant's paper bill of exchange, make of it all?

It would be too easy, however, to imagine that the Elizabethan past was a happy and innocent place, to glorify with John Stow a lost merry England. The remnants of the Elizabethan city may look tiny when we see them sitting in the shadows of the headquarters and offices of global businesses and banks. But London in the sixteenth and seventeenth century was, as I hope this book has shown, a place of formidable dynamism. Elizabethans and Jacobeans tested the moral limits of money and fortune. In their world usury became interest, and investors put their money into ventures that pushed minds, men and ships to their limits: the physical stamina and endurance it must have taken to sail across oceans, to ride across continents and to plant new territories is staggering. Today it might take computers, lawyers and accountants to dominate the world – corporate, virtual or otherwise; nearly 500 years ago it took months or years of patience, effort and travail, and with no guarantee of success. That Elizabethans and Jacobeans were able to do what they did is by any measure extraordinary. Remarkable, too, is that out of a city whose elite prided itself on its stability and con- servatism, there arose ground-breaking endeavours like the Muscovy, East India and Virginia Companies and many others like them.

And so time has moved on, as of course it does; and we have made what once belonged to others our own. Instead of Sir Richard Haddon's 'great place' on Seething Lane, there is currently a great space – though London being London that will change soon enough. Today it is a building site, surrounded by a barrier decorated with the mysterious corporate slogan 'Where the world meets the world': meaningless in almost all contexts, but oddly appropriate for the site of what was once Muscovy House, that point of encounter between London and Russia, where London merchants planned embassies to Moscow and Anthony Jenkinson reported on his travels to the court of the shah of Persia.

Upon this tiny nook of the city, very close to the Tower of London, there lies a thick patina of a long history. It is still called Seething Lane. In St Olave, Hart Street, the naval civil servant and diarist Samuel Pepys worshipped and was buried; the memorial bust of Elizabeth Pepys, apparently animated in conversation, still looks down at their pew. During the Great Fire, Pepys and Sir William Penn (the father of the William Penn who founded Pennsylvania) helped to save this portion of the city by blowing up houses with gunpowder in order to make a fire break. The churchyard was Charles Dickens's favourite in London, and in honour of its macabre gateway – one Samuel Pepys would have known well – he nicknamed it:

This gate is ornamented with skulls and cross-bones, larger than the life, wrought in stone; but it likewise came into the mind of Saint Ghastly Grim, that to stick iron spikes a-top of the stone skulls, as though they were impaled, would be a pleasant device. Therefore the skulls grin aloft horribly, thrust through and through with iron spears. Hence, there is attraction of repulsion for me in Saint Ghastly Grim, and, having often contemplated it in the daylight and the dark, I once felt drawn towards it in a thunderstorm at midnight. 'Why not?' I said, in self-excuse.[27]

St Olave, Hart Street, has been a lucky survivor. Severely damaged by bombing in 1940, it was pieced back together in the 1950s. Against all the odds, Sir Richard Haddon's memorial survives, just to the south of the altar; his image within it has long disappeared, though his two wives, Anne and Katherine, still pray for his soul. Paul Bayning, splendid in scarlet with a high, neat Jacobean ruff, kneels in front of his brother Andrew. In life they looked to the Levant and the East Indies: in death Paul looks, with brow furrowed, earnestly to heaven.

Here the past exists encapsulated in the present: a history so easy to forget in the noise and busyness of today, and yet somehow the essence of the place, indelibly part of its texture, like the weave of the merchant's cloth.

Notes

Manuscripts are cited by the call numbers in the relevant archive or library. In citing manuscripts (by folio or page) or printed books (by page or signature), series and journals, the following abbreviations are used:

Bannerman, *St Olave*	*The registers of St Olave, Hart Street, London, 1563–1700*, ed. W. Bruce Bannerman (London, 1916)
Beaven	*The aldermen of the city of London*, ed. A. B. Beaven, 2 vols (London, 1908–13)
BL	British Library, London
Dekker, *Plague*	*The plague pamphlets of Thomas Dekker*, ed. F. P. Wilson (Oxford, 1925)
EcHR	*Economic History Review*
EHR	*English Historical Review*
Freshfield, *Account books*	*The account books of the parish of St Bartholomew Exchange in the city of London, 1596–1698*, ed. Edwin Freshfield (London, 1895)
Freshfield, *Minute books*	*The vestry minute books of the parish of St Bartholomew Exchange in the city of London, 1567–1676*, ed. Edwin Freshfield (London, 1890)

HLQ	*Huntington Library Quarterly*
Jonson	*The Cambridge edition of the works of Ben Jonson*, ed. David Bevington, Martin Butler and Ian Donaldson, 7 vols (Cambridge, 2012)
Kingsford	*A survey of London by John Stow: reprinted from the text of 1603*, ed. Charles Lethbridge Kingsford, 2 vols (Oxford, 1908)
ODNB	*Oxford Dictionary of National Biography*, online or in print, ed. H. C. G. Matthew and Brian Harrison, 60 vols (Oxford, 2004)
PN1	Richard Hakluyt, *The principall navigations, voiages and discoveries of the English nation, made by sea or over land, to the most remote and farthest distant quarters of the earth at any time within the compasse of these 1500. yeeres* (STC 12625, London, 1589)
PN2	Richard Hakluyt, *The principal navigations, voiages, traffiques and discoveries of the English nation, made by sea or over-land, to the remote and farthest distant quarters of the earth, at any time within the compasse of these 1500. yeeres*, 3 vols (STC 12626, London, 1598–1600)
STC	*A short-title catalogue of English books, 1475–1640*, ed. W. A. Jackson, F. S. Ferguson and Katharine F. Pantzer, 3 vols (Bibliographical Society, London, 1986–91)
Stow, *Chronicles*	*Three fifteenth-century chronicles, with historical memoranda by John Stowe, the*

antiquary, ed. James Gairdner (Camden Society, second series, vol. 28, London, 1880)

Taylor, *Geography*   E. G. R. Taylor, *Tudor geography, 1485–1583* (London, 1930)

Taylor, *Richard Hakluyts*   *The original writings and correspondence of the two Richard Hakluyts*, ed. E. G. R. Taylor, 2 vols (Hakluyt Society, second series, nos. 76, 77, London, 1935, repr. 1967)

TRP   *Tudor royal proclamations*, ed. Paul L. Hughes and J. F. Larkin, 3 vols (New Haven, CT and London, 1964–9)

WP   Richard Hakluyt, *A particuler discourse . . . known as a Discourse of Western planting*, ed. David B. Quinn and Alison M. Quinn (Hakluyt Society, extra series, no. 45, London, 1993)

Manuscripts preserved in the United Kingdom's National Archives at Kew in London are quoted by the call number there in use. The descriptions of the classes referred to are as follows:

PC 2   Privy Council Registers

PROB 11   Prerogative Court of Canterbury, Registered Copy Wills

SP 1   State Papers, Henry VIII, General Series

SP 10   State Papers, Domestic, Edward VI

SP 11   State Papers, Domestic, Mary I

SP 12   State Papers, Domestic, Elizabeth I

SP 15   State Papers, Domestic, Addenda, Edward VI to James I

SP 68	State Papers, Foreign, Edward VI
SP 69	State Papers, Foreign, Mary I
SP 70	State Papers, Foreign, Elizabeth I (1558–77)
SP 91	State Papers, Foreign, Russia (from 1589)
SP 94	State Papers, Foreign, Spain (from 1577)
SP 97	State Papers, Foreign, Turkey (from 1577)

CHAPTER 1: A MERCHANT'S WORLD

1 The originals of the murals have disappeared. Certainly *The Triumph of Riches* was destroyed by fire in Germany in 1752, though the original sketch for it survives in the Musée du Louvre (with a copy in the British Museum), as well as an etching published in Antwerp in 1561, now in the Kunstmuseum Basel. See Paul Ganz, *The paintings of Hans Holbein: first complete edition* (London, 1950), pp. 284–8; John Rowlands, *Holbein: the paintings of Hans Holbein the Younger; complete edition* (Oxford, 1985), pp. 223–4; Susan Foister, *Holbein and England* (New Haven, CT, and London, 2004), pp. 130–37; and Susan Foister, *Holbein in England* (London, 2006), pp. 69–71.

2 PROB 11/12/28.

3 Caroline M. Barron, *London in the later middle ages: government and people, 1200–1500* (Oxford, 2004), pp. 346–8.

4 John Guy, *Thomas Becket: warrior, priest, rebel, victim* (London, 2012), p. 1.

5 *Acts of court of the Mercers' Company*, ed. Laetitia Lyell and Frank D. Watney (Cambridge, 1936), p. 131.

6 *Acts of court*, ed. Lyell and Watney, p. 130.

7 *Acts of court*, ed. Lyell and Watney, pp. 125, 130–34.

8 D. J. Keene and Vanessa Harding, *Historical gazetteer of London before the Great Fire* (Cambridge, 1987), pp. 351–63; *Materials for a history of the reign of Henry VII*, ed. William Campbell, 2 vols (London, 1873), vol. I, pp. 107, 182, 565, 570; vol. II, pp. 12, 342, 404, 438, 540; Alwyn Ruddock, 'London capitalists and the decline of Southampton in the early Tudor period', *EcHR*, second series, 2 (1949), p. 142; Beaven, vol. I, p. 130.

NOTES

9 Kingsford, vol. I, p. 252.

10 John Weever, *Ancient funerall monuments within the united Monarchie of Great Britaine, Ireland, and the Islands adjacent* (STC 25223, London, 1631), pp. 402–3; Kingsford, vol. I, p. 252.

11 'For the buriall of Aldermen', in *The ordre of my Lord Mayor, the Aldermen & the Shiriffes, for their metings and wearynge of theyr apparell throughout the yeare* (STC 16705.7, London, 1568), sig. B4-v.

12 Anne F. Sutton, *The mercery of London: trade, goods and people, 1130–1578* (Farnham, 2005), p. 382.

13 PROB 11/15/41; *Calendar of wills proved and enrolled in the Court of Husting, London, 1358–1688*, ed. Reginald R. Sharpe (London, 1890), p. 611; John Watney, *Some account of the hospital of St Thomas of Acon* (London, 1906), p. 179; *Acts of court*, ed. Lyell and Watney, pp. 263, 273, 308–9.

14 Sylvia Thrupp, *The merchant class of medieval London* (Chicago, 1948), p. 347; Sutton, *Mercery of London*, pp. 537–8.

15 PROB 11/21/281; Sutton, *Mercery of London*, pp. 537–8.

CHAPTER 2: LONDONERS

1 Jeremy Boulton, 'London 1540–1700', in *The Cambridge urban history of Britain, 1540–1840*, ed. Peter Clark (Cambridge, 2000), pp. 315–17.

2 Caroline M. Barron, *London in the later middle ages: government and people, 1200–1500* (Oxford, 2004), pp. 238–40.

3 Steve Rappaport, *Worlds within worlds: structures of life in sixteenth-century London* (Cambridge, 1989), pp. 51, 68, 391–2.

4 Rappaport, *Worlds within worlds*, p. 67; Boulton, 'London 1540–1700', pp. 316–17; Barron, *London in the later middle ages*, p. 239; Paul Slack, 'Metropolitan government in crisis: the response to plague', in *London 1500–1700: the making of the metropolis*, ed. A. L. Beier and Roger Finlay (Harlow, 1986), p. 62.

5 Rappaport, *Worlds within worlds*, pp. 78–9.

6 Kingsford, vol. II, p. 199.

7 *The city of London from prehistoric times to c. 1520*, ed. Mary D. Lobel (Oxford, 1991), p. 83.

8 *The views of the hosts of alien merchants, 1440–1444*, ed. Helen Bradley (London Record Society, vol. 46, Woodbridge, 2012), p. xxv.

9 Charles Nicholl, *The lodger: Shakespeare on Silver Street* (London, 2008), pp. 186–7.

10 Bannerman, *St Olave*, pp. 121, 123.

11 *The A to Z of Elizabethan London*, ed. Adrian Prockter, Robert Taylor and John Fisher (London Topographical Society, no. 122, London, 1979), p. ix; John Schofield, *Medieval London houses* (New Haven, CT, and London, 2003), pp. 87–8.

12 *London consistory court wills, 1492–1547*, ed. Ida Darlington (London Record Society, London, 1967), pp. 102–6, 114–16, 117–18.

13 Bannerman, *St Olave*, pp. 1–2.

14 Tarnya Cooper, *Citizen portrait: portrait painting and the urban elite of Tudor and Jacobean England and Wales* (New Haven, CT, and London, 2012), pp. 76–8.

15 *London consistory court wills*, ed. Darlington, pp. 2, 60.

16 *London consistory court wills*, ed. Darlington, pp. 44–5.

17 Martha Carlin, '"What say you to a piece of beef and mustard?": the evolution of public dining in medieval and Tudor London', *HLQ*, 71 (2008), pp. 199–217, at pp. 199, 214; *A bioarchaeological study of medieval burials on the site of St Mary Spital*, ed. B. Connell, A. G. Jones, R. Redfern and D. Walker (London, 2012), p. 161.

18 Stow, *Chronicles*, p. 142.

19 Andrew Boorde, *Hereafter foloweth a compendyous Regyment or a dyetary of Helth* (STC 3378.5, London, 1542), sig. F2-v.

20 A. J. Hoenselaars, *Images of Englishmen and foreigners in the drama of Shakespeare and his contemporaries* (London and Toronto, 1992), p. 115.

21 *English historical documents, 1558–1603*, ed. Ian W. Archer and F. Douglas Price (London and New York, 2011), pp. 735–8; BL, Cotton MS, Faustina C.II, fos. 170–87v.

22 *TRP*, vol. III, p. 182.

23 *St Mary Spital*, ed. Connell, Jones, Redfern and Walker, pp. 149–54.

24 Hatfield House, Hertfordshire, Cecil Papers 151/144.

25 Ernest L. Sabine, 'Latrines and cesspools of mediaeval London', *Speculum*, 9 (1934), pp. 306, 307.

26 A reference I owe to the kindness of Professor Martin Butler: 'And I could wish for their eternized sakes / My muse had ploughed with his that sung

A-JAX': 'On the Famous Voyage' (*c.* 1612), in Jonson, vol. V, pp. 190–98, at p. 198.

27 *News from Gravesend: Sent to Nobody* by Thomas Dekker and Thomas Middleton, in *Thomas Middleton: the collected works*, ed. Gary Taylor and John Lavagnino (New York, 2007), p. 140, lines 537–42; *Newes from Graves-end: Sent to Nobody* (STC 12199, London, 1604), sig. C4.

28 Thomas Rogers Forbes, *Chronicle from Aldgate: life and death in Shakespeare's London* (New Haven, CT, and London, 1971), pp. 100, 124–35.

29 Slack, 'Metropolitan government in crisis', p. 62. See also the Corporation of London's *Analytical index to the series of records known as the Remembrancia, 1579–1664* (London, 1878), pp. 329–38.

30 John Caius, *A boke, or counseill against the disease commonly called the sweate, or sweatyng sicknesse* (STC 4343, London, 1552), fo. 8v (sig. A8v).

31 Bannerman, *St Olave*, pp. 1, 105–6, 247.

32 *The booke of Common Prayer, and administracion of the Sacramentes, and other Rites and Ceremonies in the Churche of England* (STC 16293.3, London, 1559), sig. U1v.

33 Thomas Nashe, 'In Time of Pestilence 1593', in Forbes, *Chronicle from Aldgate*, p. 133.

34 SP 12/125, no. 21.

35 John Field, *A godly exhortation, by occasion of the late judgement of God, shewed at Parris-garden* (STC 10844.8, London, 1583), sigs. C1v–C4v, at sig. C4-v; BL, Lansdowne MS 37, fo. 8.

36 Field, *Godly exhortation*, sig. B5v.

37 Corporation of London, *Remembrancia*, p. 337.

38 Ruth Mazo Karras, 'The regulation of brothels in late medieval England', *Signs*, 14 (1989), p. 420; Paul Griffiths, 'The structure of prostitution in Elizabethan London', *Continuity and Change*, 8 (1993), p. 43. See also Henry Ansgar Kelly, 'Bishop, prioress, and bawd in the stews of Southwark', *Speculum*, 75 (2000), pp. 342–88.

39 *English historical documents*, ed. Archer and Price, pp. 711–13.

40 Jonson, vol. III, p. 562.

41 *The Elizabethan underworld*, ed. A. V. Judges (London, 1965), pp. 407–10, at p. 410.

42 *TRP*, vol. III, pp. 196–7.

CHAPTER 3: LANDMARKS

1 Wynkyn de Worde, *Here begynneth a shorte & a breve table on these cronycles* (STC 9996, Westminster, [1497]), sig. c2r.

2 Kingsford, vol. I, p. 1.

3 Ralph Merrifield, 'Roman London', in *The city of London from pre-historic times to c. 1520*, ed. Mary D. Lobel (Oxford, 1991), p. 11; Kingsford, vol. I, p. 4.

4 'The Ruin', in *A choice of Anglo-Saxon verse*, ed. Richard Hamer (London, 1990), p. 27.

5 *The Wonderfull yeare* (1603), in Dekker, *Plague*, p. 33.

6 *The panorama of London circa 1544 by Anthonis van den Wyngaerde*, ed. Howard Colvin and Susan Foister (London Topographical Society, no. 151, London, 1996).

7 James Pilkington, *The true report of the burnyng of the Steple and Churche of Poules in London* (STC 19930, London, 1561), sig. A8.

8 Thomas Middleton, *The Meeting of Gallants at an Ordinarie: or The Walke in Powles* (STC 17781, London, 1604), sig. B3-v; *Thomas Middleton: the collected works*, ed. Gary Taylor and John Lavagnino (Oxford, 2007), pp. 183–5; Eleanor Lowe, '"My cloak's a stranger; he was made but yesterday": clothing, language, and the construction of theatre in Middleton', in *The Oxford handbook of Thomas Middleton*, ed. Gary Taylor and Trish Thomas Henley (Oxford, 2012), p. 199.

9 Pierre Du Ploiche, *A treatise in English and Frenche right necessary and proffitable for al young children* (STC 7363, London, 1551), sig. H1.

10 Kingsford, vol. II, p. 2; *City of London*, ed. Lobel, p. 77.

CHAPTER 4: IN ANTWERP'S SHADOW

1 Ian Blanchard, *The international economy in the 'age of discoveries', 1470–1570* (Stuttgart, 2009); J. L. Bolton and Francesco Guidi Boscoli, 'When did Antwerp replace Bruges as the commercial and financial centre of north-western Europe? The evidence of the Borromei ledger for 1438', *EcHR*, 61 (2008), pp. 360–79; Alison Hanham, *The Celys and their world: an English merchant family of the fifteenth century* (Cambridge, 1985), pp. 210–11; Herman van den Wee, *The growth of the Antwerp market and the European economy (fourteenth–sixteenth centuries)*, 3 vols (The Hague, 1963), vol. II, pp. 113–42; Smithsonian

Institution, *Antwerp's golden age: the metropolis of the west in the 16th and 17th centuries* (Antwerp, 1973–5); Dan Ewing, 'Marketing art in Antwerp, 1460–1560: Our Lady's *Pand*', *Art Bulletin*, 72 (1990), pp. 558–84.

2 Florence Edler, 'Winchcombe kerseys in Antwerp (1538–44)', *EcHR*, 7 (1936), pp. 58–9.

3 Richard Rowlands (Verstegan), *The post for divers partes of the world* (STC 21360, London, 1576), pp. 77–87.

4 *The Book of Privileges of the Merchant Adventurers of England, 1296–1483*, ed. Anne F. Sutton and Livia Visser-Fuchs (Oxford, 2009), p. 211.

5 Anne F. Sutton, 'The Merchant Adventurers of England: their origins and the Mercers' Company of London', *Historical Research*, 75 (2002), p. 45; *Book of Privileges*, ed. Sutton and Visser-Fuchs, pp. 294–305.

6 Guido Marnef, *Antwerp in the age of Reformation: underground Protestantism in a commercial metropolis*, trans. J. C. Grayson (Baltimore, 1996), p. 23.

7 Marnef, *Antwerp in the age of Reformation*, p. 24.

8 Kristine K. Forney, 'Music, ritual and patronage at the Church of Our Lady, Antwerp', *Early Music History*, 7 (1987), p. 27.

9 Smithsonian Institution, *Antwerp's golden age*, p. 23; Ewing, 'Marketing art in Antwerp', pp. 565–6.

10 Marnef, *Antwerp in the age of Reformation*, p. 37.

11 Marnef, *Antwerp in the age of Reformation*, p. 40.

12 *The prognostication of maister Jasper Laet* (STC 470.6, London?, 1520).

13 SP 1/197, fo. 37; W. C. Richardson, *Stephen Vaughan: financial agent of Henry VIII; a study of financial relations with the Low Countries* (Baton Rouge, 1953), p. 58.

14 *Fugger-Zeitungen: ungedruckte Briefe an das Haus Fugger aus den Jahren 1568–1605*, ed. Victor Klarwill (Vienna, 1923).

15 *A collection of state papers*, ed. Samuel Haynes (London, 1740), p. 153.

16 SP 1/78, fo. 34.

17 Ian Blanchard, 'Gresham, Sir Richard (c. 1485–1549)', *ODNB*; *The chronicle and political papers of King Edward VI*, ed. W. K. Jordan (Ithaca, NY, 1966), p. 111.

18 SP 1/21, fo. 112; SP 1/21, fo. 226.

19 SP 1/21, fo. 226.

20 BL, Cotton MS, Galba B.IX, fo. 13.

21 SP 1/104, fo. 211; John Foxe, *The first volume of the ecclesiasticall history, contayning the actes [and] monumentes of thinges passed in every kinges time* (STC 11224, London, 1576), p. 1173 (sig. KKK3).

22 SP 1/75, fo. 83; *The life and times of Sir Thomas Gresham*, ed. J. W. Burgon, 2 vols (London, 1839), vol. I, p. 23.

23 Anne F. Sutton, *The mercery of London: trade, goods and people, 1130–1578* (Farnham, 2005), p. 398.

24 Stow, *Chronicles*, p. 127.

25 *A chronicle of London, from 1089 to 1483*, ed. H. N. Nicholas (London, 1827), p. 74; Caroline M. Barron, *London in the later middle ages: government and people, 1200–1500* (Oxford, 2004), p. 157.

26 *The ordre of my Lord Mayor, the Aldermen & the Shiriffes, for their metings and wearynge of theyr apparell throughout the yeare* (STC 16705.7, London, 1568), sigs. A7v–B1v.

27 SP 1/135, fo. 8; SP 1/135, fo. 105a; *Sir Thomas Gresham*, ed. Burgon, vol. I, p. 37.

28 Jean Imray, 'The origins of the Royal Exchange', in *The Royal Exchange*, ed. Ann Saunders (London Topographical Society, no. 152, London, 1997), pp. 20–35.

CHAPTER 5: 'LOVE, SERVE AND OBEY'

1 Kingsford, vol. I, p. 275; John Weever, *Ancient funerall monuments within the united Monarchie of Great Britaine, Ireland, and the Islands adjacent* (STC 25223, London, 1631), pp. 398–9; John Guy, *A daughter's love* (London, 2008), p. 21.

2 *Biographical history of Gonville and Caius College, 1349–1897*, ed. John Venn, 3 vols (Cambridge, 1897–1901), vol. I, p. 28.

3 SP 68/12, fo. 36-v.

4 SP 1/135, fo. 244; Ian Blanchard, 'Sir Thomas Gresham c. 1518–1579', in *The Royal Exchange*, ed. Ann Saunders (London Topographical Society, no. 152, London, 1997), pp. 11–12.

5 *The courtyer of Count Baldessar Castilio divided into foure bookes*, trans. Thomas Hoby (STC 4778, London, 1561), sig. Yy4v.

6 Ian Blanchard, 'Gresham, Sir Thomas (c. 1518–1579)', *ODNB*.

7 *The life and times of Sir Thomas Gresham*, ed. J. W. Burgon, 2 vols (London, 1839), vol. I, p. 115.

NOTES

8 W. C. Richardson, *Stephen Vaughan: financial agent of Henry VIII; a study of financial relations with the Low Countries* (Baton Rouge, 1953), pp. 48–53, at p. 49; R. B. Outhwaite, 'The trials of foreign borrowing: the English Crown and the Antwerp money market', *EcHR,* 19 (1966), pp. 289–92.

9 John Guy, *Tudor England* (Oxford, 1988), p. 192; Blanchard, 'Sir Thomas Gresham', pp. 15–16.

10 *A Proclamation . . . for the prohibicion of the cariyng out of the realme of gold or silver, and of eschaunge and reeschaunge* (STC 7839, London, 10 June 1551); *A Proclamacion sette furth . . . lycencyng the Exchaunges and rechaunges of money* (STC 7844.4, London, 23 March 1552); Raymond de Roover, *Gresham on foreign exchange* (Cambridge, MA, 1949), p. 183.

11 Richard Ehrenberg, *Capital and finance in the age of the Renaissance: a study of the Fuggers and their connections,* trans. H. M. Lucas (London, 1928), p. 254.

12 *Sir Thomas Gresham,* ed. Burgon, vol. I, p. 118.

13 *Sir Thomas Gresham,* ed. Burgon, vol. I, p. 92.

14 *Sir Thomas Gresham,* ed. Burgon, vol. I, p. 117; SP 70/3, fo. 8; H. Buckley, 'Sir Thomas Gresham and the foreign exchanges', *Economic Journal,* 34 (1924), p. 597.

15 Blanchard, 'Sir Thomas Gresham', p. 16.

16 SP 70/3, fo. 8.

17 SP 10/15, no. 13; *The chronicle and political papers of King Edward VI,* ed. W. K. Jordan (Ithaca, NY, 1966), pp. 146–7.

18 de Roover, *Gresham on foreign exchange,* p. 220.

19 PC 2/4, pp. 614–15.

20 PC 2/4, p. 618; see also SP 10/15, no. 13; and PC 2/4, p. 488.

21 *Sir Thomas Gresham,* ed. Burgon, vol. I, p. 119.

22 Ehrenberg, *Capital and finance,* pp. 180–81.

23 SP 69/2, fos. 50–51.

24 SP 69/2, fo. 65.

25 Jervis Wegg, *Antwerp, 1477–1559* (London, 1916), pp. 97–8.

26 BL, Lansdowne MS 12, fo. 16v; Ehrenberg, *Capital and finance,* p. 254.

CHAPTER 6: SEARCHING FOR CATHAY

1 Sebastian Münster, *A treatyse of the newe India,* trans. Richard Eden (STC 18244, London, 1553), sig. F1; see also Richard Hakluyt, *Divers*

voyages touching the discoverie of America (STC 12624, London, 1582), sigs. B1–3; *PN1*, pp. 250–51; and *New American world: a documentary history of North America to 1612*, ed. D. B. Quinn, 5 vols (New York, 1979), vol. I, p. 181.

2 Three outstanding studies of Sebastian Cabot are Robert K. Batchelor, *London: the Selden Map and the making of a global city, 1549–1689* (Chicago, 2014), ch. 1; Alison Sandman and Eric H. Ash, 'Trading expertise: Sebastian Cabot between Spain and England', *Renaissance Quarterly*, 57 (2004), pp. 813–46; and Heather Dalton, *Merchants and explorers: Roger Barlow, Sebastian Cabot, and networks of Atlantic exchange, 1500–1560* (Oxford, 2016), esp. pp. 34–9, 72–88, 179–85.

3 Wynkyn de Worde, *Here bygynneth a lytell treatyse or booke named Johan Mandevyll knyght* (STC 17247, Westminster, 1499), sig. N5-v.

4 Münster, *Treatyse of the newe India*, sigs. F1–F5v.

5 de Worde, *Johan Mandevyll*, sigs. N5–O5v; Münster, *Treatyse of the newe India*, sigs. F1–F5v.

6 B. G. Hoffman, *Cabot to Cartier: sources for a historical ethnography of northeastern North America, 1497–1550* (Toronto, 1961), pp. 16–25; *The Cabot voyages and Bristol discovery under Henry VII*, ed. J. A. Williamson (Hakluyt Society, second series, no. 120, Cambridge, 1962), pp. 270–80, 282–91, 302–3; Sandman and Ash, 'Trading expertise', pp. 816–17.

7 Humphrey Gilbert, *A discourse of a Discoverie for a new Passage to Cataia* (STC 11881, London, 1576), sig. D3; Henry Harrisse, *John Cabot the discoverer of North-America and Sebastian his son* (London, 1896), p. 440.

8 Batchelor, *London*, p. 48.

9 PC 2/2, p. 236; Henry Harrisse, *Jean et Sébastien Cabot, leur origine et leurs voyages* (Paris, 1882), pp. 358–60; Harrisse, *John Cabot*, p. 451.

10 Harrisse, *Jean et Sébastien Cabot*, pp. 359–60.

11 Batchelor, *London*, pp. 32, 49; Dalton, *Merchants and explorers*, pp. 179–81. Dalton's work is essential for a full understanding of Cabot in the context of his earlier voyage to South America with Roger Barlow.

12 Münster, *Treatyse of the newe India*, sig. aa4v.

13 The subtitle of Pietro Martire d'Anghiera, *The decades of the newe worlde or west India*, trans. Richard Eden (STC 645–647, London, 1555).

14 Münster, *Treatyse of the newe India*, sigs. aa4, aa5.

15 BL, Lansdowne MS 118, fo. 27; T. S. Willan, *The early history of the Russia Company, 1553–1603* (Manchester, 1956), p. 41.

16 Münster, *Treatyse of the newe India*, sig. A1v.

17 *PN*1, pp. 265–6.

18 *PN*1, p. 262.

19 *PN*1, p. 262.

20 d'Anghiera, *Decades of the newe worlde*, pp. 306–9; *PN*1, pp. 263–5.

21 Batchelor, *London*, p. 32.

22 *PN*1, pp. 259–63.

23 *PN*1, pp. 268–9.

24 Marshall T. Poe, *Foreign descriptions of Muscovy: an analytic bibliography of primary and secondary sources* (University of Iowa, 2008), pp. 8–9, 41–54; Samuel H. Baron, 'Herberstein and the English "discovery" of Muscovy', *Terrae Incognitae*, 18 (1986), pp. 43–54, reprinted in his *Explorations in Muscovite history* (Aldershot, 1991); Marshall T. Poe, *"A people born to slavery": Russia in early modern European ethnography, 1476–1748* (Ithaca, NY, 2000), ch. 1. On Eden's understanding of Muscovy, see d'Anghiera, *Decades of the newe worlde*, pp. 278–306, printed in Sigismund von Herberstein, *Notes upon Russia: a translation of the earliest account of that country, entitled 'Rerum moscoviticarum commentarii'*, ed. R. H. Major, 2 vols (Hakluyt Society, original series, London, 1851–2; repr. Cambridge, 2010), vol. II, pp. 177–256.

25 SP 11/5, no. 4 (*PN*1, pp. 304–9). On the founder investors in the company, see SP 11/7, no. 39; and T. S. Willan, *The Muscovy merchants of 1555* (Manchester, 1953).

26 *PN*1, p. 284.

27 *PN*1, p. 296.

28 *PN*1, pp. 263–5.

29 *'Of the Russe Commonwealth' by Giles Fletcher 1591: facsimile edition with variants*, ed. R. Pipes and J. V. A. Fine (Cambridge, MA, 1966), fos. 9-v, 11v.

30 Robert Recorde, *The whetstone of witte, whiche is the seconde parte of Arithmetike* (STC 20820, London, 1557), sig. a3v.

31 *PN*1, p. 304.

CHAPTER 7: A RUSSIAN EMBASSY

1 Henry Harrisse, *John Cabot the discoverer of North-America and Sebastian his son* (London, 1896), pp. 458–60; Jean Taisnier, *A very necessarie and profitable Booke concerning Navigation*, trans. Richard Eden (STC 23659, London, 1575), dedicatory epistle; Richard Hakluyt, *Divers voyages touching the discoverie of America, and the Ilands adjacent unto the same* (STC 12624, London, 1582), sig. A4; Heather Dalton, *Merchants and explorers: Roger Barlow, Sebastian Cabot, and networks of Atlantic exchange, 1500–1560* (Oxford, 2016), p. 184.

2 Kingsford, vol. I, p. 131.

3 *Acts of court of the Mercers' Company*, ed. Laetitia Lyell and Frank D. Watney (Cambridge, 1936), p. 694; T. S. Willan, *The early history of the Russia Company, 1553–1603* (Manchester, 1956), pp. 28–9; Anne F. Sutton, *The mercery of London: trade, goods and people, 1130–1578* (Farnham, 2005), p. 538; Mercers' Company, London, Acts of Court 1527–1560, fos. 44, 46-v.

4 Kingsford, vol. I, pp. 134, 136; Willan, *Russia Company*, pp. 28–9.

5 *PN*1, p. 299.

6 *PN*1, pp. 299–300.

7 *PN*1, pp. 293–5, 295–9, 299–300, 385–97.

8 *The diary of Henry Machyn*, ed. J. G. Nichols (Camden Society, first series, vol. 42, London, 1848), p. 127; Samuel H. Baron, *Muscovite Russia: collected essays* (London, 1980), essay III.

9 Baron, *Muscovite Russia*, essay III, pp. 48–9.

10 *PN*1, p. 322.

11 Baron, *Muscovite Russia*, essay III, p. 45; *PN*1, p. 322.

12 PC 2/7, p. 538; *PN*1, p. 322.

13 *PN*1, p. 322.

14 *PN*1, p. 322.

15 *PN*1, p. 323; *Diary of Henry Machyn*, ed. Nichols, p. 127.

16 *PN*1, p. 323.

17 *Diary of Henry Machyn*, ed. Nichols, p. 127.

18 'Of the Russe Commonwealth' by Giles Fletcher 1591: facsimile edition with variants, ed. R. Pipes and J. V. A. Fine (Cambridge, MA, 1966), fo. 113v.

19 Stow, *Chronicles*, p. 142.

20 *PN*1, p. 323.

21 Baron, *Muscovite Russia*, essay III, p. 51; *Diary of Henry Machyn*, ed. Nichols, p. 130; *PN1*, p. 324.

22 *PN1*, p. 324.

23 SP 69/10, fos. 90–93v.

24 John Strype, *Ecclesiastical memorials, relating chiefly to religion and the reformation of it*, 3 vols (Oxford, 1822), vol. III, i, p. 522.

25 *Diary of Henry Machyn*, ed. Nichols, p. 130.

26 *PN1*, p. 324.

27 A. H. Johnson, *The history of the Worshipful Company of the Drapers of London*, 2 vols (Oxford, 1914–15), vol. II, p. 185.

28 John Schofield, *Medieval London houses* (New Haven, CT, and London, 2003), p. 225.

29 *PN1*, p. 324.

30 BL, Lansdowne MS 118, fo. 27.

31 Stephen Alford, *Burghley: William Cecil at the court of Elizabeth I* (New Haven, CT, and London, 2008), pp. 76–9.

32 *PN1*, pp. 325–6.

33 Willan, *Russia Company*, p. 41.

34 Robert Recorde, *The whetstone of witte, whiche is the seconde parte of Arithmetike* (STC 20820, London, 1557), sig. a3-v.

CHAPTER 8: THE BROTHERS ISHAM

1 *John Isham, mercer and merchant adventurer: two account books of a London merchant in the reign of Elizabeth I*, ed. G. D. Ramsay (Northamptonshire Record Society, vol. 21, Gateshead, 1962), pp. lxv, 171–3.

2 Tarnya Cooper, *Citizen portrait: portrait painting and the urban elite of Tudor and Jacobean England and Wales* (New Haven, CT, and London, 2012), p. 74.

3 *John Isham*, ed. Ramsay, pp. xv, 170.

4 *John Isham*, ed. Ramsay, p. 169.

5 *John Isham*, ed. Ramsay, pp. xiv–xv.

6 *John Isham*, ed. Ramsay, p. xv.

7 *John Isham*, ed. Ramsay, pp. 170–71.

8 PROB 11/35/45.

9 *John Isham*, ed. Ramsay, p. xvi; T. S. Willan, *The Muscovy merchants of 1555* (Manchester, 1953), p. 111.

NOTES

10 Ian W. Archer, 'Isham, John (1525–1596)', *ODNB*.

11 PROB 11/41/322.

12 Anne F. Sutton, *The mercery of London: trade, goods and people, 1130–1578* (Farnham, 2005), pp. 478–80.

13 *John Isham*, ed. Ramsay, pp. 155–65.

14 *John Isham*, ed. Ramsay, p. xvi; Kingsford, vol. I, pp. 242–3; PROB 11/41/322.

15 *John Isham*, ed. Ramsay, p. 158.

16 Hatfield House Library, Hertfordshire, Cecil Papers, Bills 1.

17 William Tyndale, *The prophete Jonas* (STC 2788, Antwerp, 1531?), sig. C5.

18 *John Isham*, ed. Ramsay, p. 160.

19 *John Isham*, ed. Ramsay, pp. 162–5.

20 Kingsford, vol. I, p. 225.

21 Bishop James Pilkington of Durham, in Kingsford, vol. II, p. 316.

22 *The port and trade of early Elizabethan London: documents*, ed. Brian Dietz (London Record Society, vol. 8, London, 1972), p. 130; Willan, *Muscovy merchants of 1555*, p. 83.

23 Herman van der Wee, *The growth of the Antwerp market and the European economy (fourteenth–sixteenth centuries)*, 3 vols (The Hague, 1963), vol. II, pp. 230–38, at p. 231.

24 PROB 11/87/356.

CHAPTER 9: 'SO FAIR A BOURSE IN LONDON'

1 Richard Ehrenberg, *Capital and finance in the age of the Renaissance*, trans. H. M. Lucas (London, 1928), p. 238; Dan Ewing, 'Marketing art in Antwerp, 1460–1560: Our Lady's *Pand*', *Art Bulletin*, 72 (1990), p. 577.

2 *Elizabeth I and her people*, ed. Tarnya Cooper (London, 2013), pp. 136–7; BL, Lansdowne MS 5, fos. 95v–96.

3 SP 70/57, fo. 56v; Ann Saunders, 'The building of the Exchange', in *The Royal Exchange*, ed. Ann Saunders (London Topographical Society, no. 152, London, 1997), p. 36.

4 Saunders, 'The building of the Exchange', pp. 37–9; Jean Imray, 'The origins of the Royal Exchange', in *Royal Exchange*, ed. Saunders, pp. 28–32; Stow, *Chronicles*, p. 135; Kingsford, vol. I, p. 193.

274

5 Kingsford, vol. I, p. 193.

6 John Earle, *Micro-cosmographie. Or, A peece of the world discovered; in essayes and characters* (STC 7441, London, 1628), no. 54.

7 Julia Gasper, 'The literary legend of Sir Thomas Gresham', in *Royal Exchange*, ed. Saunders, p. 101.

8 John Payne, *Royall exchange: To suche worshipfull Citezins/ Marchants/ Gentlemen and other occupiers of the contrey as resorte therunto* (STC 19489, Haarlem, 1597), p. 42.

9 'Les Singularitéz de Londres, 1576', trans. Gill Healey and Ann Saunders, in *Royal Exchange*, ed. Saunders, pp. 48–9.

10 Kay Staniland, 'Thomas Deane's shop in the Royal Exchange', in *Royal Exchange*, ed. Saunders, pp. 59–67; Payne, *Royall exchange*, p. 15.

11 Payne, *Royall exchange*, p. 30.

12 *The accounts of the churchwardens of the parish of St Michael, Cornhill, in the city of London, from 1456 to 1608*, ed. W. H. Overall (London, 1883), p. 167; Freshfield, *Account books*, p. 6.

13 John Awdeley, *The fraternity of vagabonds* (1575), in *The Elizabethan underworld*, ed. A. V. Judges (London, 1965), p. 57.

14 *The moste excellent and pleasaunt Booke, entituled: The treasurie of Amadis of Fraunce* (STC 545, London, [1572?]). Other books sold by Hacket 'at his shop in the Royal Exchange, at the sign of the green dragon' were Pierre Boaistuau, *Theatrum Mundi, The Theatre or rule of the worlde*, trans. John Alday (STC 3169, London, 1574), a previous printing of which, from about 1566 (STC 3168), was sold from Hacket's shop in Paul's Churchyard; and Edward Hake, *A Touchestone for this time present* (STC 12609, London, 1574).

15 SP 70/130, fo. 47.

16 *An admonition to the Parliament* (STC 10848, [Hemel Hempstead?, 1572]), article 16.

17 *Calendar of the manuscripts of the most honourable the Marquis of Salisbury preserved at Hatfield House*, 24 vols (Historical Manuscripts Commission, London, 1883–1976), vol. II, p. 55.

18 SP 12/243, no. 9.

19 Gasper, 'Literary legend of Sir Thomas Gresham', p. 101.

20 *William Haughton's Englishmen for My Money or A Woman Will Have Her Will*, ed. Albert Croll Baugh (Philadelphia, 1917), p. 113 (line 373).

21 Gasper, 'Literary legend of Sir Thomas Gresham', p. 100.

22 Richard Niccols, *The Furies: With vertues encomium. Or the image of honour. In two bookes of epigrammes, satyricall and encomiasticke* (STC 18521, London, 1614), sig. B3; Crystal Bartolovich, 'London's the thing: alienation, the market, and *Englishmen for My Money*', HLQ, 71 (2008), p. 143.

CHAPTER 10: ALIENS AND STRANGERS

1 John Oldland, 'The allocation of merchant capital in early Tudor London', *EcHR*, 63 (2010), p. 1079; PROB 11/32/429.
2 Andrew Pettegree, *Foreign Protestant communities in sixteenth-century London* (Oxford, 1986), pp. 21, 82; Fiona Kisby, 'Royal minstrels in the city and suburbs of early Tudor London: professional activities and private interests', *Early Music*, 25 (1997), p. 209; *The othe of everie free man, of the Cittie of London* (STC 16763.3, London, [1595]).
3 Lien Bich Luu, *Immigrants and the industries of London, 1500–1700* (Aldershot, 2004), pp. 104–9.
4 J. Lindeboom, *Austin Friars: history of the Dutch Reformed church in London, 1550–1950* (The Hague, 1950), pp. 198–203.
5 Kingsford, vol. I, p. 177. See also *The panorama of London circa 1544 by Anthonis van den Wyngaerde*, ed. Howard Colvin and Susan Foister (London Topographical Society, no. 151, London, 1996), pp. 28–9 (drawing VII).
6 Royal Commission on Historical Monuments (England), *An inventory of the historical monuments in London*, 5 vols (London, 1924–30), vol. IV, pp. 32–4; Lindeboom, *Austin Friars*, plate III; Pettegree, *Foreign Protestant communities*, p. 77.
7 *Register of the attestations or certificates of membership, confessions of guilt, certificates of marriages, betrothals, publications of banns . . . preserved in the Dutch Reformed church Austin Friars, London*, ed. J. H. Hessels (London and Amsterdam, 1892), p. 2.
8 *Register of . . . Austin Friars*, ed. Hessels, pp. 220–21.
9 *A treatise or sermon of Henry Bullynger* (STC 4079, London, 1549).
10 Peter W. M. Blayney, *The Stationers' Company and the printers of London, 1501–1557*, 2 vols (Cambridge, 2014), vol. II, p. 607.
11 A. J. Hoenselaars, *Images of Englishmen and foreigners in the drama of Shakespeare and his contemporaries* (London and Toronto, 1992), p. 17.

12 Thomas Dekker, *The Shoemaker's Holiday*, ed. Anthony Parr (London, 2002), p. 25.

13 Dekker, *Shoemaker's Holiday*, ed. Parr, pp. 26–7.

14 *By the Mayor. An Act of Common Councell, prohibiting all Strangers borne, and Forrainers, to use any trades, or keepe any maner of shops in any sort within this Citty, Liberties and Freedome thereof* (STC 16722, London, 1606).

15 SP 12/20, nos. 14, 15.

16 *Returns of aliens dwelling in the city and suburbs of London: from the reign of Henry VIII to that of James I*, ed. R. E. G. Kirk and Ernest F. Kirk, 4 vols (Huguenot Society of London, vol. 10, Aberdeen, 1900–1908), vol. II, p. 156.

17 SP 12/201, no. 31.

18 *Sir Thomas More*, ed. John Jowett (London, 2011), p. 43.

19 *Sir Thomas More*, ed. Vittorio Gabrieli and Giorgio Melchiori (Manchester, 1990), pp. 17–18.

20 *Returns of strangers in the metropolis, 1593, 1627, 1635, 1639: a study of an active minority*, ed. Irene Scouloudi (Huguenot Society of London, quarto series, vol. 57, London, 1985), p. 3; Charles Nicholl, *The lodger: Shakespeare on Silver Street* (London, 2008), pp. 175–80.

21 Guido Marnef, *Antwerp in the age of Reformation: underground Protestantism in a commercial metropolis, 1550–1577*, trans. J. C. Grayson (Baltimore, 1996), p. 142; *Returns of aliens*, ed. Kirk and Kirk, vol. II, p. 76; vol. III, p. 394; PROB 11/60/238.

22 PROB 11/64/371; *The marriage, baptismal, and burial registers, 1571 to 1874. . . of the Dutch Reformed church, Austin Friars, London*, ed. W. J. C. Moens (Lymington, 1884), pp. 89, 125, 211; *Returns of aliens*, ed. Kirk and Kirk, vol. II, p. 167; *Two Tudor subsidy assessment rolls for the city of London, 1541 and 1582*, ed. R. G. Lang (London Record Society, vol. 29, London, 1993), p. 261 (no. 349).

23 PROB 11/64/371; *Marriage, baptismal, and burial registers*, ed. Moens, p. 89; *Returns of aliens*, ed. Kirk and Kirk, vol. I, p. 334; *Register of . . . Austin Friars*, ed. Hessels, p. 1.

24 PROB 11/64/371.

25 Frances A. Yates, *John Florio: the life of an Italian in Shakespeare's England* (Cambridge, 1934), pp. 65–6; *Returns of strangers*, ed. Scouloudi, p. 208; *Returns of aliens*, ed. Kirk and Kirk, vol. III, pp. 51, 151.

NOTES

CHAPTER 11: 'TRAVAILS, PAINS, AND DANGERS'

1 Taylor, *Geography*, pp. 95–6, 263; John Dee, *General and rare memorials pertayning to the Perfect Arte of Navigation* (STC 6459, London, 1577), sig. 13.

2 Taylor, *Geography*, pp. 172–3, 256, 264; *Johannis, confratris et monachi Glastoniensis, chronica sive historia de rebus Glastoniensibus*, ed. Thomas Hearne (Oxford, 1726), pp. 497–556.

3 *Early voyages and travels to Russia and Persia by Anthony Jenkinson and other Englishmen*, ed. E. Delmar Morgan and C. H. Coote, 2 vols (Hakluyt Society, first series, nos. 72, 73, London, 1886), vol. I, pp. 26–7.

4 *Early voyages and travels*, ed. Morgan and Coote, vol. I, pp. 35–7, at p. 37.

5 Samuel H. Baron, 'Herberstein and the English "discovery" of Muscovy', *Terrae Incognitae*, 18 (1986), pp. 43–54, at p. 44.

6 *Early voyages and travels*, ed. Morgan and Coote, vol. I, pp. 52–3; Pietro Martire d'Anghiera, *The decades of the newe worlde or west India*, trans. Richard Eden (STC 646, London, 1555), fo. 280v (sig. AAAa4v).

7 *Early voyages and travels*, ed. Morgan and Coote, vol. I, pp. 53–9, at p. 57.

8 *Early voyages and travels*, ed. Morgan and Coote, vol. I, pp. 59–81, at p. 69.

9 *Early voyages and travels*, ed. Morgan and Coote, vol. I, pp. 87–90, at p. 88.

10 *Early voyages and travels*, ed. Morgan and Coote, vol. I, pp. 107–9.

11 John H. Appleby, 'Jenkinson, Anthony (1529–1610/11)', *ODNB*.

12 Martín Cortés, *The Arte of Navigation*, trans. Richard Eden (STC 5798, London, 1561), Preface.

13 SP 70/101, fo. 36v.

14 Krystyna Szykuła, 'Anthony Jenkinson's unique wall map of Russia (1562) and its influence on European cartography', *Belgeo*, 3–4 (2008), pp. 325–40.

15 *Early voyages and travels*, ed. Morgan and Coote, vol. I, pp. 145–6.

16 *Early voyages and travels*, ed. Morgan and Coote, vol. I, pp. 150, 157–8.

17 SP 70/75, fo. 69. On Eden as Smith's pupil, see Eden's Preface to Cortés, *Arte of Navigation*.

NOTES

18 SP 12/36, no. 60, and BL, Cotton MS, Galba D.IX, fo. 4, collated in *Early voyages and travels*, ed. Morgan and Coote, vol. I, pp. 159–66.

19 *The voyages and colonising enterprises of Sir Humphrey Gilbert*, ed. D. B. Quinn, 2 vols (Hakluyt Society, second series, nos. 83, 84, London, 1940), vol. I, pp. 105–6.

20 SP 12/42, nos. 5, 5(I); *Sir Humphrey Gilbert*, ed. Quinn, vol. I, pp. 110–11; Taylor, *Geography*, p. 268.

21 SP 70/101, fo. 33.

22 *Early voyages and travels*, ed. Morgan and Coote, vol. I, pp. ci–cii.

23 William Warner, *Albions England* (STC 25082, London, 1596), p. 283.

CHAPTER 12: FLOURISHING LANDS

1 Taylor, *Richard Hakluyts*, vol. I, pp. 2–5, 69–70.

2 *Middle Temple records*, ed. Charles Henry Hopwood and Charles Trice Martin, 4 vols (London, 1904–5), vol. I, p. 433.

3 R. N. Skelton, *Explorers' maps: chapters in the cartographic record of geographical discovery* (London, 1970), pp. 78–9, 95.

4 *PN1*, sig. *2r.

5 'John Dee his Mathematicall Præface' to *The elements of geometrie of the most auncient Philosopher Euclide of Megara* (STC 10560, London, 1570), sig. c4.

6 William Cunningham, *The cosmographical Glasse, conteinyng the pleasant Principles of Cosmographie, Geographie, Hydrographie, or Navigation* (STC 6119, London, 1559), sig. A4; Peter C. Mancall, *Hakluyt's promise: an Elizabethan's obsession for an English America* (New Haven, CT, and London, 2005), p. 19.

7 Taylor, *Richard Hakluyts*, vol. I, pp. 81–2.

8 Anthony Payne, 'Hakluyt, Richard (1552?–1616)', *ODNB*.

9 Taylor, *Geography*, p. 33; ch. 4 of Humphrey Gilbert, *A discourse of a Discoverie for a new Passage to Cataia* (STC 11881, London, 1576), sigs. E2v–F1.

10 W. P. Cumming, 'The Parreus map (1562) of French Florida', *Imago Mundi*, 17 (1963), p. 27; H. P. Biggar, 'Jean Ribaut's *Discoverye of Terra Florida*', *EHR*, 32 (1917), pp. 253–70.

11 Robert Seall, *A Commendation of the adventerus viage of the wurthy Captain. M. Thomas Stutely Esquyer and others, towards the Land called Terra florida* (STC 22139, London, [1563]).

12 Jean Ribaut, *The whole and true discoverye of Terra Florida, (englished the Florishing lande.)*, trans. Thomas Hacket (STC 20970, London, 1563), sig. A2-v.

13 Ribaut, *Terra Florida*, sig. A7v.

14 Ribaut, *Terra Florida*, sig. B1v.

15 Ribaut, *Terra Florida*, sig. B3v.

16 Ribaut, *Terra Florida*, sig. B3v.

17 Ribaut, *Terra Florida*, sig. A2v.

18 Philip Tromans, 'Thomas Hacket's publication of books about America in the 1560s', *Papers of the Bibliographical Society of America*, 109 (2015), pp. 113, 117–19.

19 André Thevet, *The new found worlde, or Antarctike*, trans. Thomas Hacket (STC 23950, London, 1568); Taylor, *Geography*, pp. 170–78; Mancall, *Hakluyt's promise*, pp. 115–20.

20 Thevet, *New found worlde*, sigs. *2v–*3r.

21 Thevet, *New found worlde*, sig. *4r.

22 SP 70/101, fos. 32–3.

23 *A true declaration of the troublesome voyadge of M. John Haukins* (STC 12961, London, 1569).

24 *PN1*, sig. *3r.

CHAPTER 13: THE UNKNOWN LIMITS

1 BL, Cotton MS, Otho E.VIII, fo. 42; *The three voyages of Sir Martin Frobisher*, ed. Richard Collinson (Hakluyt Society, first series, no. 38, London, 1867), pp. 87–8.

2 *Sir Martin Frobisher*, ed. Collinson, p. 88.

3 James McDermott, *Martin Frobisher: Elizabethan privateer* (New Haven, CT, and London, 2001), p. 109.

4 McDermott, *Martin Frobisher*, p. 112; T. S. Willan, *The early history of the Russia Company* (Manchester, 1956), pp. 26–8.

5 Samuel H. Baron, 'William Borough and the Jenkinson map of Russia, 1562', *Cartographica*, 26 (1989), pp. 72–85; the voyage of William's brother Stephen in 1556 is described in *PN1*, pp. 311–21.

6 McDermott, *Martin Frobisher*, pp. 104–5.

7 BL, Cotton MS, Otho E.VIII, fo. 42v.

8 McDermott, *Martin Frobisher*, p. 116.

9 *Sir Martin Frobisher*, ed. Collinson, pp. 89–90.

10 McDermott, *Martin Frobisher*, p. 118.

11 Sir Humphrey Gilbert, *A discourse of a Discoverie for a new Passage to Cataia* (STC 11881, London, 1576), Epistle to the reader.

12 John Dee, *General and rare memorials pertayning to the Perfect Arte of Navigation* (STC 6459, London, 1577), sig. A1v.

13 Richard I. Ruggles, 'The cartographic lure of the northwest passage: its real and imaginary geography', in *Meta Incognita: a discourse of discovery; Martin Frobisher's Arctic expeditions, 1576–1578*, ed. Thomas H. B. Symons, 2 vols (Quebec, 1999), vol. I, p. 202; James McDermott, *The navigation of the Frobisher voyages* (Hakluyt Society, London, 1998), p. 8.

14 Gilbert, *Discourse of a Discoverie*, ch. 4 (sigs. D3v–D4v); Taylor, *Geography*, p. 33.

15 McDermott, *Navigation of the Frobisher voyages*, pp. 4–5.

16 Dee, *General and rare memorials*, sig. A1v.

17 BL, Lansdowne MS 24, fo. 159.

18 George Best, *A true discourse of the late voyages of discoverie, for the finding of a passage to Cathaya, by the Northweast, under the conduct of Martin Frobisher Generall* (STC 1972, London, 1578), p. 51; McDermott, *Martin Frobisher*, p. 153.

19 McDermott, *Martin Frobisher*, p. 155.

20 PC 2/11, pp. 157–8.

21 SP 12/110, nos. 21, 22; *Sir Martin Frobisher*, ed. Collinson, pp. 111–13.

22 Pietro Martire d'Anghiera, *The History of Travayle in the West and East Indies, and other countreys lying eyther way, towardes the fruitfull and ryche Moluccaes*, trans. Richard Eden and ed. Richard Willes (STC 649, London, 1577), p. 236. See also Dionyse Settle on Cathay and America in *The three voyages of Martin Frobisher*, ed. Vilhjalmur Stefansson, 2 vols (London, 1938), vol. II, p. 11.

23 Best, *True discourse*, p. 51.

24 *Martin Frobisher*, ed. Stefansson, vol. II, pp. 99–101.

25 *Martin Frobisher*, ed. Stefansson, vol. II, p. 102.

26 Taylor, *Geography*, p. 182.

27 *Martin Frobisher*, ed. Stefansson, vol. II, pp. 14–15.

28 SP 94/1, fo. 3.

29 Settle in *Martin Frobisher*, ed. Stefansson, vol. II, pp. 16–18.

30 SP 15/25, no. 35.

31 *The third voyage of Martin Frobisher to Baffin Island, 1578*, ed. James McDermott (Hakluyt Society, third series, no. 6, London, 2001), p. 83.

32 McDermott, *Martin Frobisher*, pp. 191–2.

33 *Martin Frobisher*, ed. Stefansson, vol. II, p. 225; Taylor, *Geography*, p. 183.

34 PC 2/12, p. 27.

35 *Sir Martin Frobisher*, ed. Collinson, pp. 170–83; *Third Voyage*, ed. McDermott, p. 78.

36 *Third Voyage*, ed. McDermott, p. 78.

37 *Sir Martin Frobisher*, ed. Collinson, pp. 182–3.

38 *Third Voyage*, ed. McDermott, p. 84.

39 *Third Voyage*, ed. McDermott, p. 84.

CHAPTER 14: MASTER LOK'S DISGRACE

1 George B. Parks, 'Frobisher's third voyage', *Huntington Library Bulletin*, 7 (1935), pp. 183–4.

2 *The third voyage of Martin Frobisher to Baffin Island, 1578*, ed. James McDermott (Hakluyt Society, third series, no. 6, London, 2001), pp. 66–9.

3 *Third voyage*, ed. McDermott, pp. 58–63. See also BL, Cotton MS, Otho E.VIII, fos. 110–11.

4 *The three voyages of Martin Frobisher*, ed. Vilhjalmur Stefansson, 2 vols (London, 1938), vol. II, p. 5.

5 Kettel's portrait of Frobisher, which is in the Bodleian Libraries in the University of Oxford, is reproduced as a colour plate in *Meta Incognita: a discourse of discovery; Martin Frobisher's Arctic expeditions, 1576–1578*, ed. Thomas H. B. Symons, 2 vols (Quebec, 1999); and on the flyleaf to *Third voyage*, ed. McDermott.

6 Thomas Churchyard, *A discourse of The Queenes Majesties entertainement in Suffolk and Norffolk* (STC 5226, London, 1578), sig. L4v.

7 *Third voyage*, ed. McDermott, pp. 91–2.

8 *Third voyage*, ed. McDermott, p. 94. See also Lok's paper on Frobisher's accusations, BL, Lansdowne MS 31, fos. 191–4.

9 PC 2/12, p. 310.

10 PC 2/12, pp. 331–2.

11 *Third voyage*, ed. McDermott, pp. 97–8.

12 *Third voyage*, ed. McDermott, p. 100.

13 Churchyard, *Discourse*, sig. H3.

14 Churchyard, *Discourse*, sig. H3v.

15 Thomas Churchyard, *A Prayse, and Reporte of Maister Martyne Forboishers Voyage to Meta Incognita* (STC 5251, London, [1578]), sigs. A6v–A7.

16 Thomas Ellis, *A true report of the third and last voyage into Meta incognita: achieved by the worthie Capteine, M. Martine Frobisher Esquire. Anno 1578* (STC 7607, London, 1578), sigs. C2v–C3.

17 Ellis, *True report*, sig. B7v.

18 George Best, *A true discourse of the late voyages of discoverie, for the finding of a passage to Cathaya, by the Northweast, under the conduct of Martin Frobisher Generall* (STC 1972, London, 1578), sig. A1v.

19 Richard I. Ruggles, 'The cartographic lure of the northwest passage: its real and imaginary geography', in *Meta Incognita*, ed. Symons, vol. I, p. 214.

20 Best, *True discourse*, sig. a4-v.

21 William H. Sherman, *John Dee: the politics of reading and writing in the English Renaissance* (Amherst, MA, 1995), pp. 176–81.

22 *PN1*, p. 484; Taylor, *Richard Hakluyts*, vol. I, pp. 159–62.

23 *PN1*, p. 469.

24 BL, Lansdowne MS 122, fo. 30; see also BL, Cotton MS, Otho E.VIII, fos. 78–80v; and *PN1*, p. 459.

25 *PN1*, pp. 460–66.

26 Taylor, *Richard Hakluyts*, vol. I, pp. 152–4.

27 Taylor, *Richard Hakluyts*, vol. I, p. 155.

28 David Beers Quinn, *England and the discovery of America, 1481–1620* (London, 1974), pp. 314–15.

29 Ruggles, 'Cartographic lure', pp. 228–9.

30 Richard Hakluyt, *Divers voyages touching the discoverie of America* (STC 12624, London, 1582), dedication to Philip Sidney.

31 Christopher Carleill, *A breef and sommarie discourse upon the entended Voyage to the hethermoste partes of America* (STC 4626.5, n.p., 1583), sig. A2.

32 *The three voyages of Sir Martin Frobisher*, ed. Richard Collinson (Hakluyt Society, first series, no. 38, London, 1867), p. 79.

33 G. D. Ramsay, 'Clothworkers, merchants adventurers and Richard Hakluyt', *EHR*, 92 (1977), pp. 504–21; Peter C. Mancall, *Hakluyt's*

promise: an Elizabethan's obsession for an English America (New Haven, CT, and London, 2005), pp. 60–61; Anthony Payne, *Richard Hakluyt: a guide to his books and to those associated with him, 1580–1625* (London, 2008), pp. 3–7.

34 For the term 'proprietorial colonies', see the editors' Introduction to *WP*, p. xvi.

35 *WP*, pp. 3–7.

CHAPTER 15: SHYLOCK'S VICTORY

1 Douglas Bruster, *Drama and the market in the age of Shakespeare* (Cambridge, 1992), p. 14.

2 Sir Walter Mildmay in 1576, in R. B. Outhwaite, 'Royal borrowing in the reign of Elizabeth I: the aftermath of Antwerp', *EHR*, 86 (1971), p. 261.

3 SP 1/224, fo. 88.

4 SP 1/224, fos. 72–3v; SP 1/224, fos. 88–9v.

5 SP 70/2, fo. 7.

6 BL Lansdowne MS 12, fo. 16.

7 SP 70/14, fo. 73.

8 Gerard Malynes, 'A treatise of tripartite exchange', BL, Cotton MS, Otho E.X, fo. 94.

9 BL, Lansdowne MS 12, fos. 28–30v.

10 SP 12/19, no. 2; *The death of usury, or, the disgrace of usurers* (STC 6443, Cambridge, 1594), p. 21.

11 Outhwaite, 'Royal borrowing', pp. 252–3.

12 Norman Jones, *God and the moneylenders: usury and law in early modern England* (Oxford, 1989), pp. 34–42; Outhwaite, 'Royal borrowing', p. 253.

13 Thomas Wilson, *A discourse upon usury*, ed. R. H. Tawney (London, 1925), p. 304.

14 For a more developed study of *The Merchant of Venice*, see Michael Ferber, 'The ideology of *The Merchant of Venice*', *English Literary Renaissance*, 20 (1990), pp. 431–64.

15 *Death of usury*, p. 40.

16 Pierre de La Primaudaye, *The French Academie* (STC 15233, London, 1586), p. 527.

17 Louis Le Roy, *Aristotles Politiques, or Discourses of government* (STC 760, London, 1598), p. 52.

18 Thomas White, *A sermon preached at Pawles Cross on Sunday the thirde of November 1577. in the time of the plague* (STC 25406, London, 1578), p. 13.

19 William Wager, *A comedy or enterlude intituled, Inough is as good as feast* (STC 24933, London, [?1570]), sig. G1-v.

20 Richard Porder, *A sermon of gods fearefull threatnings for idolatrye* (STC 20117, London, [1570]), sig. A5-v.

21 For example, *The Lawes of the Markette* (STC 16704.6, London, 1562).

22 Bruster, *Drama and the market*, pp. 15–19.

23 Porder, *Sermon*, fo. 76-v (sig. L4-v).

24 George Whetstone, *A mirour for magestrates of cyties* (STC 25341, London, 1584), sig. H2.

25 Wilson, *Discourse*, ed. Tawney, p. 303.

26 Porder, *Sermon*, fos. 81v–83 (sigs. M1v–M3). See also Raymond de Roover, 'What is dry exchange? A contribution to the study of English mercantilism', *Journal of Political Economy*, 52 (1944), pp. 252–7; Raymond de Roover, *Gresham on foreign exchange* (Cambridge, MA, 1949), pp. 94–172; and T. H. Lloyd, 'Early Elizabethan investigations into exchange and the value of sterling, 1558–1568', *EcHR*, 53 (2000), pp. 60–83.

27 Jones, *God and the moneylenders*, p. 4.

28 Porder, *Sermon*, fo. 84 (sig. M4).

29 de Roover, 'What is dry exchange?', p. 258.

30 Porder, *Sermon*, fo. 85-v (sig. M5-v).

31 Porder, *Sermon*, fo. 86v (sig. M6).

32 de Roover, 'What is dry exchange?', p. 255.

33 Wilson, *Discourse*, ed. Tawney, p. 177.

34 Wilson, *Discourse*, ed. Tawney, pp. 200, 209.

35 Wilson, *Discourse*, ed. Tawney, p. 314.

36 Wilson, *Discourse*, ed. Tawney, pp. 325–6.

37 Wilson, *Discourse*, ed. Tawney, p. 249.

38 Wilson, *Discourse*, ed. Tawney, pp. 177, 200.

39 SP 12/75, no. 54; Wilson, *Discourse*, ed. Tawney, p. 155; Jones, *God and the moneylenders*, pp. 51–2.

CHAPTER 16: ST BARTHOLOMEW THE LESS

1 SP 12/245, no. 50.

2 Dekker, *Plague*, p. 33.

3 Ian W. Archer, *The pursuit of stability: social relations in Elizabethan London* (Cambridge, 1991), p. 11.

4 Jonathan Bate, *Soul of the age: the life, mind and world of William Shakespeare* (London, 2008), p. 12.

5 Henry Arthington, *Provision for the poore, now in penurie* (STC 798, London, 1597), sigs. B2–3.

6 *The Queenes Majesties Proclamation for staying of all unlawfull assemblies in and about the Citie of London, and for Orders to punish the same* (STC 8242, London, 4 July 1595).

7 *The Queenes Majesties Proclamation for suppressing of the multitudes of idle Vagabonds, and for staying of all unlawfull assemblies, especially in and about the Citie of London, and for orders to punish the same* (STC 8266, London, 9 September 1598).

8 39 Elizabeth I, c. 4, printed as *An Acte for punishment of Rogues, Vagabonds, and sturdie Beggers* (STC 8261.7, [London, 1598?]).

9 Archer, *Pursuit of stability*, p. 8.

10 *Two Tudor subsidy assessment rolls for the city of London: 1541 and 1582*, ed. R. G. Lang (London Record Society, vol. 29, London, 1993), pp. 170–71.

11 Kingsford, vol. I, p. 180.

12 Freshfield, *Minute books*, pp. xliv–xlv.

13 Freshfield, *Minute books*, p. 12.

14 Freshfield, *Minute books*, pp. 39, 40.

15 Freshfield, *Account books*, p. 3.

16 Freshfield, *Minute books*, p. 40. See also Freshfield, *Account books*, p. 3.

17 The 'Bocke of Statuttes' bought by the parish some time after February 1598 (Freshfield, *Account books*, p. 3) was STC 9492.7 (or one of its variants), where the Vagabonds Act could be found on sigs. B6-C3.

18 Freshfield, *Account books*, p.10.

19 PROB 11/81/9.

20 PROB 11/88/94.

21 Tarnya Cooper, *Citizen portrait: portrait painting and the urban elite of Tudor and Jacobean England and Wales* (New Haven, CT, and London, 2012), pp. 126–7.

22 Freshfield, *Minute books*, p. 25.

23 *Elizabeth I and her people*, ed. Tarnya Cooper (London, 2013), p. 142.

CHAPTER 17: CHANGE AND NOSTALGIA

1 Dekker, *Plague*, p. 40.

2 John Stow, *The survay of London*, ed. Anthony Munday (STC 23344, London, 1618), p. 800.

3 John Schofield, 'An introduction to the three known sheets of the Copperplate Map', in *Tudor London: a map and a view*, ed. Ann Saunders and John Schofield (London Topographical Society, no. 159, London, 2001), p. 2.

4 Bridget Gellert, 'The melancholy of Moor-ditch: a gloss of *1 Henry IV*, I. ii. 87–88', *Shakespeare Quarterly*, 18 (1967), pp. 70–71; John Taylor, *The pennyles pilgrimage* (STC 23784, London, 1618), sig. D1v.

5 Robert Anton, *The philosophers satyrs* (STC 686, London, 1616), p. 20 (sig. F2v); Gellert, 'Melancholy of Moor-ditch', pp. 70–71. See also the imposture of Brainworm as a poor gentleman-soldier begging for charity in Moorfields in Ben Jonson's *Every Man In His Humour* (1616), II. iv. 6–17, 44–7, a reference I owe to Professor Martin Butler.

6 *The travels of John Sanderson in the Levant, 1584–1602*, ed. William Foster (Hakluyt Society, second series, no. 67, London, 1931), pp. 288–9.

7 Richard Johnson, *The Pleasant Walkes of Moore-fields* (STC 14690, London, 1607), sig. A4.

8 Stow, *Survay*, ed. Munday, p. 802.

9 Johnson, *Pleasant Walkes of Moore-fields*, sig. A4.

10 Johnson, *Pleasant Walkes of Moore-fields*, sig. A2.

11 Johnson, *Pleasant Walkes of Moore-fields*, sig. A3v.

12 Johnson, *Pleasant Walkes of Moore-fields*, sig. A4.

13 John Norden, *Speculum Britanniae* (STC 18635, London, 1593), p. 36.

14 Kingsford, vol. I, p. 72; Stow, *Survay*, ed. Munday, p. 794.

15 Kingsford, vol. I, p. 126.

16 *TRP*, vol. II, p. 466.

17 Lena Cowen Orlin, 'Temporary lives in London lodgings', *HLQ*, 71 (2008), pp. 219–42. See also her *Locating privacy in Tudor London* (Oxford, 2007).

18 Kingsford, vol. II, p. 368.

19 Kingsford, vol. II, p. 73; *Survay*, ed. Munday, p. 795.

20 Ian W. Archer, *The pursuit of stability: social relations in Elizabethan London* (Cambridge, 1991), p. 81.

21 Orlin, 'Temporary lives', p. 220.

22 Patrick Collinson, 'John Stow and nostalgic antiquarianism', in *Imagining early modern London: perceptions and portrayals of the city from Stow to Strype, 1598–1720*, ed. J. F. Merritt (Cambridge, 2001), pp. 27–51.

23 Ian W. Archer, 'The arts and acts of memorialization in early modern London', in *Imagining early modern London*, ed. Merritt, pp. 89–113.

24 Kingsford, vol. II, p. 17.

25 Kingsford, vol. II, p. 72.

26 Kingsford, vol. I, p. 126.

27 Kingsford, vol. II, p. 213.

28 *PN2*, vol. I (1598), sig. *4.

29 *PN2*, vol. I (1598), sig. *4.

30 *PN2*, vol. I (1598), sig. *4.

31 *PN2*, vol. I (1598), sig. *5v.

32 *PN2*, vol. I (1598), pp. 124–5.

33 Kingsford, vol. I, p. 4.

CHAPTER 18: TO THE EAST INDIES

1 *The travels of John Sanderson in the Levant, 1584–1602*, ed. William Foster (Hakluyt Society, second series, no. 67, London, 1931), p. 255.

2 *Travels of John Sanderson*, ed. Foster, p. 3.

3 *The policy of the Turkish Empire* (STC 24335, London, 1597), sig. A3.

4 'The praise of the red herring' (1599), in *The works of Thomas Nashe*, ed. Ronald B. McKerrow and F. P. Wilson, 5 vols (Oxford, 1966), vol. III, p. 173.

5 SP 97/2, fo. 66; *Travels of John Sanderson*, ed. Foster, p. xii.

6 *Works of Thomas Nashe*, ed. McKerrow and Wilson, vol. III, p. 173.

7 *PN2*, vol. II (1599), i, pp. 141–4.

8 *A collection of state papers*, ed. William Murdin (London, 1759), p. 781; Alfred C. Wood, *A history of the Levant Company* (London, 1964), p. 17.

9 Wood, *Levant Company*, p. 17.

10 SP 97/2, fo. 235; Wood, *Levant Company*, p. 13.

11 *PN2*, vol. II (1599), i, pp. 295–303.

12 *PN2*, vol. II (1599), i, pp. 250–65; Trevor Dickie, 'Fitch, Ralph (1550?–1611)', *ODNB*.

13 *PN2*, vol. II (1599), i, pp. 250–51.

14 *PN2*, vol. II (1599), i, p. 296.

15 *PN2*, vol. II (1599), i, p. 297; SP 97/2, fo. 159.

16 *The voyages of Sir James Lancaster to Brazil and the East Indies, 1591–1603*, ed. William Foster (Hakluyt Society, second series, no. 85, London, 1940), pp. 1–30; and Kenneth R. Andrews, *Elizabethan privateering: English privateering during the Spanish war, 1585–1603* (Cambridge, 1964), pp. 214–16.

17 Andrews, *Elizabethan privateering*, p. 216.

18 *PN2*, vol. II (1599), i, p. 250.

19 Om Prakash, 'The English East India Company and India', in *The worlds of the East India Company*, ed. H. V. Bowen, Margarette Lincoln and Nigel Rigby (Woodbridge, 2002), p. 2.

20 *The voyage of Sir Henry Middleton to the Moluccas, 1604–1606*, ed. William Foster (Hakluyt Society, second series, no. 88, London, 1943), pp. 199–201; R. A. Skelton, *Explorers' maps: chapters in the cartographic record of geographical discovery* (London, 1970), pp. 148, 156; P. J. Marshall, 'The English in Asia to 1700', in *The origins of empire: British overseas enterprise to the close of the seventeenth century*, ed. Nicholas Canny (Oxford, 1998), p. 269.

21 *A true report of the gainefull, prosperous and speedy voiage to Java in the East Indies, performed by a fleete of eight ships of Amsterdam* (STC 14478, London, [1599?]), p. 23 (sig. D2).

22 *Travels of John Sanderson*, ed. Foster, p. 180.

23 SP 12/253, no. 118.

24 *Travels of John Sanderson*, ed. Foster, p. 184.

25 *Travels of John Sanderson*, ed. Foster, p. 190.

26 *Travels of John Sanderson*, ed. Foster, p. 186.

27 *The dawn of British trade as recorded in the court minutes of the East India Company, 1599–1603*, ed. Henry Stevens (London, 1886), p. 270; Wood, *Levant Company*, p. 31.

28 *Dawn of British trade*, ed. Stevens, pp. 5–7.

29 *Dawn of British trade*, ed. Stevens, p. 8.

30 *Dawn of British trade*, ed. Stevens, pp. 10–11.

31 Those Levant merchants appointed as directors of the East India voyage were Thomas Cordall, William Garaway, Thomas Simonds, Richard Staper and Nicholas Leate: *PN2*, vol. II (1599), i, p. 296; *Select charters of trading companies, 1530–1707*, ed. Cecil T. Carr (Selden Society, London,

NOTES

1913), pp. 31–2; Theodore K. Rabb, *Enterprise and empire: merchant and gentry investment in the expansion of England, 1575–1630* (Cambridge, MA, 1967), alphabetical list of names; Robert Brenner, *Merchants and revolution: commercial change, political conflict, and London's overseas traders, 1550–1653* (Cambridge, 1993), pp. 21–2, 77–9. For the charter members of 1605, see Mortimer Epstein, *The early history of the Levant Company* (London, 1908), pp. 158–60.

32 *The register of letters etc. of the Governor and Company of Merchants of London trading into the East Indies*, ed. George Birdwood and William Foster (London, 1893, repr. 1965), pp. 163–89; *Select charters*, ed. Carr, pp. 30–43.

33 *Register of letters*, ed. Birdwood and Foster, p. 204.

34 *Register of letters*, ed. Birdwood and Foster, p. 198.

35 Dudley Digges, *The defence of trade. In a Letter to Sir Thomas Smith Knight, Governour of the East-India Companie, &c.* (STC 6845, London, 1615), p. 42.

36 K. N. Chaudhuri, *The English East India Company: the study of an early joint-stock company, 1600–1640* (London, 1965), p. 8.

37 *Register of letters*, ed. Birdwood and Foster, p. 180.

38 Marshall, 'English in Asia', p. 269; Chaudhuri, *East India Company*, p. 117. See also *Register of letters*, ed. Birdwood and Foster, pp. 196–9.

39 Digges, *Defence of trade*, pp. 19–22.

40 *The English factories in India: a calendar of documents in the India Office, British Museum and Public Record Office*, ed. William Foster, 13 vols (Oxford, 1906–27), vol. I.

41 *The lawes or Standing Orders of the East India Company* (STC 7447, [London], 1621), pp. 50–51.

42 Prakash, 'English East India Company', p. 3.

43 *Dawn of British trade*, ed. Stevens, pp. 123–4; Peter C. Mancall, *Hakluyt's promise: an Elizabethan's obsession for an English America* (New Haven, CT, and London, 2007), pp. 237–43; Heidi Brayman Hackel and Peter C. Mancall, 'Richard Hakluyt the Younger's notes for the East India Company in 1601: a transcription of Huntington Library Manuscript EL 2360', *HLQ*, 67 (2004), pp. 423–36.

44 Taylor, *Richard Hakluyts*, vol. II, pp. 487–8; *The Hakluyt handbook*, ed. D. B. Quinn, 2 vols (Hakluyt Society, second series, nos. 144, 145, London, 1974), vol. I, pp. 305–6, 311, 313; Mancall, *Hakluyt's*

promise, pp. 240–41; Hackel and Mancall, 'Richard Hakluyt the Younger's notes', p. 425; Jan Huygen van Linschoten, *Itinerario, voyage ofte schipvaert van Jan Huygen van Linschoten* (Amsterdam, 1596); *John Huighen van Linschoten his Discours of Voyages into the Easte & West Indies* (STC 15691, London, [1598]), on which see Skelton, *Explorers' maps*, pp. 146–7; Juan Gonzáles de Mendoza, *The Historie of the great and mightie kingdome of China, and the situation thereof*, trans. Robert Parke (STC 12003, London, 1588).

45 *Dawn of British trade*, ed. Stevens, p. 143; Taylor, *Richard Hakluyts*, vol. II, pp. 465–8, 476–82; Mancall and Hackel, 'Richard Hakluyt the Younger's notes', pp. 431–5.

CHAPTER 19: VIRGINIA RICHLY VALUED

1 SP 91/1, fo. 171-v; T. S. Willan, *The early history of the Russia Company, 1553–1603* (Manchester, 1956), p. 256.

2 Freshfield, *Account books*, p. 4.

3 SP 91/1, fo. 194.

4 BL, Lansdowne MS 112, fos. 134–5v, printed in '*Of the Russe Commonwealth' by Giles Fletcher 1591: a facsimile edition with variants*, ed. Richard Pipes and J. V. A. Fine (Cambridge, MA, 1966), pp. 61–4. See also *The English works of Giles Fletcher, the elder*, ed. Lloyd E. Berry (Madison, WI, 1964), pp. 150–53; Felicity J. Stout, '"The strange and wonderfull discoverie of Russia": Hakluyt and censorship', in *Richard Hakluyt and travel writing in early modern Europe*, ed. Daniel Carey and Claire Jowitt (Hakluyt Society, extra series, no. 47, Farnham, 2012), p. 160; and Felicity J. Stout, *Exploring Russia in the Elizabethan commonwealth: the Muscovy Company and Giles Fletcher, the elder (1546–1611)* (Manchester, 2015), pp. 189–98.

5 *Sir Thomas Smithes voiage and Entertainment in Rushia* (STC 22869, London, 1605), sig. B1v.

6 SP 91/1, fos. 196–8v, at fo. 196.

7 Karen Hearn, 'Merchant-class portraiture in Tudor London: "Customer" Smith's commission, 1579/80', in *Treasures of the royal courts: Tudors, Stuarts and the Russian tsars*, ed. Olga Dmitrieva and Tessa Murdoch (London, 2013), pp. 37–43. See also Kingsford, vol. I, p. 174.

8 SP 12/278, no. 57.

9 T. S. Willan, *The Muscovy merchants of 1555* (Manchester, 1953), pp. 105–6; Beaven, vol. I, p. 158; vol. II, p. 47.

10 *PN2*, vol. III (1600), sigs. (A2), (A3).

11 *PN2*, vol. III (1600), sig. (A3).

12 *PN1*, p. 728.

13 Taylor, *Richard Hakluyts*, vol. II, p. 332; John Brereton, *A Briefe and true Relation of the Discoverie of the North part of Virginia, being a most pleasant, fruitfull and commodious soile* (STC 3611, London, 1602), p. 30 (sig. D3v).

14 John Guy, *Elizabeth: the forgotten years* (London, 2016), pp. 68–75, at p. 73.

15 *PN1*, pp. 770–71; Thomas Harriot, *A briefe and true report of the new found land of Virginia* (STC 12785, London, 1588); David Beers Quinn, *England and the discovery of America, 1481–1620* (London, 1974), pp. 283–5.

16 *The English New England voyages, 1602–1608*, ed. David B. Quinn and Alison M. Quinn (Hakluyt Society, second series, no. 161, London, 1983), p. 207.

17 John Brereton, *A Briefe and true Relation of the Discoverie of the North part of Virginia* (STC 3610, London, 1602), pp. 15, 23. On Brereton's pamphlet (STC 3610) and its expanded reissue (STC 3611), see *The Hakluyt handbook*, ed. D. B. Quinn, 2 vols (Hakluyt Society, second series, nos. 144, 145, London, 1974), vol. I, p. 319.

18 *Sir Thomas Smithes voiage*, sig. B1.

19 'To the Virginian voyage', in Michael Drayton, *Poemes Lyrick and pastorall* (STC 72255, London, [1606]), sigs. C4–C5.

20 George Chapman, Ben Jonson and John Marston, *Eastward Hoe* (STC 4973, London, 1605), sig. E1-v; Peter C. Mancall, *Hakluyt's promise: an Elizabethan's obsession for an English America* (New Haven, CT, and London, 2007), pp. 257–8. For the verbal similarities between *Eastward Hoe* and *Utopia*, see Thomas More, *A fruteful, and a pleasaunt worke of the beste state of a publyque weale, and of the newe yle called Utopia* (STC 18094, London, 1551), sig. K7-v, a reference I owe to the kindness of Professor John Guy.

21 Virginia Company of London, *A true and sincere declaration of the purpose and ends of the Plantation begun in Virginia . . . Sett forth by the authority of the Governors and Councellors established for that Plantation* (STC 24832, London, 1610), p. 6.

22 *Hakluyt handbook*, ed. Quinn, vol. I, p. 317.

23 *The Jamestown voyages under the first charter, 1606–1609*, ed. Philip L. Barbour, 2 vols (Hakluyt Society, second series, nos. 136, 137, Cambridge, 1969), vol. I, pp. xxiv–xxviii.

24 *The great frost. Cold doings in London, except it be at the loterrie* (STC 11403, London, 1608), esp. sigs. B2v–B3; Malcolm Gaskill, *Between two worlds: how the English became Americans* (Oxford, 2014), ch. 1.

25 STC 24830.4, which is the certificate for £25 of Richard Widows, a London goldsmith: *The records of the Virginia Company of London*, ed. Susan Myra Kingsbury, 4 vols (Washington, DC, 1906–35), vol. III, p. 89.

26 *The genesis of the United States*, ed. Alexander Brown, 2 vols (Boston and New York, 1890), vol. I, pp. 257–8, 277–82, 291–3, 302–7.

27 Richard Hakluyt, *Virginia richly valued, By the description of the maine land of Florida, her next neighbour* (STC 22938, London, 1609), sig. A4-v.

28 Robert Johnson, *Nova Britannia: offering most excellent fruites by Planting in Virginia. Exciting all such as be well affected to further the same* (STC 14699.5, London, 1609).

29 Virginia Company of London, *For the Plantation in Virginia. Or Nova Britannia* (STC 24831, London, 1609).

30 STC 24830.9.

31 William Symonds, *Virginia. A sermon preached at White-Chappel, In The presence of many, Honourable and Worshipfull, the Adventurers and Planters for Virginia. 25. April. 1609. Published for the benefit And Use of the Colony, Planted, And to bee Planted there, and for the Advancement of their Christian Purpose* (STC 23594, London, 1609), p. 1.

32 Robert Gray, *A good speed to Virginia* (STC 12204, London, 1609), sig. B2v.

33 Symonds, *Virginia*, p. 54.

CHAPTER 20: TIME PAST, TIME PRESENT

1 Peter Barber, *London: a history in maps*, ed. Laurence Worms, Roger Cline and Ann Saunders (London Topographical Society, no. 173, London, 2012), pp. 22–3.

2 Barrett L. Beer, 'Stow [Stowe], John (1524/5–1605)', *ODNB*.

3 Taylor, *Richard Hakluyts*, vol. II, p. 509.

4 Minnie Reddan and Alfred W. Clapham, *The church of St Helen, Bishopsgate* (vol. IX of London County Council's *Survey of London*, ed. Sir James Bird and Philip Norman, London, 1924), p. 52 and plates 62–5.

5 Alfred Povah, *The annals of the parishes of St Olave Hart Street and Allhallows Staining, in the city of London* (London, 1894), pp. 58, 66–8.

6 Povah, *St Olave Hart Street*, pp. 89–91; Mortimer Epstein, *The early history of the Levant Company* (London, 1908), pp. 159, 255, 257, 258, 261; Alfred C. Wood, *A history of the Levant Company* (London, 1964), p. 22; *The dawn of British trade as recorded in the court minutes of the East India Company, 1599–1603*, ed. Henry Stevens (London, 1886), pp. 54, 56–8, 74–6, 98, 116, 167, 187, 249, 254, 263.

7 Staper's monument was moved from St Martin Outwich to St Helen, Bishopsgate, in the late eighteenth or early nineteenth century: *The registers of St Martin Outwich*, ed. W. Bruce Bannerman (London, 1905), pp. v–vi; Reddan and Clapham, *St Helen Bishopsgate*, p. 71, plates 94–5.

8 PC 2/13, p. 419.

9 SP 12/187, no. 77.

10 Immanuel Bourne, *The godly mans guide: with a direction for all; especially, merchants and tradsmen, shewing how they may so buy, and sell, and get gaine, that they may gaine heaven* (STC 3417, London, 1620), p. 19.

11 Bannerman, *St Olave*, p. 123.

12 Charles Dickens, *The uncommercial traveller and reprinted pieces etc.* (Oxford, 1987), pp. 233–40.

13 Freshfield, *Account books*, pp. 62–3.

14 *The marriage, baptismal, and burial registers, 1571 to 1874 . . . of the Dutch Reformed church, Austin Friars, London*, ed. W. J. C. Moens, (Lymington, 1884), pp. xxxi–xxxii.

15 *The English factories in India: a calendar of documents in the India Office, British Museum and Public Record Office*, ed. William Foster et al., 13 vols (Oxford, 1906–27), vol. I, pp. 183–6.

16 *The records of the Virginia Company of London*, ed. Susan Myra Kingsbury, 4 vols (Washington, DC, 1906–35), vol. I, p. 398.

17 Council for Virginia, *A declaration of the state of the Colonie and Affaires in Virginia: with the Names of the Adventurors, and Summes adventured in that Action* (STC 24841.4, London, 1620), p. 1.

18 Council for Virginia, *Declaration of the state of the Colonie*, pp. 3–4.

19 *By the King. A Proclamation for the restraint of the disordered trading for Tobacco* (STC 8637, London, 1620).

20 *Virginia Company*, ed. Kingsbury, vol. I, pp. 402–3.

21 Barber, *London: a history in maps*, pp. 36–9.

22 *The diary of John Evelyn*, ed. William Bray, 2 vols (New York and London, 1901), vol. II, p. 21.

23 Barber, *London: a history in maps*, p. 52.

24 J. Lindeboom, *Austin Friars: history of the Dutch Reformed church in London, 1550–1950* (The Hague, 1950), pp. 191–2.

25 Kingsford, vol. I, p. 143.

26 Kingsford, vol. I, p. xcviii.

27 Dickens, *Uncommercial traveller*, p. 234.

List of Illustrations and Maps

ILLUSTRATIONS

297

Maps

All maps are details from Richard Hakluyt, *The principal navigations, voiages, traffiques and discoveries of the English nation*, 1598–1600 (Reproduced by courtesy of the Department of Special Collections, University of Leiden. Shelf Mark: 1370 C 10-12)

Acknowledgements

The persuasive nudge to write this book came from Peter Robinson, and the initial idea and prospectus for it has since been shaped and nurtured into existence by Simon Winder at Penguin, George Gibson at Bloomsbury USA and George Lucas at Inkwell Management. Peter has a spooky talent for apparently knowing what I want to write about before I quite do myself, and Simon, George and George have helped enormously in giving to the project direction and purpose. To all four I owe substantial debts of gratitude. I must also thank the team at Penguin (most especially Maria Bedford, Richard Duguid and Marina Kemp) for their unfailing help, Jane Robertson for her superb copy-editing and Cecilia Mackay for her skill in locating and securing so many wonderful images for the illustrations.

The first draft of the book was read by Dr Sara Barker, Professor Martin Butler and Professor John Guy, whose comments, corrections and suggestions (some but by no means all of which are recorded in the Notes) have improved it no end. Needless to say, in the conventional scholarly caveat, any mistakes or oddities in this final version are entirely my own. To John Guy I owe a further and special debt: twenty years ago he taught me my trade as a historian, and his scholarship and writing is a continuing inspiration.

I am grateful indeed to my colleagues in the School of History at Leeds for allowing me a term of study leave after three-and-a-half busy teaching years, months in early 2016 that gave me the peace and silence necessary to finish the book. Professor Ian Wood deserves particular thanks for sharing with me his own extensive Elizabethan interests. The research that underpins this book owes a very great deal to the professionalism and courtesy of the staffs of the Brotherton and

ACKNOWLEDGEMENTS

Laidlaw libraries in Leeds, of Cambridge University Library, of the London Metropolitan Archives and of the Special Collections reading room of the Universiteitsbibliotheek in Leiden.

Not a word of this book would be in print without the unfailing love of Max, always my best supporter and most perceptive critic, and our darling Matilda, from whom I learn so much every day, and whose joy of life makes everything worthwhile. It is dedicated with love to my parents, Jennifer and Tony Alford, who have always encouraged me on a historical journey that began a long time ago with pitched battles at Weston Park, L. du Garde Peach's *Oliver Cromwell*, and the Roman ruins that sit in the long shadow of the Wrekin.

Stephen Alford
Gargrave
December 2016

Index

Locations such as streets and buildings are in London, except where otherwise stated

INDEX

INDEX

Ivan IV ('the Terrible'), Tsar 74, 76, 81, 82, 86, 90, 130, 131, 132, 133–4, 135, 140, 141

Jacobs, Gillis 119
James brewhouse 19
James I (VI of Scotland), King 133, 234–5, 241, 251, 253
Jamuna, river 222
Japan xi, 161, 226, 230, 234, 241
Java 224, 226, 230, 231, 232
Jenkinson, Anthony xvii, 130–41, 142, 146, 147, 148, 151, 157, 159–64, 168, 186, 215, 216, 219, 235, 248, 257
Jenkinson, Judith (née Marshe) 140, 142
Jenyns, Stephen 3
Jerusalem 141
Jewel (ship) 221
Jews 16, 184
John the Evangelist (ship) 132
Johnson, Richard, *The Pleasant Walkes of Moore-fields* 207–8
Johnson, Richard and Robert (of Muscovy Company) 134
Jonson, Ben 20, 114
  The Alchemist 23
  Bartholomew Fair 114, 207
  Catiline, His Conspiracy 23, 208
  Every Man in his Humour 113, 115, 196, 221
Judde, Sir Andrew 236
Judith (ship) 168
Justice, Elizabeth 201

Kara Sea 176
Katherine of Aragon, Queen 36, 55
Katherine Wheel Alley 210
Kazan 134
Ketel, Cornelis 169, 235
Kholmogory 82, 87
Killingworth, George 81, 82, 83
Knightrider Street 34, 37
Knights of St Thomas of Acre 4
Knights Templar 4
Knightsbridge 28

Knowles, Thomas 9
Kosityn, Mikhail Grigor'ev 86
Kyd, Thomas, *The Spanish Tragedy* 195, 202

Labrador Sea 155, 163
Laet, Jaspar, *Prognostication* 44
Lambeth 89
Lamport Hall, Northamptonshire 104
Lancashire 14
Lancaster, James 223, 231
languages 34, 54, 71, 74, 76, 86, 144
Lapland 162
Latin (language) xii, 34, 54, 71, 74, 133, 147
Leadenhall 20
Leadenhall Building 256
Legg Alley 199
Leo X, Pope (Giovanni di Lorenzo de' Medici) xii
Leonardo da Vinci xii
Levant Company 222–3, 226–9, 237, 249
Limehouse 160
Lisbon 13
Little Carter Lane 30
Little Hall Island 163
livery companies 3–4, 14, 244
Livy (Titus Livius) 26
Llewelyn, John 6–7
Lok, John 157
Lok, Michael 154, 157–67, 168–71, 175, 177–8, 180, 216, 219, 236, 248
Lok, Michael (younger) 248
Lok, William 46, 157
Lok family 95
Lok's Land 174
Lombard Street 42, 50, 106, 108, 110, 115, 148
London:
  Bishop of 30, 32
  Great Fire xvii, 53, 254–5
  as Londinium 26–7, 255
  Mint 40
  mortality in 14
  population xi, 13–14, 42

INDEX

INDEX

Queenhithe 1, 27, 33, 86

Ralegh, Sir Walter xvii, 179, 216, 239, 240, 241
Randolph, Thomas 160
Recorde, Robert 77, 91, 131, 147
  Castle of Knowledge 161–2
Red Lion theatre 22
Red Sea xi, 221, 229, 230
Reformation xiv–xv, 35, 86, 198, 248
Regensburg 40
Reigate 255
Revett, Thomas 102
Reynolds, Sir Joshua 255
Reynolds, Nicholas 137
Ribault, Jean 151–2
  Terra Florida 149–51, 153, 181
Richard II, King 49
Richmond Palace 169
Rivers, Elizabeth (née Barne) 77–8
Rivers, John 77
Roanoke Island 240, 243
Rochdale, Lancashire 94
Roebuck (ship) 233
Rogers, Daniel 106–7
Romans 26–7
Romney, Sir William 242
Rose theatre, Southwark 22
Rosetta 219
Rotterdam 224
Royal Commission on Historical Monuments 211
Royal Exchange 37, 102, 105–15, 127, 148, 164, 199, 200–1, 203, 207, 211, 219, 249, 250, 254
Royal Exchange (ship) 221
Russia (Muscovy) xi, 15, 74–9, 81–91, 103, 130–37, 139–41, 151, 153, 159, 162, 172, 176, 178, 220, 223, 229, 230, 234, 252, 257
Rutland, Earl of 102

St Andrew Hubbard 245
St Andrew Undershaft 248, 256
St Antholin's 2–3, 5, 8–10, 94, 254
St Bartholomew the Less (St Bartholomew near the Exchange), church and parish of 128, 197–201, 205, 233–4, 251
St Bartholomew's Hospital 24, 36
St Benet Sherehog 126
St Botolph without Aldgate 21
St Dunstan in the East (parish) 76, 81, 153
St Giles-without-Cripplegate 35
St Gregory by St Paul's 30, 34
St Helen, Bishopsgate 248, 250, 256
St James's Palace 28
St Katherine, hospital of 189
St Laurence Lane 5
St Lawrence Jewry 5, 34, 39, 53, 64, 254
St Magnus the Martyr 37
St Martin Outwich 249
St Martin's 120
30 St Mary Axe ('The Gherkin') 256
St Mary le Bow 34
St Mary's Spital 50
St Matthew's church, near Cheapside 18
St Michael Cornhill 211, 250
St Michael Paternoster 99, 101
St Michael (Wood Street) 140
St Nicholas Lane 127
St Nicholas (port) 74, 76, 82, 83, 132
St Olave, Hart Street 16, 21, 37, 80, 165, 249, 251, 257–8
St Paul's Cathedral 4, 29–31, 88, 102, 105, 106, 109, 110, 112, 218, 254, 255
St Paul's Churchyard (St Paul's Cross) 31–3, 33, 43, 106, 109, 120, 137, 148, 150, 151, 161, 164, 172, 186, 194, 226, 250
St Paul's School 33, 120, 200, 218
St Peter Le Poor 34
St Peter's Cornhill 186, 189
St Sepulchre-without-Newgate 35
St Sithe's Lane 94
St Stephen Walbrook 27
St Thomas of Acon 254
  hospital 4–5, 10, 50
  mercers' chapel 81, 96
St Thomas' Hospital 24